see comment
by Lacey p. 92.

The Perils of Federalism

The Perils of Federalism

Race, Poverty, and the Politics
of Crime Control

Lisa L. Miller

OXFORD

UNIVERSITY PRESS

2008

OXFORD
UNIVERSITY PRESS

Oxford University Press, Inc., publishes works that further
Oxford University's objective of excellence
in research, scholarship, and education.

Oxford   New York
Auckland   Cape Town   Dar es Salaam   Hong Kong   Karachi
Kuala Lumpur   Madrid   Melbourne   Mexico City   Nairobi
New Delhi   Shanghai   Taipei   Toronto

With offices in
Argentina   Austria   Brazil   Chile   Czech Republic   France   Greece
Guatemala   Hungary   Italy   Japan   Poland   Portugal   Singapore
South Korea   Switzerland   Thailand   Turkey   Ukraine   Vietnam

Copyright © 2008 by Oxford University Press, Inc.

Published by Oxford University Press, Inc.
198 Madison Avenue, New York, New York 10016

www.oup.com

Oxford is a registered trademark of Oxford University Press

Library of Congress Cataloging-in-Publication Data
Miller, Lisa Lynn.
The perils of federalism : race, poverty, and the politics
of crime control / Lisa L. Miller.
p.   cm.
Includes bibliographical references and index.
ISBN 978-0-19-533168-4
1. Crime prevention—United States—Citizen participation.   2. Crime prevention—
Pennsylvania—Citizen participation.   3. Federal government—United States.   4. Pressure
groups—United States.   5. Pressure groups—Pennsylvania.   6. African Americans—Crimes
against—Prevention—Citizen participation.   7. Poor—Crimes against—United States—
Prevention—Citizen participation.   I. Title.
HV7431.M552 2008
364.40973—dc22   2008006017

1 3 5 7 9 8 6 4 2

Printed in the United States of America
on acid-free paper

PREFACE

I first began thinking about how federalism might structure crime, law, and policy in the 1990s when I conducted research on a Department of Justice policy called Weed and Seed. The program provided federal funding for urban areas to target particular high-crime neighborhoods. The strategy was to weed out the criminal element and seed the area with social services and other programs designed to revitalize communities. Weed and Seed inspired a great deal of opposition in Seattle and other locales where it was to be implemented, and in the course of my research on the program, I was struck by the differences between the Justice Department's program goals and the goals of local community leaders. Their problem definitions, understanding of the origins of crime, solutions for crime problems, and implementation strategies were virtually polar opposites of one another. Had community leaders in Seattle been part of the policy design process, I mused, this program might have been called "Seed, Mulch, and Carefully Weed."

Why was the Justice Department's program so thoroughly disconnected from the objectives and preferences of local organizations and community groups, some of whom openly refused to take the seed money out of protest? How much urban mobilization around crime and public safety exists, and does it differ from the political mobilization around crime in other venues? How could urban communities with high rates of serious crime effectively pressure democratic institutions to respond to their quality of life and public safety needs? I began to wonder how the range of interest groups that participate in crime and justice policy-making varied across levels of government and whether different types of groups offered different messages about crime and its origins. This pursuit of the relationship between democratic accountability and social control led to an interesting, important and largely neglected question in the study of politics: how does federalism structure group representation, policy environments, and democratic participation? Most scholars have pointed to the democracy-enhancing features of our federal system, as the porous nature of the policy process creates multiple avenues of access. As I discovered in my research on crime control, however, this process has a darker side for democratic politics. By opening up many avenues for policymaking, U.S. federalism systematically advantages highly organized groups with specific and sometimes very narrow policy interests. As a result, citizens with deep and abiding concerns about quality of life, but few resources and policy ideas to match, are disadvantaged. The story that unfolds in this book focuses primarily on the intersection of race and poverty, but the implications go well beyond crime and race to implicate federalism more generally as limiting the representational capacity of diffuse citizen interests. It is my hope that this book will inspire additional research into other policy domains across legislative venues and also into the variability of perspectives and policy ideas about crime and violence that flourish in local contexts.

I would never have come to this topic or completed this book were it not for the intellectual support and encouragement of several scholars in particular. The foundation for this book was initially formed when I was a graduate student working with Stuart Scheingold. His important works on the politics of crime and criminal justice and our ongoing conversations about the relationship between political institutions and social control were the initial inspiration for my research. I continue to refer to and teach those works, and they form the foundation of my interests in state responses to crime and violence. I am deeply indebted to Stuart for his scholarship, intellectual encouragement, and friendship. The project in its current form would probably not have come to fruition were not for the many conversations I had with Frank Baumgartner while I was at Penn State. Frank listened patiently as I wrestled with the book's central premise, he nurtured my initial impulse for the book, and he suggested the phrase "representational bias," which crystallized the book's core ideas. I am extremely grateful to him for his generous time and support throughout the project, as well as his ongoing collegiality and intellectual nourishment.

Research of this sort is highly dependent on individuals working in government institutions who can navigate complex record-keeping systems. Latisha Taylor in Pittsburgh and Michael Decker in Philadelphia were particularly helpful in providing transcripts of city council hearings and repeatedly explaining to me the way each locale maintained records. In the Pennsylvania General Assembly, Judy Sedesse, Peggy Nissly, and Jackie Jumper were absolutely indispensable. It is because of the public records obtained with the help of these individuals that I am able to make the meaningful comparisons this project required. I would also like to thank the legislators in Harrisburg, Philadelphia, and Pittsburgh, to whom I have promised confidentiality, for taking time from their busy schedules to speak candidly with me. I am deeply indebted to all of these individuals for their contributions to this research project.

Friends and colleagues during my years at Penn State were also enormously helpful. Holloway Sparks, Ange-Marie Hancock, and Marnina Gronick were invaluable in encouraging the project from the beginning. They know just how much support was needed in those early years, and they offered it freely and generously. Several graduate students at Penn State provided invaluable assistance throughout the course of this project. Alison Cares's tireless work on witnesses at congressional hearings was particularly crucial in helping me analyze the congressional data. She and her husband, Todd, also provided helpful child care at crucial moments in this project! Brent Teasdale and Chris Scheitle provided enormous logistical help, which made it possible for me to manage the wide range of data this project utilized. The Baumgartner and Jones Policy Agendas Project forms the foundation of chapter 3, and I am very grateful for their research as well as their willingness to create public archives that allow other scholars to access the data. The Research and Graduate Studies Office at Penn State University supported the initial research for this project, providing the means by which I was able to travel to Philadelphia, Pittsburgh, and Harrisburg to conduct interviews. The Political Science Department at Rutgers University provided additional support that allowed me to obtain archival records from the Pennsylvania General Assembly. The anonymous reviewers who read initial chapters and the full manuscript proved extremely helpful in expanding the book's theoretical frames, pointing out conceptual and analytic inconsistencies and suggesting additional literatures. I am very grateful for their time and efforts.

My colleagues at Rutgers University have been wonderful, providing mentoring and support in a variety of ways, including the time and opportunity to complete this project. I am particularly grateful to Jane Junn, Beth Leech, and Dan Tichenor for the many hours of conversation about the project and their feedback on specific portions of the manuscript.

On a more personal level, Regina Lawrence, Michael McCann, Sarah Pralle, Lennie Feldman, and Tom Birkland are all counted as mentors and friends, and they all contributed, in some way or another, to the strength of this project. Of course, they also did not hesitate to point out its limitations, and to the extent that I have failed to address them, I take full responsibility for the book's shortcomings.

I am also grateful to live in a spirited, supportive community where friends and neighbors regularly help one another cope with professional obligations and active family lives. Grace and Paul Lanaris, Liliana Sanchez and Jose Camacho, Cami Townsend and John Nolan, Elissa Rozov and David Copperman, Nancy Isenberg and Max Likin, and Vicki and Jim Zarra, among many others too numerous to name, have all offered family support, intellectual stimulation, and countless relaxing hours of conversation and friendship. I also deeply appreciative of my local chiropractor, Dr. Bruce Grossman, whose care and advice have helped me to continue the long hours of reading and writing this work requires without suffering significant back and neck pain.

Finally, my family has and continues to be a source of strength, pride, intellectual growth, and challenge. My parents, Elmer and Lois Miller, and in-laws, Don and Carole McCrone, have all engaged in long conversations about crime, race, law, and democracy and I am deeply appreciative of their perspectives and support. My sister, Rosina, graciously shared her insights into the urban experience and helped shape some of my own thinking about political mobilization in that context. My children, Annie and Jacob, and my step-daughter, Fiona, all deserve thanks for the time and energy they allowed me to put into this project.

I reserve my most sincere and deeply held gratitude for my best friend and husband, Jamie. He nurtures my intellectual development, supports my professional interests, and makes Herculean contributions to a healthy and happy home life. On top of all that, he is the undisputed best chef around.

CONTENTS

ABBREVIATIONS OF GROUP NAMES

The following abbreviations are used for names of groups throughout the text:

ACLU	American Civil Liberties Union
ACORN	Association of Community Organizations for Reform Now
ADL	Anti-Defamation League
MADD	Mothers Against Drunk Driving
NAACP	National Association for the Advancement of Colored People
PCADV	Pennsylvania Coalition Against Domestic Violence
NRA	National Rifle Association
PCAR	Pennsylvania Coalition Against Rape
WOAR	Women Organized Against Rape

The Perils of Federalism

One

INTERESTS, VENUES, AND
GROUP PARTICIPATION

> The central political fact in a free society is the tremendous contagiousness
> of conflict.... The outcome of all conflict is determined by the scope of
> its contagion. The number of people involved in any conflict determines
> what happens; *every change in the number of participants, every increase
> or reduction in the number of participants, affects the result.*
> —E. E. Schattschneider, *The Semi-Sovereign People*

In November 2000, the Philadelphia city council passed Bill
No. 000659, amending the Philadelphia Code by adding
a section entitled "Reporting Requirements upon the Application or
Renewal of a License to Carry a Firearm." The amendment required all
applicants for concealed weapons permits in Philadelphia to list on the
application all of the weapons they owned. The purpose of the bill was
to provide police with a tool for tracking guns that were used to commit
crimes in the city. In 2006, four out of five homicides in Philadelphia
were committed with firearms, and almost 6,000 robberies were committed with a gun.[1]

While support for tracking guns was high among local officials and
residents of crime-ridden areas, particularly African American neighborhoods, state legislators had taken a dim view of similar previous
efforts. Within a year of Philadelphia and Pittsburgh approving bills banning certain assault rifles within their city limits in 1993, for example,
the General Assembly of Pennsylvania enacted a preemption law, voiding the weapons ban. The law amended the state's Uniform Firearms Act
to provide that

no county, municipality or township may in any manner regulate the lawful ownership, possession, transfer or transportation of firearms, ammunition or ammunition components when carried or transported for the purposes not prohibited by the laws of this Commonwealth. (PA C.S. 6101–6124)[2]

A legal challenge to the state law ensued, led by a broad coalition of interested parties, including the city of Pittsburgh, three Philadelphia city council members, two local ward leaders, the district council president of the American Federation of State, County and Municipal Employees (AFSCME), the vice president of Albert Einstein Medical Services in Philadelphia, the president of the Philadelphia chapter of the National Congress of Puerto Rican Rights and Fellowship Commission, and a Democratic candidate for the state legislature. Calling the plaintiffs' arguments "frivolous" and "without merit," the Supreme Court of Pennsylvania affirmed a lower court's 1996 decision and dismissed the challenge.[3]

Despite this setback, Philadelphia was at it again in 2000, trying a new tactic for gun registrations. In a city council hearing about the bill, one of the bill's cosponsors who represented a predominately African American area of the city with high rates of gun crime revealed his frustration with the outcome of the city's previous efforts:

> I'm not going to continue to allow some state legislator from Lacka-
> wanna County or East Giblip County to tell us what we can do in the
> City of Philadelphia. . . . I'm sick and tired of the State dictating to
> the City . . . and I'm telling you I'm not going to continue to go home
> to my constituents and tell them that because of some state law we
> can't do something to stem the tide of these guns.[4]

This conflict represents an interesting and relatively unexplored problem in crime control politics specifically and American politics more generally. Policies widely supported by local officials and citizen alliances are sometimes thwarted by legislators representing much larger constituencies with little or no connection to local problems and much less connection to serious crime. There is an enormous range of policy options for addressing crime and violence, and there is no shortage of groups mobilized to present policy alternatives. Why are local crime policy preferences not more successful in state and national politics? What do the policy environments for crime and justice policy look like across legislative venues?

These questions strike at the core of democratic participation and citizenship. The criminal law, and the justice system that implements it, represent the state's monopoly on the use of force—sometimes lethal—and the extent of democratic representation and political accountability that inheres in these institutions are crucial areas of study for scholars of law, policy, and politics. This book argues that U.S. federalism shapes the representation of group interests and the policy environments at each level of government in ways that severely underrepresent the interests of citizens facing serious crime victimization—most frequently the poor and racial minorities. In doing so, the book offers a rich discussion of an important causal mechanism shaping crime politics—the representation of group interests—and provides a foundation for understanding massive variation in crime policy outcomes across the political landscape. In addition, it presents a framework for understanding how federalism structures interest group representation and how that representation interacts with institutions and issues to create important variation in policy environments across levels of government.

Federalism and Group Participation: An Important Puzzle

Jurisdictional conflicts between the national and state governments were one of the central political problems at the founding of the republic.[5] Early in the nation's history, each level of government retained primary control over specific policy areas that were largely out of reach for other legislative venues. But a wide range of domestic and international factors has led to the spreading of policy issues across all three legislative venues—beginning with the Civil War and continuing in the early to mid–twentieth century, with a rapid increase following World War II.[6] The result is that many, if not most, policy issues are addressed at the local, state, and national levels of government simultaneously. Few scholars have explored the implications of this development for studies of American politics and sociolegal scholarship.[7] I refer to this as the *federalization* of policy issues and argue that it raises fundamental questions at the heart of democratic politics with important implications for interest group representation, democratic participation, political accountability, and the rule of law.[8]

How does federalism shape the representation of interest groups on a given policy issue? Does the federalization of issues across legislative venues enhance or diminish democratic participation? What types of groups have the greatest mobilization capacity for migrating across legislative venues? The conventional political science wisdom suggests that smaller scale political conflicts—those in regional and local arenas—are often monopolized by parochial interests and that broader citizen interests can be vindicated primarily through expanding a conflict's scope to include additional interests.[9] This set of scholarship, much of which emerged from the civil rights movement, emphasized the limited capacity of groups representing broad citizen interests to counter the pressures of highly mobilized groups with narrow and material interests at stake at the subnational levels. Indeed, E. E. Schattschneider's well-known observation that "the scope of the conflict" determines public policy outcomes served as a foundation for this research by suggesting that governments representing larger constituencies were most likely to include groups with broad public interest goals.[10]

But the stories about crime politics that open this chapter suggest that this assessment is incomplete. The centralization of crime policy in state and national governments and the institutionalization of crime policy agendas limit the voice of groups who are most affected by crime and who frame crime as a public interest problem. While some citizen groups seem to fare well on the national level, others—for example neighborhood associations, community-based organizations, ex-offenders groups, mothers' and parents' groups—are deeply embedded in local contexts and often resource-poor, making it difficult to migrate across multiple legislative venues. They may also have a character and purpose—for example, diffuse policy interests—that are difficult to convey in more formalized policy contexts. Long histories of tension between police and black neighborhoods in some urban areas also help shape the crime control politics of the locale. In addition, citizens groups from these neighborhoods often have a view of crime that is intermingled with the other social and economic conditions in which they live. Prior research on local crime politics suggests that unique race and ethnic tensions, community organizations, and coalitions of ad hoc groups with quality-of-life concerns are frequently participants in the local policy process.[11] Indeed, as chapters 3 and 4 will illustrate, while local political venues have been criticized for their parochial character, sometimes state and national venues can exhibit similarly narrow policy environments while the local level provides a wider range of group participants and policy ideas.

Thus, while the growth of organized interests at the state and federal level and the increasing size of the federal bureaucracy over the past 50 years have expanded opportunities for groups to press their claims, these developments may have also served to further marginalize groups that lack the organizational capacity to compete for attention at the state and federal levels, not to mention all three levels of government simultaneously.[12] Policymakers at the higher levels seem largely insulated from the policy priorities of these groups, despite their persistent and occasionally successful organizing efforts at the local level. As chapters 5 and 6 will illustrate, some of these groups are likely to be very loosely organized, which makes them able to work their way into local politics through less conventional means, but less likely to engage in the kind of collective action required for a presence on the state or national scene. Thus, the collective action problem usually at work with poor people's movements and groups advocating broad public goods is exacerbated by federalism because it further diffuses and balkanizes mobilization efforts.[13]

Meanwhile, the bureaucratic institutions that provide the backbone of the criminal process (law enforcement, prosecutors, probation, corrections officers, and judges) and a few highly mobilized citizen groups (for example, the National Rifle Association [NRA], Mothers Against Drunk Driving [MADD], the Coalition Against Rape, and the American Civil Liberties Union [ACLU]) occupy a space in crime politics across all levels of government but form a particularly strong and routine component in state and national crime politics. This is consistent with research in American politics that illustrates how the politicization of issues generates institutional arrangements that linger long after the public has turned its attention elsewhere and suggests that more legislative venues may sometimes result in less competitive policy venues.[14] Few have applied these theoretical and empirical insights to the domain of crime policy. But doing so suggests that groups that develop access to state and national crime agendas, and the institutions that respond to those interests, are often unrepresentative of objective crime victimization risk and can even be representative of opposing policy priorities and problem definitions that depoliticize the causes and consequences of crime.

Thus, a major theme that emerges as this book unfolds is that the *federalization* of crime control—that is, the presence of crime control as an active agenda item at all three levels of government—generates a systematic bias in the interest group environment across levels of government. Highly active single-issue interest groups and crime control bureaucracies are mobilized *into* the political process at the state and national levels while broad citizen groups and other groups with more diffuse interests—particularly those representing citizens who experience serious crime risks and exposure to the criminal justice apparatus—are mobilized *out* of it. Of particular interest here are urban blacks, who face criminal victimization *and* interaction with the criminal justice system at substantially higher rates than whites. As crime becomes a regular part of legislative agendas that are geographically and psychologically distanced from crime problems and require more formal resources, these groups are unable to maintain a presence in the routine policy process; nor are they in a position to ally with similarly situated groups in other urban areas because of the fragmented nature of the American political system.

Paul Peterson has noted that cities, states, and national governments "differ in their essential character," and argues persuasively that cities operate under specific structural and institutional constraints that have important implications for policy options at the local level.[15] I suggest here that state and national governments also operate under structural constraints that can sometimes promote a much narrower range of problem definitions and policy solutions than are apparent in cities. In fact, while cities clearly have strong structural incentives to emphasize economic growth and efficiency over equality and quality-of-life concerns, state and national governments also have structural incentives to narrow citizen concerns to issues that fall into focused and manageable conflicts. Some policy issues, however, such as crime, transportation, neighborhood blight, and public services, are deeply intertwined, and citizen pressure to address these issues becomes difficult to translate into legislative venues that are more formalized and require specific policy solutions.

Interest Groups, Pluralism, and Crime Control in American Politics

In *The Politics of Street Crime*, Stuart Scheingold noted that "the politics of the criminal process at the national level is more about authority than policy, while the converse is true at the local level."[16] Local officials are simply unable to ignore the complex realities of crime; nor are they able to focus on monocausality in the way national officials can. This is true, in part, because local officials must actually respond to victims of crime and constituents who live with the daily threat of victimization as well as the collateral consequences of crime policies. At times, these constituents make almost hysterical pleas for help that local lawmakers can hardly ignore, even if they have strong incentives to do so. Thus, on the local level, pragmatism is likely to factor into crime politics, while moral panics and pressure from vested interests are likely to play into levels of government that are farther removed from the day-to-day realities of crime and violence. Embedded within this discussion is a clear claim about the role of group interests. National elected officials face a different set of constituent pressures than local ones because of their geographic and electoral isolation from the problem and, I suggest, because this isolation allows for the emergence of single-issue groups with narrow interests whose problem definitions and issue frames intersect with prosecutors and police around punishing offenders. This is strikingly dissimilar from—and sometimes even oppositional to—the emphasis on harm reduction and community building proposed by citizens facing daily risks of crime victimization.

This thesis forms a powerful starting point for this study. Group theorists have long understood that the array of interests in a policy venue has important consequences for how social problems are defined and the types of policy proposals that are available.[17] Theories of interest group formation and maintenance also recognize that not all interests are created equal. When group benefits are diffuse, many people will free ride rather than participate, whereas when benefits are aimed narrowly, pressure groups will be more easily formed and maintained. More recent research has documented the dramatic growth of citizens' groups, suggesting that early critics of pluralism underestimated the likelihood of group formation when nonmaterial interests were at stake.[18] However, we know little about whether the range of groups that participate in governmental activity accurately reflects the underlying array of citizen interests in society or whether preference intensity directs citizens groups to reflect the most extreme positions, rather than the most widely held ones.[19] By neglecting the structural context in which interest group formation and activity takes place in the United States, we miss the opportunity to understand more fully the relationship between institutions and interests.

Another critic of pluralism, E. E. Schattschneider, has offered a more nuanced insight into groups and the policy process by suggesting that the very formation of groups—the mobilization of interests—is itself a form of bias that privileges some types of problem definitions and solutions over others. This is a particularly important because it suggests that the way groups form and are able to sustain themselves in the policy process necessarily closes off some forms of organization, issue frames, and problem definitions. My approach borrows this concept from Schattschneider by applying the insights of mobilization bias to the federal system, in which group formation not only biases problem definitions and solutions but also has consequences for which groups are most likely to have access to which policy venues.

Cutting across these debates are scholars whose primary interest is in understanding the representation of the public interest in American democratic politics. How well are broad public interests represented in the policy process? How do groups whose primary purpose is addressing public interest concerns fare in the political process? On the heels of the massive social movements of the 1960s, political scientists largely embraced James Madison's framework offered in *Federalist* 10: smaller constituencies are more likely to create nefarious and damaging factions while larger constituencies are made up of a wider range of interests such that control by a narrow band of groups is less likely.[20]

While there are good theoretical and empirical bases for this presumption, the actual relationship between legislative policy venues and the range of interest groups on a given policy issue is an empirical question, and more recent research has taken a closer look at the relationship between federalism, social movements, public policy, and interest group activity.[21] The civil rights movement probably played a disproportionate role in solidifying the Madisonian assumption that larger policy environments were more likely to protect the public interest than smaller ones; but the civil rights problem was itself at the heart of the constitutional compromises that generated the federal system in the first place. Given the dramatic changes to the political process over the course of the nation's history—the increase in the nature and scope of state and congressional lawmaking, the emergence of specialized committees, the growth of professional legislatures and lobbyists, the role of mass media in politics, to name just a few—it is increasingly important to direct empirical attention toward understanding pluralism across all levels of government.[22]

In addition, as new institutionalists have reminded us, interests do not act in a vacuum but, rather, interact with institutional contexts that can vary across time, across issues, and, of course, cross-nationally. While a growing body of literature addresses the growth of legislative venues for participation, the strategies groups use to venue shop, and the impact of these strategies on policy outcomes, few have paid systematic attention to how policy environments vary across levels on the same issue, examined pressure groups beyond the state and national levels, or included group activity that is ad hoc or more informal than the lobby-intensive groups that populate Washington, D.C.[23] Comparing group activity on the same issue across levels not only addresses the gap in our understanding of the crime policy process but also contributes to the study of group politics more generally. In particular, it illustrates the surprising array of groups that participate in local politics but are unable to migrate across venues. Many scholars have assumed quiescence and demobilization among urban minorities, but the research presented here shows a citizenry that is active and engaged, albeit in a fragmented and sporadic way. It also demonstrates how problem definitions and policy alternatives vary across levels of government, partly as a function of the groups that bring very different perspectives on problems and solutions and their interaction with institutional venues. For example, the emphasis of urban groups representing black neighborhoods on restoring families and neighborhoods torn apart by gun violence contrasts sharply with the state emphasis on punishing offenders.

The primary thesis of this book is that variation in policy environments across levels of government has significant implications for political representation and accountability and also for understanding how institutions and interests interact to create substantially different policy agendas, legal alternatives, and potential solutions. At the state and national levels, the presence of criminal justice agencies and a few single-issue citizen groups creates a policy environment in which punishing offenders becomes the focal point of policy objectives. This turns out to be particularly true at the state level, where the interests of prosecutors and citizen groups focused on victims more readily intersect. The dominance of these groups creates and reinforces a policy environment best described as regulatory and distributive: intensely organized but highly specialized interests vie for legislative resources but only infrequently come into direct conflict with one another.[24] In this context, where police, prosecutors, and narrow single-issue citizen groups stake out claims for resources, offenders are central to problem definitions and solutions—a somewhat surprising outcome, given the growing emphasis on responding to victims over the past 30 years.[25] The resultant policy process reinforces existing problem definitions and policy frames into which existing groups can easily fit their claims. State and national political institutions are particularly responsive to pressure groups that frame policy solutions in ways that are consistent with existing programmatic efforts, and the professionalized nature of contemporary policy advocates makes it possible for highly resourced groups to feed into existing policy programs.[26] The pressure to increase funding for courts and prosecutors at the congressional level, for example, has implications for these organizational priorities at other levels. These feedback effects, then, occur not only *within* legislative venues but *across* them, contributing to a process in which "policy begets participation begets policy in a cycle that results not in equal protection of interests, but in outcomes biased towards the politically active."[27]

At the local level, however, where broad citizen groups—for example, Mothers United Against Tragedy, Ex-Offenders Incorporated, the Garfield Neighborhood Association, Congreso de Latinos Unidos, Parents Against Violence, and the Association of Community Organizations for Reform Now (ACORN), to name just a few—represent the poor, racial minorities, and a wide range of quality-of-life concerns, a substantially different policy arena emerges, one in which the crime issue is framed less around distributing resources to various crime-fighting organizations and more around redistribution of resources to help ailing communities and reduce individual suffering. The nature of crime itself, its potential causes, and its preferred solutions become contested political terrain and create opportunities for engaging in local political life, promoting civic attention to social problems, and creating pathways of access to political institutions and the policy process.[28] This policy environment, however, is disconnected from other, similar environments across the political landscape, and grassroots mobilization becomes difficult to sustain, particularly in the face of highly professionalized groups that migrate across venues.[29] Thus, the potential mobilization of bias in crime control as a function of federalism has implications for both local political life and for policy outcomes.

Crime Politics across Legislative Venues

Crime as a policy issue is well overdue for analysis by scholars interested in democratic participation and accountability. As Robert Cover noted, when citizens act within the context of state institutions that exercise authoritative use of force, they act without the normal inhibitions against violence and control that typically bound their actions.[30] In this sense, the relationship between the state-sanctioned use of force that inheres in criminal law and criminal justice practices and the robustness of democratic institutions is a crucial area of study for law and policy scholars. At the foundation of the criminal law is violence—explicit coercion and the implicit threat of force. Without a clear sense of the *process* through which the state arrives at legal rules determining deviant behavior, and the norms and practices governing the institutions designed to address that behavior, our understanding of democratic accountability is limited.

Several aspects of crime control make the issue particularly ripe for study.[31] Spending on crime control has increased dramatically over the past 30 years, even in relation to spending on other social issues such as education and health.[32] The most dramatic growth has been at the national and state levels, where justice spending has increased nearly sixfold over the past 20 years (as compared to a more modest but still substantial growth of three-and-a-half-fold at the local level).[33] Incarceration rates have also exploded, more than tripling since 1980, such that the United States now has the highest incarceration rate in the industrialized world.[34] Despite this growth, we know little about the process by which government attempts to address the roughly 1 million aggravated assaults, 350,000 violent crimes with firearms, and 16,000 homicides that are committed each year.[35] Nor do we have much to say about how U.S. governments end up depriving nearly 2 million American citizens of their liberty and sending dozens more to execution annually.[36]

Another aspect of crime control that makes it a particularly important policy area for analysis is that serious crime victimization is not randomly distributed but is more common among blacks and Latinos, the poor, the urban, and males (particularly as these groups intersect). Homicide rates for black teenage boys, for example, are over seven times those for white teenage boys, and black teenage girls are three and a half times more likely to be murdered than white teenage girls.[37] Similarly, Latinos and African Americans are robbery victims at more than twice the rate of whites.[38] Men of all racial groups are victims of homicide more often than women, and robbery rates are almost double for men.[39] Furthermore, people living in urban areas experience more violent victimization than suburban and rural dwellers, and for all race and ethnic groups violent victimization is most prevalent among the very poor.[40] Urban minorities experience violent victimization at especially high rates.[41] Serious crime, then, is a salient issue for only a portion of the public on a day-to-day basis. While we are all *potential* victims of serious crime, the empirical reality is that real victimization is experienced by some populations at much higher rates than others and varies systematically by race, age, gender, income, and residential location. In fact, decreases in crime rates over the past 20 years have benefited higher-income households far more than the poor, which also means that whites as a group have benefited from this decline more than African Americans or Latinos.[42] Thus, crime-control politics at all three levels of government raise important questions of race and ethnic participation in the policy process, the role of poor people's perspectives in politics, the connection between urban social problems and state and national policy making, and the degree to which those with a significant stake in policy outcomes are represented in the policymaking process.

Of course, it is now widely known that blacks and Latinos are also significantly more likely to be incarcerated than whites and that even white incarceration rates are at their highest point in U.S. history. A number of scholars have used the term "mass incarceration" to refer to America's current crime control regime, and a great deal of scholarship over the past few years has deftly explored the impact of mass incarceration on citizens, particularly as it disproportionately affects minorities and the poor.[43] In addition to high incarceration rates, blacks are substantially more likely to come into contact with virtually every aspect of the justice system, including police, juvenile justice, parole and probation officers, courts, and prisons, and tend to have a far more negative view of the police than whites, even when class status and residential location are taken into account.[44] Because of their socioeconomic condition, the poor and racial minorities also experience the collateral consequences of imprisonment—such as limitations on federal aid for public housing and social welfare, the absence of breadwinners in the family, and the impact on parent-child relations—in more profound and long-lasting ways than other groups.[45]

Much of the extant literature on contemporary crime policy focuses on the national level, and a substantial portion of this literature comes from legal scholars whose primary interests are in the constitutionality of congressional involvement in criminal law, the interaction between actors in different parts of the legal system (i.e., federal and local prosecutors), and recent crime bills in Congress.[46] Frequently, research on crime control treats it as a unique policy arena, operating in isolation from the routine elements of American political processes that drive other issues on and off legislative agendas. In this framework, crime control policy is a bellwether of governmental legitimacy, a proxy for underlying anxieties about economic or social issues, a window into the degree of moralizing in politics, and a measure of elite control of government institutions and lower-class populations.[47] These macro-analyses have provided important sociological analyses of broad trends in social control and the discursive frames in which law-and-order policy making takes place. In particular,

Garland (2001) and Simon (2006) offer compelling arguments about an important shift in the nature and tone of policy making such that crime victims become a kind of citizen-subject and social control becomes an overarching frame in which policy making of all kinds takes place, thus limiting the scope of problems to be addressed and the range of possible solutions. The research presented here provides some support for these claims, as it reveals the deep inroads into policymaking and legal narratives that prosecutors, police, and single-issue citizen groups (often representing victims) have made over the past 40 years.

These analyses, however, reveal less about the day-to-day process by which actual crime policies are conceptualized, are proposed, are modified, and become law, not to mention the ways they may be substantially altered in their implementation.[48] Furthermore, there is an enormous range of crime policy outcomes, from lengthy sentences for drug offenses, severe gun control provisions, and Three Strikes You're Out to community supervision, decriminalization of medical marijuana, and alternatives to incarceration for drug offenders and the mentally ill. Macro-level analyses of changing patterns in crime policy typically focus only on one level of government (e.g., national) and one aspect of the criminal process (e.g., incarceration), making them likely to miss the abundance of policies that exist at other levels of government and the multitude of crime policy agendas that legislators regularly confront.[49]

Some recent scholarship does take up the midrange between macro-theorizing and micro-empirical studies of criminal courts and policing, through an examination of the importance of state political structures and political cultures, the role of social movements, and the receptivity of legislative institutions to particular crime control agendas.[50] I situate my own project in these traditions, which largely treat the crime policy domain as part of the political process, one that is influenced by the same forces that drive the policy process in other issue areas, rather than as a product of larger, macro-level social forces that are exogenous to the day-to-day realities of political institutions. This does not preclude additional, *unique* aspects of the crime issue that need to be addressed (e.g., its valence status, for example), but crime is not the only issue that has these idiosyncratic elements. By taking as a starting point the fact that crime policy operates within a legislative process that scholars have long studied, we have an opportunity to identify how key elements of that process influence crime policy specifically. In addition, my focus is on the agenda setting, problem definition, and policy formulation phase of the policy process, rather than the crafting of bills to address a single crime problem, the passage of specific legislation, or the implementation process.[51] I begin from this starting point because it offers an opportunity to gain some empirical footing for understanding broader claims about crime policy making.

By systematically mapping the quantity and quality of group participation at each level of government, and how the interaction of groups and legislative venues produces unique policy environments, this book offers a detailed understanding of the crime policy process.

The Approach of This Book

The primary research focus here is a key causal mechanism in the policy process: identifying the range of groups that participate in the policy process across legislative venues and comparing the policy environments that result from the interaction of groups and legislative institutions. In particular, this book forges new ground in identifying the full spectrum of citizen groups, professional associations, and government agencies that participate in the policy process and makes important distinctions among them, particularly different types of citizen groups.

Participation in the political process has a direct impact on policy outcomes.[52] Thus, at the core of this project is a simple, fundamental question: who is represented in government at the local, state, and national levels on crime and justice policy issues? Taking a historical lens and drawing on public policy, interest group, legal, and criminological literature, I establish a framework for understanding the range of groups that participate in crime policy debates. This framework harnesses multiple data sources and develops a rich empirical picture of variation in crime politics across local, state, and national legislative agendas. This variation is linked to the development of institutions and policies at each level of government that generate unique political landscapes, patterns of access, and hence policy environments.

Thus, my approach builds on previous social control research yet differs in several important ways. First, and foremost, it brings *interest groups* squarely into the analysis. Crime mobilizes a wide range of different social movement actors, including "traditional, conservative, law and order constituencies mobilized around punitive policies like three strikes; feminist movements organized against rape and domestic violence; gay and lesbian groups advocating for hate crimes legislation; million moms march pushing for gun control."[53] We know little, however, about the full range of groups and the extent of their participation in day-to-day crime policy making.[54] It turns out that just a few highly active single-issue groups—for example, the ACLU, the NRA, Women Against Rape, and MADD—make up the dominant type of citizen group and occupy an enormous amount of citizen group space in the policy environment. Most research on crime policy also neglects other potentially important group actors, beyond victims' groups and civil libertarians. Criminal justice agents themselves, for example, have become central participants in the policy process, helping to shape how issues are defined, policy alternatives are formulated, and policy outcomes adopted.[55] Indeed, these actors are particularly important, as chapters 2, 3, 4, and 5 demonstrate, because they often reference their own internal priorities and goals when advocating for their interests in legislative arenas.[56]

Similarly, we know little about the extent of participation by less formal groups, for example urban crime victims, neighborhood organizations, and urban public interest organizations. Less formally organized groups are often neglected by policy scholars, and as a result, a great deal of research on interest groups is conducted at the national and state levels. Because participation in these venues requires a fairly high level of organizational capacity, interest group research is heavily skewed toward lobbyists for whom formal organization is de rigueur.[57] However, focusing almost exclusively on formally organized groups or groups with paid lobbyists makes it difficult to determine whether the range of groups that are actively pressuring government reflects the range of group interests arrayed in society.[58] Rather, this research tells us that, *among the highly organized*, some groups are more significant players than others.

In contrast, I see loosely organized groups, ad hoc coalitions, and informal associations as an important part of the policy process generally and crime politics in particular.[59] Indeed, recent research on local groups illustrates the high frequency with which neighborhood organizations, for example, participate in local politics.[60] Because crime victimization is highly skewed on the basis of race, class, and locale, it is not surprising that one would find few highly mobilized, well-financed groups representing the interests of people at high risk of victimization. Nor would we expect criminal defendants or those at risk of interacting with the criminal justice system to be particularly well organized. This does not mean, however, that these populations have no group representation or are not active participants in the policy process. I treat informally structured coalitions as organized groups (rather than latent social movements) because they represent people with a common set of interests and because they participate in the policy process with both insider strategies (e.g., appearances at legislative hearings) and outsider ones (e.g., mass protests, rallies, vigils). Chapters 5 and 6 will illustrate that these groups offer substantially different problem definitions and policy formulations than other groups, and therefore their absence from the political process is an important component in the resulting policy environments at the state and national levels. Indeed, my approach provides an opportunity to compare the problem definitions and issue frames that more and less formal groups bring to the policy process. There are a range of other group participants as well—including religious groups, educational associations, social service organizations—about which we have little understanding.

A second area where this study diverges from previous analyses of crime control—indeed, from previous analyses in any policy area—is in comparing policy environments across all three levels of government. While comparisons across time or issue are now a routine part of research on groups, what I have termed the federalization of policy issues has been much less frequently studied. Crime, education, social welfare, the environment, and health care, for example, are all issues that have an active presence on all three legislative agendas simultaneously, yet few have compared group activity on the same issue across all three levels of government. Doing so not only addresses the gap in our understanding of the underlying range of group interests, as articulated by Scholzman (1984) and Lowery and Gray (2004), it helps determine the level of government that is most pluralistic on a given policy issue, and it provides an opportunity to understand the dynamics of less formally organized groups. By examining just one level of government, we risk creating monolithic pictures of policy and drawing inferences about a policy domain as a whole that do not accurately reflect policy processes at another level.

For example, by observing just one level of government we may understate or miss altogether the role that some very active groups play across the three policy venues, thus increasing the likelihood that policies in at least one venue will reflect their interests. Recent research on education and environmental policy illustrate how policy entrepreneurs capitalize on federalism by seeking out the venue in which they are most likely to be victorious.[61] Groups that are active in more than one venue, for example the NRA or the ACLU, not only increase their likelihood of success but can also learn to target the level of government on specific policy issues where they have found legislative success in the past. The NRA, for example, has been very effective in targeting state legislatures for preemption laws that prohibit localities from enacting any new gun legislation, and recent analysis of the gun issue in American politics has centered on the difficulty gun control advocates have had in exploiting the exigencies of federalism as well as the NRA.[62] In addition, bureaucratic agencies, such as prosecutors or law enforcement agents, may have more in common with their counterparts at other levels of government than they do with other actors at their own level.[63] As a result, groups representing bureaucratic interests may find it valuable to participate in venues that are not their own but that might support their counterparts' interests.

Another illustration of the problem of a singular focus on one level of government is that while urban areas have long been hotbeds of racism, exclusion, and violence against racial and ethnic minorities, the same groups have also used local political arenas to agitate for greater inclusion in the American political process. As a result, they have generated well-worn paths of resistance and mobilization that have sometimes resulted in substantial changes to local policies. In addition, crime policies developed at one level can have implications for legislative venues at other levels, as when community policing emerged from the tense and sometimes violent conflicts between police and citizen groups at the local level and became a national agenda item in the 1990s. Or, conversely, the heavy emphasis on punishing offenders at the state level has made offender reentry into local communities a significant local policy issue, while substantially narrowing the range of policy options local governments have for addressing it. In fact, crime policies appear to be getting more and more interactive as law enforcement and prosecutorial interaction is promoted and traditional criminal jurisdictions between local, state, and national governments are eroded.[64] Thus, an exploration of crime policy at a single level of government risks over- or understating a particular set of interests and institutional arrangements and missing other important mechanisms that shape policy outcomes.

My approach here differs from the extant literature in a third way: I suggest that the *historical reach* of most of scholarship on criminal justice policy is not long enough.[65] Most research on crime policy takes a snapshot of one policy or a brief period of time.[66] But social and political processes unfold over time and are embedded in specific institutional contexts. Insufficient attention to temporality can lead to biases in research design because they neglect the specific policy pathways that have been forged in earlier time periods.[67] For example, crime policy proposals have often served as symbolic levers as much as they have reflected underlying risks of victimization. A focus on a narrow slice of history may *overstate* the salience of existing political conflicts to the crime agenda, for example racial tensions during the 1960s, while understating the gradual development of crime as a national policy issue over the nation's history (see chapter 2). Similarly, while the relationship between crime rates and legislative attention to crime is tenuous, a historical approach reveals a long history of spikes in attention to crime when underlying social conditions changed in dramatic and unsettling ways. Which groups are currently able to capitalize on legislative interest in crime depends, in part, on the earlier development of institutional arrangements that smoothed the paths of access for some groups more than others.

This approach puts into perspective claims that crime became a key national and state agenda item in the 1960s when Republicans engaged in a systematic effort to use crime as a proxy for racial prejudice, focusing white fears of racial integration and keeping crime on the national agenda as a means by which to drive the civil rights agenda out of the picture. There is substantial evidence for this claim; at least a portion of the Republican leadership during the 1968 presidential campaign and during the early years of the Nixon presidency made a concerted effort to equate black Americans with crime and black civil rights with black violence.[68] However, the melding of racial and ethnic minorities with crime and violence in the public imagination is hardly a new phenomenon in American politics. Crime as a proxy for fears of racial integration is a consistent theme. Antiimmigrant bias is well documented, and the Chinese Exclusion Act, the Harrison Narcotics Act, and the White Slavery Act are all illustrations of federal crime policies were initiated, at least in part, as a result of racial or ethnic bias.[69] Thus, the racialization of crime issues during the late 1960s is of interest less for its novelty than for its magnitude and staying power. As chapter 2 shows, biases in group representation in national crime politics have a long tradition in American politics, but the 1960s provided a unique political context for institutionalizing these biases.

More important, these approaches do not specify how national political priorities affected policy environments at other levels of government. The monocausal story of racial politics and crime policy is misleading because it both overstates and understates the role of race in the policy process. A careful analysis of groups and institutions reveals less a direct racial bias toward criminal offenders than a deeply embedded set of institutional arrangements that privilege white victims over black ones and underrepresent urban minority constituents.

The Race and Crime Question

In fact, the centrality of my concerns with African American mobilization around crime issues will quickly become apparent. This stems from a longstanding interest in the political and economic marginalization of blacks, and few issues illustrate this reality more than crime and punishment. Two points are worth noting here about this underlying theme. First, while a great deal is known about the effect of race on contemporary political and social outcomes, far less is known about the causal mechanisms that produce those effects. How, exactly, does race matter for policy outcomes? We know that whites often express open hostility toward black interests and that whites who are prejudiced are less likely to support policies they perceive will help blacks.[70] Scholars have also demonstrated the connection between blacks and criminality in the white imagination and that this has an impact on whites' attitudes toward punishment and the causes of crime; and there is a substantial body of literature drawing clear causal connections between the racial composition of a region and its relative punitiveness.[71] Others have drawn attention to broad shifts in attitudes about crime and criminals and the centrality of racial hierarchy to those attitudes.[72]

Far less is known, however, about *how* these racial attitudes or racial demographics come into play in the policy process and generate legal rules and institutional processes that have such a negative impact on African Americans. A crucial component of understanding race in American politics is to document the specific ways that policy making is shaped by racially stratified access to power, resources, and wealth.[73] Indeed, scholars have only limited understanding of how specific institutional arrangements around crime may, as Paul Frymer notes, "provide rules and procedures that motivate people to behave in a racist manner or to behave in a manner that motivates others to do so."[74] Part of my aim in this study is to move beyond the traditional examination of the *effect* of race on some dependent crime variable (policies, attitudes, sentencing) to assess the *processes* or *mechanisms* through which race continues to play a role in contemporary American law and politics. What institutional arrangements operate to help maintain racial differences as a factor in crime policy? What causal mechanisms produce the vast racial disparities in the impact of the criminal law on citizens? By examining the policy process, I illustrate how groups representing those at greatest risk of victimization—disproportionately racial minorities—have the greatest access to the legislative process at the local level, which is the policy venue with the least capacity to shape major policy outcomes. In addition, the policy environments at the state and national level decouple crime from broader economic and social issues, such as housing, blight, education, city services, and other quality-of-life concerns, which have an enormous impact on the life chances of racial minorities but which local governments are structurally ill equipped to address.[75]

A second reason race figures into this discussion is that the study of the intersection of race and the criminal law is often disconnected from broader analyses of American politics. But understandings of the dynamics of race and crime control, as well as theoretical frameworks for understanding the policy process, would benefit from more intersectionality between these two types of research. For example, attention to substantial racial differences in interest group representation raises important questions about existing understandings of group theory. Resources clearly play a role in the frequency and strength of lobbying potential for various social groups, for example. But at least in the crime policy domain, the challenges of political mobilization may extend beyond the resource problem to longstanding and deeply embedded pathways of access to the policy process in which perceptions of worthy victims (whites) and likely offenders (racial minorities) linger.[76] Thus, attention to the racial dimensions of interest group representation across levels of government in this study provides an opportunity to rethink the foundations of group theory. Similarly, there is an enormous body of literature focused on understanding the differential policy impact of the criminal justice system on whites as compared to blacks and Latinos, but few of these studies make use of established public policy frameworks.[77] By bringing these frameworks to bear on the intersection of race and crime control politics, we can observe the ways "racism, like other behaviors in society, can be analyzed as a political act."[78]

Research Design

The primary aim of this study is to assess how federalism shapes the representation of group interests in the development of the criminal law and crime and justice policies. At its core, it is concerned with the agenda-setting aspect of the policy process. The fundamental question under examination is: what is the relationship between the level of government at which the crime issue is salient and the range of interest groups that are represented in the policy process?[79]

Because data on the full range of groups that participate in legislative policy discussions are not readily available or comparable across all levels of government, I adopt a case-oriented approach that allows me to triangulate data on groups participating in the policy process from a variety of sources.[80] No single source of data on its own offers sufficient opportunity for inference, but pooling data from several sources can provide a rich picture of the group environment. Thus, the research design provides an opportunity to gain an understanding of how the group environments vary across levels of government. This is crucial, since the key aim is to gain a comparative understanding of the full range of group types and the extent of their participation across levels, an analysis that is largely absent from the crime policy arena and is exceedingly rare in public policy and law more generally. This approach will result in a framework of group types that can be utilized to assess participation across all three levels of government in different issue areas.

The research design involves detailed analysis of three cases: two urban areas (Philadelphia and Pittsburgh), a state legislature (Pennsylvania), and Congress. Each case contains between 60 and 500 observations and analyses of several hundred to several thousand witnesses from public legislative hearings and interviews. The data are drawn from five sources: hundreds of legislative hearings on crime and justice (local, state, national); dozens of interviews with legislators and their aides (local, state); witness testimony at legislative hearings (local, state, and national); lobby disclosure reports and other lists of group participants (local, state, and national); and government lists and media coverage of nonprofit organizations (local). (Readers interested in details of the data collection and comprehensive descriptions of the datasets should see the appendices.)[81]

A Preliminary Typology of Interest
Groups in Crime Control Policy

I adopt a broad definition of *interest group*: "an association of individuals or organizations or a public or private institution that, on the basis of one or more shared concerns, attempts to influence public policy in its favor."[82] By making distinctions among different types of groups, it is possible to observe the interests that are most likely to be represented or are most frequently represented. The most common distinction policy scholars draw is between groups whose members participate because of their professional interests—such as business, professional, and trade organizations—and citizen groups, whose members join because of some shared interest that is distinct from their professional concerns.[83] These two primary types are often further refined by comparing membership associations to institutional associations, or public interest groups to single-issue citizen groups. I rely on many of these distinctions in this analysis, but I also adapt them to the research questions of particular interest here. Primarily, I make distinctions within the citizen group category to disaggregate single-issue groups from broad citizen organizations, which I define as groups with diffuse interests—beyond one issue, one aspect of the political process, or one element of the justice system. This distinction is similar to the public interest/single issue distinction, except that I do not require that members of broad citizen groups be without a stake in the outcomes of their particular priorities.

The distinction I seek is more fundamental. I am interested in distinguishing between groups that are focused on a single aspect of the policy process (police or prisons, for example, or the death penalty) or a single crime issue (rape, for example, or drunk driving or homicide) from groups that organize around general, broad quality-of-life concerns, including but not limited to crime or the justice system. Why make this distinction? Some research over the past decade suggests that single-issue citizen groups may dominate the citizen group category of interests but may not be all that representative of citizen concerns. Single-issue groups tend to draw in the most passionate, most preference-intense citizens, who may also be the most extreme in their views.[84] Furthermore, groups with a single focus may have an easier time migrating across legislative agendas when they see an opportunity arise. Broad citizen groups, on the other hand, have more diffuse interests, spanning a range of quality-of-life concerns beyond specific crimes or institutions. Because they form to address a broader range of public safety or quality-of-life issues, they are more likely to represent a wide range of citizen interests and may be less likely to propose specific, concrete policy options. As such, they may have more difficulty overcoming collective action problems, and their presence or absence from different legislative agendas reflects the impact of federalism on collective action and group representation. These groups are also of particular interest in crime control because they are most likely to represent interests that are decoupled from bureaucratic imperatives or highly charged emotional responses to criminal behavior. They are also likely to capture groups representing citizens whose crime victimization is coupled with concern for community members who may be caught up in anticrime strategies. I also create a separate category for civil liberties groups. While the interests of these groups can be quite broad (the ACLU, for example) they tend to focus narrowly on legal responses to problems in the justice system. I discuss the limitations of civil liberties groups for representing the interests of the urban poor and urban minorities in chapters 4 and 7.

To be clear, my definition of broad citizen groups does not refer to how broadly or widely groups are supported but rather to the breadth of interests and concerns they bring to the policy process. Thus, for example, while some victims' rights groups, such as the Jacob Wetterling Foundation, may be seen as having a broad public mandate, I consider these groups to be single-issue ones because of their singular focus on one type of crime (child sexual assault) or on increasing punishment. I make this distinction because, as the empirical chapters will demonstrate, some of the groups that appear to have broad public appeal, for example MADD, the NRA, and groups focused on child sex crimes, are actually quite narrow in terms of the populations they directly represent, as well as in their problem definitions and policy proposals.

In addition to these distinctions among citizen groups, I bring representatives of the criminal justice system—police, prosecutors, judges, corrections officers, probation and parole agents, crime victims' compensation boards—into the analysis and treat them as another group participant in the policy process. While bureaucrats are not interest groups in the traditional sense, they clearly play a role in the political process and operate in much in the same way as interest groups.[85] They are a clear and effective presence that lobbies for the interests of professionals involved in the criminal justice system. Their ongoing and increasing presence in crime policy warrants attention, and to the extent that they bring policy goals and preferences to the policy process, they are interests that compete with other groups for problem definitions and policy solutions.[86]

Thus, the interest groups are analyzed on the basis of the following categories:

- *Government groups*
  - o *Criminal justice agencies:* Includes the professional associations that represent these agency interests, e.g., the Pennsylvania

District Attorneys Association, the Correctional Association of America, the International Association of Police Chiefs

- *Prosecutors*: e.g., district attorneys, district attorneys' associations, prosecuting attorneys, attorneys general, U.S. attorneys
- *Law enforcement*: local, state, and federal law enforcement departments, sheriff's associations, county constable associations, Fraternal Order of Police
- *Other criminal justice agents*: prison administrators and staff, judges, probation officers, parole boards, wardens, corrections officers, crime prevention commissions, sentencing commissions
  - o *Government (noncriminal justice) agencies:* elected officials, municipal and state governments, e.g., state legislators, U.S. Senators, city council members, Department of Human Services, Department of Health and Public Welfare, etc.; includes organizations representing government employees, e.g., AFSCME
- *Professional, business, and trade associations and organizations:* groups focused on the issues that relate to their members' professional affiliations
  - o *Legal:* law-related organizations, law firms, law schools, associations of private attorneys, e.g., American Bar Association, county bar associations, law schools
  - o *Medical:* medical organizations, hospitals, health-care associations, medical schools, e.g., American Medical Association, Hospital Association of America.
  - o *Educational:* universities, elementary and secondary schools, and teachers' unions, e.g., School Boards Association, National Education Association
  - o *Religious:* religious institutions and religious associations, e.g., Evangelical Lutheran Church of America, Concerned Jewish Women of America
  - o *Social service:* private sector organizations dedicated to providing social services, including youth services, drug and alcohol treatment services, senior assistance services, e.g., Children's Advocacy Centers, Adoption Councils[87]
  - o *Business:* private businesses, e.g., Liberty Management Systems, Behavior Technology, Inc.
  - o *Unions:* Traditional labor unions, e.g., AFL-CIO, AFSCME
- *Citizen organizations:* any group in which membership is not based on the professional, vocational, or business interests of its members
  - o *Single-issue groups:* groups focused on one particular crime or one institutions of the criminal justice system: NRA, MADD, Pennsylvania Coalition Against Rape (PCAR), Drug Policy

TABLE 1.1. A Typology of Interest Group Participation in Policymaking

Type of mobilization	National	State	Local
Hyper	Yes	Yes	Yes
Top-heavy	Yes	Yes	No
Split	Yes	No	Yes
National	Yes	No	No
State	No	Yes	No
Bottom-heavy	No	Yes	Yes
Local	No	No	Yes
Unmobilized	No	No	No

Alliance, Families Against Mandatory Minimums, Sentencing Project, Mothers for Police Accountability
- o *Broad groups:* focused more broadly on the criminal justice system or related social, economic, political issues: the National Association for the Advancement of Colored People (NAACP), Kensington Neighbors Association, Urban League, ACORN, Parents Against Violence, neighborhood associations, community councils[88]
- o *Civil liberties groups:* ACLU
• *Individual citizens:* individuals who appear at a hearing but are unaffiliated with any group

In order to assess the range of groups participating in crime policy at each legislative venue, I develop a typology of interest group representation that identifies the relative strength of group participation at each level of government (table 1.1). When groups are mobilized at each level, for example, I call this hypermobilization, whereas when groups are active in only national and local levels I refer to this as split mobilization.

This typological frame will allow me to assess group participation in crime policy making at each level of government. I suggest that professional interests (including criminal justice agencies) and single-issue citizen groups will be hypermobilized or top-heavy whereas broad citizen groups will be largely locally mobilized or, in a few specific instances, bottom-heavy. Other groups, professional associations, government agencies (noncriminal justice), and individuals will vary by substantive topic area but will be largely top-heavy.

Summary of the Chapters

The goals of this book are threefold. First, I offer an empirical mapping of the range of interests across all three levels of government in an important policy domain. Second, I move beyond the limits of current theoretical and empirical work on crime policy to develop a conceptual frame for understanding variation in crime policy environments in a federal political system. Finally, this project provides a foundation for assessing our historical and current understandings of the nature of U.S. federalism and the position of citizen groups with broad quality-of-life concerns within them.

Chapters 2 and 3 offer extensive analysis of interest group activity in Congress. Chapter 2 focuses on a political history of crime on the congressional agenda. I do this in part because there has been so much attention to national crime agendas beginning in the 1960s that a closer look at the longer institutional development is warranted. This chapter provides an important historical context for the emergence of crime as a major policy issue in Congress and reveals a gradual process that was sometimes punctuated by rapid change as crime emerged as a national policy issue. By the end of World War II, much of the scaffolding for what would later become the national crime agenda was already erected: well-worn paths of access for policy entrepreneurs and interest groups addressing high-profile crimes against women and children, executive institutions aimed at attacking crime through aggressive law enforcement, limited pathways of access for blacks as victims, and a decoupling of crime from broader racial and economic inequalities.

Chapter 3 picks up where chapter 2 left off and provides extensive data analysis of crime on the congressional agenda and of witnesses at legislative hearings from World War II through 2002. This chapter demonstrates the rise of criminal justice agencies and single-issue citizen groups as central players in the national policy process.[89] A few broad citizen groups, such as the NAACP, Operation PUSH (People United to Serve Humanity), and United Puerto Ricans of Greater Miami, made their way into the congressional policy process during the particularly politicized decade of the late 1960s to mid-1970s, but after the frenzied attention to law and order waned and the policy environment settled into a more stable pattern, all but a few of these types of groups fell off the legislative agenda entirely. A wide range of professional associations contributed to the policy environment, but they primarily represented highly organized elites, for example research and policy analysts and national social service organizations. The analysis ranges across the spectrum of crime issues, from substantive crime concerns such as guns, drugs, and domestic violence to procedural and oversight concerns such as policing strategies and sentencing rules.

Chapter 4, following a similar path, traces the development of crime in state legislatures and then zeroes in on crime on the legislative agenda in Pennsylvania. Utilizing an innovative, original dataset of legislative hearings, the analysis reveals the deep convergence of interests between criminal justice agencies—particularly prosecutors—and single-issue citizen groups. In fact, even fewer citizen groups make their way into the state crime policy process than the national one. The process is dominated by criminal justice agencies and a few high-profile groups, such as the ACLU, the NRA, MADD, and women's antiviolence groups. Professional groups are heavily skewed toward legal organizations, for example public defender and bar associations.

Chapters 5 and 6 explore the two local sites, Philadelphia and Pittsburgh, paying particular attention to the quantity and quality of citizen group access. Chapter 5 illustrates the dramatic participation of urban citizen groups, particularly broad groups—for example neighborhood associations, community reform groups, mothers organizations, ex-offender groups, block watches, and civic organizations—for whom crime is one social problem among many that they must confront. These groups participate in local politics at an impressive rate, accounting for large portions of the witnesses at hearings and the dominant groups mentioned by legislators. This chapter also analyzes the strength of these groups' presence in local political activity on the basis of whether they were to be found on the Internal Revenue Service's List of Charitable Organizations, in local newspaper stories, or on the Internet. Chapter 6 delves into the type of problem frames and solutions these groups bring to the policy process and contrasts them with the standard messages transmitted to policymakers by police and prosecutors. This chapter demonstrates how the mobilization of bias operates to crowd out groups with diffuse interests that have far more nuanced and practical policy concerns than can be easily articulated at the state and national levels.

Chapter 7 concludes with a discussion of the significance of the mobilization of bias in federalism for the crime policy process and policy outcomes and for democratic politics more generally. Here, I draw together literature on crime, urban politics, race, and federalism to develop a framework for assessing the participation of various types of groups across legislative venues. This chapter also discusses how the representational biases of federalism may apply to other policy venues and the implications for understanding democratic representation and accountability. As this chapter demonstrates, this book is not a defense of localism. Rather, its purpose is call attention to how federalism divides democratic participation and state accountability in ways that strengthen existing power differentials and disadvantage those groups already marginalized in the political process. Federalism divides and conquers, opening up pathways for highly mobilized, resource-rich groups to dominate aspects of the policy process while simultaneously limiting the capacity of groups with diffuse interests to take part in the policy process.

Two

A POLITICAL HISTORY OF CRIME
ON THE CONGRESSIONAL AGENDA

"How did you go bankrupt?" Bill asked.

"Two ways," Mike answered. "Gradually and then suddenly."

—Ernest Hemingway, *The Sun Also Rises*

L egal scholars and social scientists writing about crime policy at the national level have focused primarily on the sudden growth in federal criminal jurisdiction over the past 40 years.[1] While this growth is indisputable, the emphasis on recent years misstates the slow development of crime as a national policy issue over the course of the nation's history. A more accurate picture reflects something of Mike's answer to the question of his financial ruin in *The Sun Also Rises*. How has federal jurisdiction over ordinary crimes grown so large? *Gradually* over the course of the nation's first 150 years, and then *suddenly* in the wake of social upheavals, increasing crime rates, racial prejudice, and dramatic changes to the structure of American politics. This perspective on crime in national politics is consistent with recent research on the dramatic increases in incarceration rates in the 1970s and 1980s and also with more general American politics scholarship illustrating that attention to social problems can evolve both gradually and suddenly.[2] Each process has important implications for how issues are framed, the groups that participate in the policy process, and the institutions that emerge as a result of agenda attention.

There are several limitations to short-term analyses of national crime policy. First and foremost, they miss an opportunity to see how paths of access to policy making become smoothed in favor of specific actors and policy entrepreneurs over a long period of time. The interaction between institutional arrangements and group participation can strengthen those groups and lead to the salience of their specific policy frames, reinforcing the initial group dynamics.[3] Second, the post-1960s analysis often treats crime control as exogenous to the routine political processes that shape other policy domains. In this formulation, national crime policy emerges from what Naomi Murakawa aptly calls a "*zeitgeist* that does not account for the mechanisms that translate sensibility into policy," or "a set of actions without actors."[4] As a result, we know little about the specific aspects of the policy process that drive crime policy agendas at the congressional level. Finally, a longer historical view reveals that the racial dynamics of national crime policy have roots far deeper than the racial tensions of the 1960s, and that the racialized nature of national crime debates is deeply intertwined with the dynamic shifts in jurisdiction and power between state and national governments through the nineteenth and early twentieth centuries. Dramatic changes to the economy, technology, and demographics not only pushed old institutions to pursue new goals (such as congressional efforts to regulate new crimes) but also generated new political institutions (such as the Bureau of Investigation) and innovative political pressure groups (such as the women's prohibition movement). Because this book's primary concern is causal mechanisms, which can emerge from long-standing institutional patterns and interaction with organized interests, a historic understanding of crime on the congressional agenda has direct bearing on the contemporary policy environment.

My discussion of congressional crime politics unfolds in two chapters, beginning here with a political history of the nationalization of crime and justice. I argue that the groundwork for today's congressional attention to crime was laid not in the volatile 1960s but in mundane political processes as well as the dramatic responses to social problems that riddle American political history.[5] Most research on the history of crime on the national political scene minimizes congressional and executive involvement in crime control prior to the 1960s. But by taking seriously the institution-building and policy frames generated in these earlier time periods, one can see how each point of attention contributed to a scaffolding of groups, policies, legal rules, and institutions that were poised to coalesce into the modern national policymaking process of the late twentieth century. As Marie Gottschalk notes:

> With each campaign for "law and order" and against certain crimes and vices, state capacity accrued. As each campaign receded, the institutions it created did not necessarily disappear. As the institutional capacity of the government expanded over time, the periodic calls for law and order and attacks on the designated vices of the

moment were more likely to result in concrete policies with real ramifications. The politics of law and order became less symbolic and more substantive. The propensity of politicians since the 1960s to use calls for law and order as a political mobilization strategy is distinct not because it is a new phenomenon but because it has had different consequences.[6]

These gradual developments were intertwined with race, class, and gender anxieties but were also heavily dependent on the institutional infrastructure—in particular the shifting relationship between federal and state jurisdictions—in which politicization was taking place. As a result of fluid congressional jurisdiction on crime—a direct result of federalism—paths of access to policymakers have been long established for groups with single-issue, high-profile crime concerns that resonate with the voting electorate, for example crimes against the affluent, whites, or women. In addition, the institutional dynamics of Congress decoupled the crime issue from broader race and class conflicts in ways that would have consequences for group access to the national policy process. Drawing on legal history, congressional hearings, and literature on crime on the congressional agenda, this chapter describes the gradual development of the crime issue as a national political agenda item and how the institutional paths of access have roots back to the Civil War. In particular, I emphasize the gradual erosion of distinctions between federal and state policy jurisdiction in a range of issue areas; the deep roots of Congress's interest in responding to violence; the growth of national institutions aimed at addressing crime and violence; and the role of policy entrepreneurs in maintaining congressional attention to crime and justice, each of which has created structural conditions more amenable to narrow law-and-order interests than broad citizen concerns about public safety and quality of life.

Federal Criminal Law and the Early Republic

Efforts to bring the power of the centralized government to bear on criminal behavior are nearly as old as the republic.[7] Not long after the ratification of the Constitution, Congress embarked on a process of creating, expanding, and revising the federal criminal code that continues today.[8] In fact, one of the central weaknesses of the Articles of Confederation was its inability to impose penalties for crimes against the new nation, such as counterfeiting, treason, and privacy. The Constitution itself, then, grants Congress some authority over criminal behavior. Article 1, section 8 authorizes Congress to punish "counterfeiting the Securities and current Coin of the United States," as well as "piracies and Felonies, committed on the high Seas, and Offences against the Law of Nations." Article 3, section 3 provides that "Congress shall have the power to declare the punishment of treason" and article 4, section 2 requires states to return felons from other states to their respective homes.

Congress wasted little time in creating the federal courts and adopting the first set of federal criminal laws. The Judiciary Act of 1789 established the three-tiered federal court system, and in 1790 Congress adopted the first federal crimes act, which targeted treason, murder, robbery and disfigurement on the high seas, and crimes committed on federal property (such as post offices or Indian reservations) or against the nation's emerging financial institutions.[9] Subsequent crime bills mirrored these concerns. The 1810 Postal Act, for example, criminalized the wounding of a mail carrier in the commission of a robbery, operating a competing postal system, counterfeiting, mutilating a mail bag, and obstructing the mail.[10] An 1824 act criminalized rape on the high seas, and in 1825, Congress passed another Federal Crimes Act, which included provisions for prosecuting any crime committed on federal property that was prohibited by the state in which the federal property lay, regardless of whether the action was explicitly prohibited by federal law.[11]

What is striking about these actions is Congress's willingness to regulate a wide range of substantive criminal behavior. The limitation on congressional authority in this area was largely jurisdictional, not substantive.[12] Murder, rape, larceny, assault, robbery, conspiracy, and even vandalism (note the Postal Act) were all punishable under federal law within decades of the nation's founding, and Congress seemed to have little difficulty embracing a regular role for the federal government in addressing criminal behavior. That these actions were generally restricted to geographic areas over which the national government had specific jurisdiction indicates Congress's general unwillingness to move beyond traditional jurisdictional boundaries. Nonetheless, some did advocate such a move. In 1822, James Buchanan, serving as a first-term member of the House of Representatives, may have been the first national representative to call for greater congressional involvement in crime control by advocating that "the Committee on the Judiciary be instructed to inquire whether there be any, and, if any, what, crimes not now punishable by [federal] law, to which punishments ought to be affixed."[13]

In fact, a brief but vigorous debate raged in the early nineteenth century as to whether the federal courts ought to adopt a U.S. version of English common law that would allow the central government to prosecute citizens for crimes not expressly listed in the federal criminal code. In 1812, the Supreme Court determined that the federal courts had essentially no criminal jurisdiction over common law cases, and while some representatives continued to press Congress to establish such jurisdiction, it refused to do so as the Court repeatedly reaffirmed the federal courts' limited jurisdiction.[14] Prior to the Civil War, then, given the narrow jurisdiction of the federal criminal law, congressional activity on crime was infrequent, and when it did occur, it dealt primarily with creating a federal code that could address criminal behavior on federal property, by federal employees, or on the high seas or could confront criminal law issues with an explicit national focus, such as slavery and war.[15]

A series of additional court decisions confirmed that the jurisdiction of federal courts would be confined primarily to geographic locations belonging to the nation as a whole, rather than individual states. Most notably, Chief Justice John Marshall affirmed that a seaman charged with murder while aboard the U.S. ship of war *Independence* as it was anchored in Boston harbor was not "cognizable in the circuit court for the District of Massachussetts."[16] Nonetheless, the range of actual criminal behaviors that federal criminal laws targeted was bounded largely by the narrow jurisdiction of national government at the time. Concurrent jurisdiction for certain types of actions, as in the 1798 Bank Act, which punished forgery of currency from the Bank of the United States but did not preclude states from prosecuting such acts as well, had already been established by the late eighteenth century.[17]

Shifting Jurisdictional Terrain

In permanently rearranging the jurisdictional boundaries between the national and state governments, the Civil War began a process of rewriting the U.S. political landscape that would continue with the New Deal, the aftermath of World War II, and the Great Society programs of the 1960s. The incremental institutionalization of crime on the national legislative agenda was punctuated by these dramatic changes that left permanent legacies on the institutional infrastructure of America politics. With the enactment of the Thirteenth, Fourteenth, and Fifteenth Amendments to the Constitution and the massive initial efforts at Reconstruction, Congress embraced a new national policymaking role. Emboldened by the Union victory and the Civil War Amendments, Congress claimed the authority to protect civil rights by imposing criminal liability on the deprivation of the rights granted to all citizens. Though much of this legislation was struck down by the Supreme Court, the claim nonetheless demonstrates Congress's willingness as an institution to push the boundaries of its existing powers to enact federal criminal statutes.[18] In particular, it illustrates that as jurisdictional boundaries began to shift in the aftermath of the Civil War, Congress quickly stepped into the breach to create new areas of federal criminal law.

Between the end of the Civil War and the Great Depression, Congress held hundreds of hearings on a wide range of crime topics, including riots and disorders, homicide, juvenile delinquency, drugs, rape, arson, prostitution, fraud, robbery, law enforcement, smuggling, bootlegging, corruption, and bribery.[19] By far, the most common hearings involved corruption, bribery, and fraud, with nearly 200 hearings on fraud alone by 1917. Presidents' State of the Union addresses and party platforms from the same era reveal a similar national crime agenda focused heavily on fraud and corruption.[20] Toward the end of the nineteenth century, these issues took on new urgency as the increasing mobility of goods and services generated fresh opportunities for deceit and corruption. The Post Office Act of 1872 forbidding the use of the mail system for the purposes of defrauding citizens illustrates the twin concerns of fraud and mobility.

Despite the emphasis on fraud, concerns over violence also have a long, if sporadic, history on the congressional agenda, and the Civil War and its aftermath helped shape the quantity and quality of congressional attention to crime and violence.[21] Riots and disorders were the subject of more than 80 hearings between 1867 and 1920, with over 2,000 witnesses appearing. Many of these involved post–Civil War disputes in the Reconstruction South, including 15 hearings in the 1870s about election outcomes in South Carolina, Louisiana, and Florida and 25 hearings on the East St. Louis riots alone.[22] An additional 19 hearings were on labor disputes in Michigan, Colorado, and West Virginia. Several familiar national interest groups appeared at these hearings—the Women's Christian Temperance Union, the American Bar Association, the American Drug Manufacturing Company, the Council of Jewish Women, the United Garment Workers of America. Prosecutors and police appeared regularly at these hearings as well. Most of the witnesses, however, were individuals representing their professional obligation or themselves as citizens, including railroad workers, printers, farmers, carpenters, and just plain residents. A few hearings even had representation from the most enduring and dangerous organized interest group in American history, the Ku Klux Klan.[23]

Congress's Reconstruction efforts were all but undone by the former confederate states' increasing resistance to civil rights legislation, the Supreme Court's complicity in the undermining of congressional civil rights goals, and the contested presidential election of 1876, wherein white segregationists accepted the presidency of Rutherford B. Hayes in exchange for removal of federal troops from southern states.[24] The end of Reconstruction and the reentrenchment of white supremacy in the South were important developments for national crime politics because they contributed to a blocking of pathways for black leaders to draw congressional attention to the problems of black victimization and to a process where blacks as victims of racist violence were largely written out of the national policy process. The Supreme Court participated in this counterrevolution by gutting the Fourteenth Amendment's privileges and immunities clause in *Slaughter-House Cases*, refusing to recognize any new, affirmative rights in the Civil War Amendments in *U.S. v. Cruickshank*, voiding the criminal conspiracy section of the Ku Klux Klan Act of 1871 (*U.S. v. Harris* 1882), and, in culmination, completely repudiating congressional authority to enact legislation aimed at protecting individual citizens against the discriminatory actions of other citizens in the *Civil Rights Cases* in 1883.[25] In his lengthy dissenting opinion, Justice John Marshall Harlan articulates the majority position and his opposition to it:

> The opinion of the court, as I have said, proceeds upon the ground that the power of congress to legislate for the protection of the rights and privileges secured by the 14th amendment cannot be brought into activity except with the view, and as it may become necessary, to correct and annul state laws and state proceedings in hostility to such rights and privileges. In the absence of state laws or state action, adverse to such rights and privileges, the nation may not actively interfere for their protection and security. Such I understand to be the position of my brethren [the majority]....I venture, with all respect for the opinion of others, to insist that the national legislature may, without transcending the limits of the constitution, do for human liberty and the fundamental rights of American citizenship, what it did, with the sanction of this court, for the protection of slavery and the rights of the masters of fugitive slaves.[26]

A majority of the court and an increasingly large number of legislators disagreed, narrowly defining Congress's remedial powers and limiting the scope of black protection from white violence for another 75 years. These developments illustrate how the stunted efforts to assist black victims of violence and intimidation contributed to a political landscape in which many national lawmakers were unwilling to see blacks as victims. Equally as important, the institutional context in which these lawmakers found themselves made it almost impossible to do so.

In fact, the majority opinion in *Cruickshank* illustrates the framework of national crime politics with respect to black victims that would remain dominant for the next century. *Cruickshank* involved white defendants charged with conspiring to keep blacks from peaceable assembly, bearing arms, and voting. The court determined that the black citizens were not protected from infringement by private citizens on any of these actions. The First and Second Amendments merely restricted *Congress's* ability to limit the right of citizens to assembly or to bear arms, and no such protections from the actions of private citizens, the Court ruled, existed under Louisiana state law. Furthermore, the Fifteenth Amendment did not guarantee the right to vote; it simply barred states from basing the franchise on race, color, or creed. Consistent with the blind eye Congress would turn toward black victimization over the next 80 years, the majority in *Cruickshank* determined that

> there is no allegation that this was done because of the race or color of the persons conspired against. When stripped of its verbiage, the case as presented amounts to nothing more than that the defendants conspired to prevent certain citizens of the United States, being within the State of Louisiana, from enjoying the equal protection of the laws of the State and of the United States.[27]

The Supreme Court's opinion clearly delineates the powers of Congress and the states, which would remain in dramatic and sometimes violent conflict with one another well into the twentieth century.

By the late nineteenth and early twentieth century, Congress's crime focus began shifting away from civil rights enforcement and labor strife to crimes involving white women, drugs, and obscenity. Fraud and deception also continued to occupy congressional attention and occasionally intersected with moral concerns, resulting in legislation designed to regulate, control, or otherwise manage the growing mobility and ease of communication that made criminal conspiracies more likely. Emboldened by the Supreme Court decision in *Champion v. Ames*, 1902, which upheld Congress's plan to prohibit the interstate transportation of lottery tickets, Congress continued its expansion of regulations against allegedly dangerous products through its commerce and postal powers.[28] Driven in part by moral entrepreneurs like Anthony Comstock and the Society for the Suppression of Vice, initial attention centered on sexuality and moral depravity. In an early example of the interaction between a single-issue group interest and government institutions, the Comstock Law brought together a growing bureaucratic agency, the Post Office, with a highly mobilized group of purity activists who successfully shoehorned antiobscenity legislation into Congress's interstate commerce powers.[29] The Comstock Law, passed in 1873, resulted in Comstock's appointment as a special agent of the Post Office, which allowed him to travel the country identifying and confiscating obscene materials. Despite opposition to the federal law, which began almost immediately after it was passed and grew rapidly, as Morone notes, "Comstock was still racking up legal victories into the 1910s, long after obscenity had given way to entirely different kinds of panics."[30]

The juxtaposition of two important pieces of legislation in the early 1900s illustrates both the way institutional arrangements provided more opportunities for whites than blacks to access the growing congressional jurisdiction over crime and the interaction between race and federalism. The Mann Act, which criminalized the transportation of women across state lines for any sexual activity, passed in 1910, despite objections that it interfered with traditional boundaries of congressional and state regulatory powers.[31] Drawing on the emergence of the aforementioned congressional legislation that was aimed at ferreting out corruption, fraud, and criminal enterprises benefiting from the new communication and transportation technologies, the Mann Act was not so far afield from other recent federal legislation. Many of the arguments made in favor of the Act, however, could have easily been used to support the antilynching legislation that black civil rights leaders and some members of Congress favored at the time. Lynchings, while not exclusively used against blacks, were frequently used to terrorize blacks and prevent them from exercising their newly proffered civil rights.[32] Of course, white segregationists and virtually all of the southern delegation to Congress opposed such legislation. But antilynching legislation faced additional obstacles because it challenged the delicate balance between congressional and state sovereignty that remained extremely fragile after the Civil War. Supporters of antilynching legislation argued that U.S. citizens deserved the protection of the federal law when states refused to enforce fundamental rights such as equal protection. Congress had passed several pieces of legislation during Reconstruction that criminalized conspiracies to deprive citizens of constitutional rights.[33] Opponents argued that Congress had no power to criminalize the behavior of private citizens, even if those citizens were attempting to deprive blacks of their civil rights. The "state action doctrine" articulated most clearly by the Supreme Court in the *Civil Rights Cases* narrowed the range of discriminatory actions that Congress could address by reading the Fourteenth Amendment's equal protection clause to apply only to discriminatory actions implemented by the states, which essentially excluded actions taken by private parties, such as lynch mobs.

The central problem for antilynching law advocates thus lay with the claim that blacks were being denied equal protection of the law by the states' refusal to protect them from white lynch mobs. Opponents argued that the Fourteenth Amendment did not give Congress the authority to act since lynch mobs were private citizens, though it was widely known that they often operated under the color of the local law enforcement or, at least, with its implicit sanction.[34] A series of federal court cases strengthened this position. In *Hodges v. U.S.*, for example, the Supreme Court denied the government's claim that the Thirteenth Amendment, banning involuntary servitude, gave Congress the power to prohibit private action that interfered with black civil rights.[35] The Court ruled that the Thirteenth Amendment applied to all citizens, not just blacks, and then kept the scope of the Amendment's prohibition on involuntary servitude narrow. Opponents of antilynching legislation also openly invoked racial prejudice. With vivid racial imagery, Representative Benjamin Tillman of South Carolina argued that an antilynching bill proposed by Representative Dyer would eliminate the state and

> substitute for the starry banner of the Republic, a black flag of tyrannical centralized government, a black flag indeed, black as melted midnight, black as the dust on the hinges to the gates of hell, black as the face and heart of the rapist.[36]

The juxtaposition of the Mann Act and antilynching legislation illustrates the long-standing patterns of access, problem definitions, and institutional arrangements that characterized congressional attention to crime in the early twentieth century. Anxieties over an increasingly mobile world in which young women might be whisked away by strange and dangerous men actually meshed reasonably well with growing federal jurisdiction over criminal activity that crossed states lines. While the underlying problem—"white slavery"—was probably quite limited in scope, particularly relative to the claims made by proponents of the bill, the problem, as least hypothetically, was nonetheless one Congress was arguably well situated to address with its interstate commerce powers. The Comstock Law had already established precedent for Congress to regulate the use of the interstate mail system to send obscene materials across the states, so the notion that moving actual people across state lines for "obscene" or "immoral" purposes would be within Congress's commerce clause powers was not so much of a stretch.[37]

Antilynching legislation, however, posed a different set of problems. On the one hand, there is the inescapable fact that racial prejudice and the invisibility of blacks as victims made it difficult for lawmakers to grasp the scope of the problem. One congressional delegate from Congress complained that floor debates in the House had degenerated into debates over "the constitutional right to burn fellow citizens alive."[38] The ongoing anxieties of white southerners that they would be overrun by free blacks if Congress were given authority to fully enforce equal protection of the laws animated the South's response to a great many congressional policy proposals in the twentieth century. The antilynching legislation anchors one end of that century and illustrates the deep racial animosity that limited the extent of protection black victims could expect from their national lawmakers.

It would be misleading, however, to characterize the differences between the Mann Act and the anti-lynching bills as hinging entirely on race. In fact, the anti-lynching bill did pose constitutional problems at the time that were not so easily resolved and were less apparent in the Mann

Act with its interstate component. In the late nineteenth and early twentieth centuries, the federal courts were actively striking down congressional statutes aimed at breaking up corporate trusts, limiting child labor, and other aspects of commercial activity, which were arguably even more connected to Congress's enumerated powers than criminal legislation.[39] And congressional power to enact criminal legislation was being challenged in federal court, with the Supreme Court clearly articulating in 1876 that Congress did not have the power to make murder a punishable crime under federal law, absent some clear federal jurisdictional issue.[40] And it wasn't just the judiciary that resisted congressional encroachment into traditional state police powers. States themselves came into conflict with Congress over its attempts to expand its jurisdiction, particularly over legislation such as Prohibition and even the Mann Act. Antilynching legislation thus raised the stakes by proposing to grant federal jurisdiction over criminal activity that had traditionally fallen wholly within the power of state criminal courts.

One strategy antilynching advocates proposed was for Congress to use its war powers to grant the executive branch the authority to prosecute lynching as an interference with the war effort in Europe. At a 1918 hearing on antilynching legislation, an exchange between Representative William Igoe, a Democrat from Missouri, and two representatives from Military Intelligence illustrates the tension between state and federal jurisdiction over criminal matters:

> REP. IGOE: Have you ever considered the other side of this question, and that is the possible resentment on the part of States against a law which might interfere with the jurisdiction of the State courts in the prosecution of crimes?
>
> MAJOR SPRINGARN: Well, sir, in answer to that I should say, first, that it was to avoid any semblance of such action or any semblance of the idea that it was directed against any section or State that the bill was drafted under the war powers and not under the Fourteenth Amendment...
>
> [LATER] REP. IGOE: do you think that we could go beyond [protecting] those who are in the service or are liable to service in the army?
>
> MAJOR SPRINGARN: I think so, in the same way that you are providing the war-risk insurance act for the families of the men you have called into service.
>
> REP. IGOE: But in doing so under the war-risk insurance act we are not interfering with the States, or taking any jurisdiction away from them. We have the right, of course, to provide for the men in the military service and their dependents out of the Treasury of the US. There is no question about that.

CAPT. HORNBLOWER: But it grows out of the war powers of Congress. The only power expressly granted you by the Constitution to do that is under the war power.

MR. IGOE: There is a great distinction there between paying money out of the Treasury of the U.S. to certain classes of people and this case where we would be invading the jurisdiction of the States themselves.

CAPT. HORNBLOWER: You gentlemen felt that it was constitutional to provide that the federal government should punish a man in a State who would turn to somebody on the street corner and say, "Don't you go in and register for military service; don't do it; it is a bad thing to do." You punish such a man under the Federal law.

MR. IGOE: That would be interfering with the registration of soldiers or recruiting the Army.

CAPT. HORNBLOWER: Maj. Springarn is here to testify that the situation which now exists may interfere with the recruiting of enlisted men or the service of the U.S. and may seriously interfere with the morale of a large body of people from whom soldiers are drawn.[41]

In fact, antilynching legislation did reflect something qualitatively different from the other war powers to which Captain Hornblower refers. On those matters, states simply had no jurisdiction, and Congress was empowered to act through its constitutionally derived war powers. Violence that had not taken place on federal property, involved federal employees, or crossed state lines, however, had long been reserved to states and localities, and the Supreme Court had recently determined that Congress did not have general police powers over crimes such as homicide. Clearly state and local governments were turning a blind eye toward lynchings (indeed, often encouraging them), but the larger question of federal jurisdiction remained, at least for another two decades.

To be sure, Representative Igoe's queries no doubt reflected a desire to keep the federal government out of southern affairs wherever blacks were concerned, but they also reflected the uneasy balance of power between states and the federal government. Indeed, debates about the Mann Act reflected similar concerns, and Representative Mann himself took care to make the boundaries of the legislation clear:

The legislation is not needed or intended as an aid to the states in the exercise of their police powers in the suppression or regulation of immorality in general. It does not attempt to regulate the practice of voluntary prostitution, but aims solely to prevent panderers and procurers from compelling thousands of women and girls against their will and desire to enter and continue in a life of prostitution.[42]

Unlike antilynching legislation, the Mann Act also came on the heels of an international agreement to break up worldwide prostitution rings to which the United States was a signatory, and even in that context legal scholars at the time and in subsequent years condemned the Mann Act for its overreach.[43]

Antilynching legislation thus came onto the congressional agenda at a time of great conflict between the national and southern states over the extent of congressional power and in the aftermath of the atrophying of congressional authority to enforce civil rights and criminalize actions by those standing in the way of those rights. In the ensuing web of conflicting legislation and court decision making, black victims of racist violence were conveniently written out of the national crime problem. The existing political structure, in which the national government's power was limited by constitutional design and by advocates of state sovereignty, helped to successfully frame the lynching issue as a function of private actions wholly internal to individual states.[44] In this view, acts of criminal violence against blacks, as well as the poor generally, were disconnected from larger economic and political forces—including but not limited to racial hierarchies—that contributed to violence and its aftermath. As the discussion between Representative Igoe and Major Springarn illustrates, some members of Congress simply could not—or would not—view violence against blacks as an outgrowth of racial hierarchies that had national political, social, and economic origins and implications. Thus, two legacies of the institutional development of congressional power regarding the criminal law during this era are the atrophied access of black leaders to congressional policy making at just the moment when lynching and other forms of segregationist violence were keeping blacks out of state and local policy making, and the decoupling of crime and criminal violence from larger, structural conditions of white supremacy and black disenfranchisement.

The other dimension of these two bills that illustrates the intersection of race and institutional power dynamics is the contrast between victims of "white slave traffickers" and victims of lynchings. While the former were fairly consistently labeled as innocents in the legislative process, the latter were routinely *relabeled* as offenders or potential offenders by southern whites who were disinclined to support greater congressional involvement in southern states' affairs, particularly—though not exclusively—if it involved blacks.[45] The opposition to lynching legislation that was offered in Congress presupposed a dangerous and uncontrollable black population (especially men) that could not be controlled by traditional legal institutions but required extralegal action.[46] At a 1921 hearing on an antilynching bill, for example, in response to allegations that black soldiers returning from the war had been lynched for wearing soldiers' uniforms, Representative Fred Dominick (D, South Carolina) denied that such an event ever took place while simultaneously implying that if it did, the behavior of colored soldiers justified white violence.

> They [colored soldiers] were just discharged from the Army; they received a bonus of $60 from Congress under the law; and they wore their uniforms around there and did not do any work. Some people undoubtedly hoped that the uniforms would soon be worn out, that their $60 bonus would soon be spent, and that "Cuffee" would get hungry, so that they could have somebody to perform labor there.[47]

Thus, white supremacists determined that the alleged victim of a lynching was not, in fact, a victim at all but at best a layabout or at worst a dangerous criminal or even just an unfortunate casualty of the larger program of social control that was necessary to keep free blacks from threatening the social order. Black victims and offenders were merged in ways that made it difficult for lawmakers, who were already on edge about the potential consequences of congressional interference into state territory, to actively and openly support legislation that was an even greater extension of Congress's power than it had previously adopted. This was particularly significant when members of Congress had little testimony from black victims—or other racial groups who were the target of lynchings—to buttress their claims for the legislation's importance. In fact, none of the five congressional hearings on antilynching legislation between 1918 and 1921 included families of lynching victims or individuals threatened with lynching, though references to them exist.[48] Only four witnesses appeared across the five hearings, with two of the hearings having no witnesses at all. A June 16, 1918, hearing before the House of Representatives Committee on the Judiciary included the two military personnel mentioned earlier.[49] On June 18, 1921, a hearing took the testimony of Representative Merrill Moores, who wrote the antilynching bill, and two days later another hearing had testimony from G. D. Goff, assistant to the U.S. attorney general.[50] The NAACP was deliberately cautious in not lobbying overtly for the bill, as it was mindful of the appearance of the bill being beneficial to blacks, which would make its passage even less likely.[51] Thus, congressional debates about black victimization took place with little commentary from the victims themselves. This transformation of victims to offenders was revisited in the 1960s when Congress considered sweeping anticrime proposals alongside civil rights legislation.[52] By that point, the eclipsing of black victims by black offenders had significant consequences for how the crime problem was defined and which interests gained access to the policy process. But as the foregoing discussion illustrates, the linkage between black victims and offenders is as much a legacy of the Civil War and the federal constitutional system as of the politics of the 1960s.

A final and crucial point about the increasing use of congressional authority to address crime problems with white or middle-class victims (such as the Dyer Act of 1919, which criminalized interstate auto theft, the Lindbergh Act of 1932, which criminalized kidnapping across state lines, and the Mann Act) concerns the institutions that are generated as a result. The Department of Justice was created in 1870.[53] But it was relatively inactive until the early twentieth century, when it began to expand as a result of new federal criminal laws and responsibilities. For example, the Bureau of Investigation, the precursor of the Federal Bureau of Investigation, was formed in 1908, largely in response to the growing number of criminal fraud, corruption, and interstate criminal investigations the Justice Department was undertaking. At the time, the department hired secret service agents from the Treasury Department to conduct these investigations, but this became an increasingly expensive and inefficient way of getting things done. Then Attorney General Charles Bonaparte made an appeal to Congress to establish a small investigative bureau within the Department of Justice.[54] Much of this investigative work involved fraud, specifically land fraud in western territories.

The Bureau of Investigation was eventually charged with enforcing both the Mann and auto-theft bills, which contributed to growth in its jurisdiction, staff, financing, and autonomy. Indeed, the Mann Act itself grew in scope to encompass not just coercive acts of prostitution but any transportation of women across state lines for immoral purposes. Despite the controversy over the Act, once it was established and began to be utilized, its scope and application grew.[55] The use of the law in this manner was upheld by the Supreme Court and allowed federal prosecutors to increase the number of convictions over the next 20 years.[56] The kidnapping and murder of Charles and Anne Lindbergh's son led to the passage of federal kidnapping laws and further charged the bureau, then headed by J. Edgar Hoover, with the responsibility of investigating interstate kidnappings.[57]

Around the same time as the antilynching debates, Congress was also pursuing antinarcotics legislation, basing its authority to regulate cocaine, heroin, and marijuana in its taxation powers, which consolidated the authority of yet another federal agency. The Harrison Narcotics Tax Act (1914) emerged from the conflicts over the international opium trade that emerged at the end of the Spanish-American War.[58] Both U.S. traders and missionaries in the Philippines, now under U.S. authority, complained about the British and Chinese opium trade, and an international conference on the topic resulted in the Hague Convention of 1912. The Harrison

Act was the U.S. response to these international efforts and was largely intended to create an orderly market in opium. However, the Treasury Department's Bureau of Narcotics quickly began to use the Act against doctors prescribing heroin for addicts. In 1923, the Treasury Department Narcotics Division banned all legal narcotics sales. Furthermore, the Volstead Act, which drew on racial prejudice to garner support for amending the Constitution to ban liquor sales, generated the Bureau of Prohibition, which originated in the Internal Revenue Bureau and then moved to the Treasury Department.[59]

The Bureaus of Narcotics, Prohibition, and Investigation would finally be collapsed into the Federal Bureau of Investigation (FBI) under the authority of the Justice Department. The evolution of the bureau would eventually lead to investigations into a long list of real and alleged subversive forces, including gangsters, communists, Nazi sympathizers, civil rights and antiwar activists, and drug conspiracies.[60] Hoover's relationship with the congressional subcommittees that were responsible for funding and oversight of the FBI was largely positive as Hoover was scrupulously attentive to public perceptions of the bureau and maintaining bureau autonomy. According to one analyst, Hoover's obsession with public support initially led him to resist investigations into subversive political activity, which he thought was beneath the bureau's skilled agents. This also meant that bureau activity would focus most heavily on criminal activities that garnered substantial public attention, such as vice, fraud, and political corruption.[61] The reorganization of the Justice Department in 1933 and its expansion in 1940 to include the Immigration and Naturalization Service (which had previously been housed in the Department of Labor) also contributed to the Department's growth.[62] Meanwhile, the revenue collectors in the Bureau of Prohibition became the Alcohol Tax Unit after the repeal of Prohibition, and this agency eventually became the Bureau of Alcohol, Tobacco and Firearms.

Of course, the New Deal introduced massive and sweeping changes to Congress's limited police powers as well. By the time the Supreme Court finally reversed 60 years of limitations on Congress's commerce power in *NLRB v. Jones* in 1937, Congress had already successfully passed several major pieces of criminal legislation (discussed previously). The New Deal and the Court's constitutional sanction of it smoothed the path for dozens more crime bills aimed at addressing the causes and consequences of the depression, including the federal criminalization of bank robbery, extortion using telephones, telegraph, or radio, transportation of stolen property across state lines, fleeing from one state to another to avoid prosecution for crimes of violence (and a few others), as well as a national firearms act.[63] The Supreme Court, with its new standard of deference to congressional decision making, generally upheld this legislation, and

Congress and the executive wasted little time in enacting and enforcing new criminal laws.[64] J. Edgar Hoover's Bureau of Investigation was at the heart of many new enforcement efforts, and the entire Department of Justice had undergone substantial reorganization and consolidation that centralized civil and criminal investigations and prosecutions.[65]

Pathways of Access to National Policymaking

Thus, on the eve of World War II, the aftermath of which would contribute to yet another dramatic transformation of domestic policy making, several important aspects of the national crime policy scaffolding had already been erected. *First*, Congress's propensity to enact criminal laws had roots deep in the nation's infrastructure and was bound only by the narrow jurisdictional terrain of national institutions during the first 80 years of the country's existence. As the federal government grew in size and scope from the Civil War to the New Deal, congressional inclinations to enact criminal law did not ebb but in fact grew along with the expanding jurisdictional boundaries in many other policy areas. In some respects, the growth of congressional jurisdiction over the criminal law is an illustration of the nationalization of a wide range of social issues in the first half of the twentieth century.[66]

Second, while corruption and fraud were the primary concerns of members of Congress between the Civil War and World War II, the national government was no stranger to other crime topics, including violence and vice, which had occupied a consistent portion of the congressional agenda since the Civil War, including hearings on obscenity, riots, labor disputes, homicide, kidnapping, arson, and even rape. Indeed, Lawrence Friedman suggests that crimes emerge on the federal docket in fits and starts: "Prohibition came and went. The effort to catch auto thieves came and went. The Mann Act came and went. Today, drug offenses have taken over these empty nests. . . . Federal criminal justice, then, has been more subject to the changing winds of politics, to fashions and movements, than the state systems; it has been more ancillary, less fundamental in focus."[67] But congressional attention to violent crime extends back into the late eighteenth century when Congress made its first efforts to address murder and rape on federal property.

Third, and related, Congress has been particularly responsive to powerful issue entrepreneurs who have pursued their interests in national politics and have taken advantage of policy windows when they have become available. This has meant that crimes in which the health and welfare of the status quo citizenry has been at stake have been more likely to gain attention than crimes involving victims from disenfranchised, marginalized, or otherwise suspicious groups. The Comstock Law and Prohibition targeted the behavior of the growing masses of immigrants flooding the nation's shores as white segregationist violence flourished in the South. Federal kidnapping legislation and auto theft prohibitions were rooted in Congress's interstate commerce clause powers and were aimed at criminal activity agitating the more affluent segments of society. The heightened public anxieties and media frenzy that the Lindbergh baby kidnapping generated, for example, were different not so much in *kind* as in *scale* from similar furors that contemporary issues, such as the Columbine school shootings in 1999, have stirred up.[68] Thus, the selective nationalization of crime contributed to the creation of a policy environment that some groups have found more hospitable to their interests than others. This has created a feedback process in which benefits to these types of groups accrue, generating more opportunities for them to participate, and further atrophying the prospects for excluded groups to get into the game.[69] Baumgartner and Jones (1993) refer to this as a positive feedback process that reinforces existing institutional arrangements, paths of access, and policy frames, making it difficult for groups that were not involved early on to gain a seat at the policymaking table.

Because of this fluid and reactive nature of congressional jurisdiction over crime, the national crime agenda has long been sensitive to policy entrepreneurs who press their cases before Congress, picking up the crime issue du jour—particularly, it seems, if the alleged criminal behavior threatens economic stability, established interests, or white women. That much of the national crime agenda emerged from white majorities' resistance to the integration of immigrants and former slaves into mainstream political and economic life is an important element in the resultant institution-building. Congressional attention to interstate crime and crimes against white women gained more traction than run-of-the-mill criminal activity within the traditional reach of state legislatures. Even with the growth of congressional jurisdiction over a wide range of social issues, local and state police powers remained, creating a context in which some crime issues would be addressed by Congress but the vast majority remained at the regional levels. As the foregoing discussion illustrates, this vast expanse of potential policy issues is not equally accessible to all interested parties. When issues expand onto the national legislative arena, prevailing stereotypes about race, class, and gender can actually distort policy environments in ways that limit access for minorities and the poor.[70]

Fourth, national institutions to address crime and violence were limited in the late nineteenth and early twentieth centuries but were rapidly increasing in scope and poised to expand their jurisdiction under the right internally or externally driven circumstances. Increasing congressional attention to crime generated bureaucratic agencies—the FBI and a formally organized Justice Department, as well as more professionalized state and local law enforcement—that have emerged as central players in contemporary national crime policy agenda setting and implementation. In fact, Prohibition itself, though eventually repealed, contributed substantially to the national criminal justice agenda. "Prohibition would rewrite American federalism, criminal justice, the courts, civil liberties, crime-fighting, crime families, and national attitudes. Americans still live with its legacy."[71] It is also probably the first time that federal law enforcement and prosecutors engaged in formal, organized cooperation with their state and local counterparts.[72] As scholars of bureaucratic developments have noted, incrementalism typically characterizes changes in the scope and resources of government agencies, and the gradual expansion of federal crime-fighting authority over the course of the twentieth century is a crucial component of the institutional arrangements that characterize the national crime policy environment today. Herb Jacob notes that this incremental process helps explain the growth in municipal police expenditures in the second half of the twentieth century, and the federal budget reveals similar patterns.[73] Indeed, at the end of World War II, federal expenditures on law enforcement, prosecutions, and the federal judiciary were still relatively small, with money for policing, prosecutions, and judges accounting for less than two-tenths of 1 percent of the federal budget. Once these agencies had gained a foothold in the federal budget, however, and spending on all kinds of activity began to grown in the 1950s and 1960s, these agencies rarely slipped back to the status quo.[74] Exogenous shocks to the system, such as the growth in crime rates, race riots, and political violence during the 1960s and 1970s did not create these agencies but certainly contributed to expansions in their scope and resources. Their mere existence has generated opportunities for attention and for policy agendas that have emphasized law enforcement, interdiction, arrests, and investigation.

Finally, the race and gender dynamics of Congress's attention to crime were well entrenched long before World War II. The juxtaposition of the Mann Act and antilynching legislation illustrates how the paths of access for congressional attention to crime were smoothed for middle-class and white victims relative to nonwhites and the poor. As important, if not more so, the emphasis on white victims decoupled the crime problem from the race and class stratification that so clearly marked the first half of the twentieth century. While some explanations for racially divisive outcomes are rooted in straightforward racial bias explanations, others also emerge because of institutional dynamics that make it difficult to address issues at the intersection of race and class.[75] While racial bias clearly played a role in opposition to antilynching legislation, the challenge that such legislation posed to the federal nature of the U.S. political system contributed to a policy environment in which advocates who wished to link lynching to more systematic white supremacy efforts were highly constrained in their ability to do so. The victimization of blacks in former confederate states, for example, was difficult to make visible in the policy debates in Congress. Members of Congress who were supportive of the legislation had a difficult enough time overcoming the constitutional challenges, not to mention grappling with the larger issues of equality and justice that the systematic violence and intimidation of blacks raised. It was far more consistent with Congress's constitutional mandate and institutional structure to focus on interstate crime, over which much of the public was agitated, than to address long-standing social and political inequalities that required rethinking the constitutional balance of power, not to mention dismantling 200 years of social inequities. As others have shown, racial divisions and white supremacy were not merely in the hearts and minds of individuals but were at the very core of U.S. federal constitutional design and political ideologies.[76] These developments also illustrated how easily efforts to call attention to black victimization in Congress evolved into debates about black criminality. This process would gain momentum again in the 1960s, as rising crime rates and urban riots gave Republicans and southern Democrats even more traction to make such links.

Crime has been an intermittent issue on the congressional agenda since the early days of the Republic. Federal law enforcement has occupied a central role in the development of some key crime legislation during the twentieth century. The FBI, for example, became a regular and significant player in national crime politics not only as a result of several high-profile cases but also as a function of the expansion of government powers under the New Deal.[77] The Justice Department, more generally, is arguably the most central group presence in the national crime policy process, and one research project identified it as just about the only lobbyist to participate in drafting criminal law at the congressional level.[78] Though few scholars have systematically examined interest group activity in national crime legislation, there is a general consensus about the centrality of criminal justice agencies.[79]

An important theme of the interest group environment in national crime politics is the periodic emergence of moral panics or antisin crusades throughout American history and their role in shaping crime agendas.[80] National anticrime agendas have often addressed a single vice issue that has mobilized specific segments of society—those opposing prostitution, liquor, drugs, obscenity, or urban riots, for example. This is particularly noteworthy because as the political dynamics of group participation in national politics shifted in the 1960s to include a greater number of citizen organizations, the pathways of access to the policy process have been easier for groups with such high-profile vice constituencies than for groups without them. Indeed, Gottschalk (2006) and Morone (2003) both illustrate the importance of social movements and policy entrepreneurs in generating specific policy goals and normative frameworks in which crime and violence have been addressed. In particular, Gottschalk identifies the women's, victims', and prisoners' rights movements as contributing to an increasingly punitive national discourse on crime. This suggests that policy entrepreneurs—groups with a focus on high-profile crimes and race, class, and gender dynamics—are all potentially important aspects of the congressional crime policy environment. Thus, just prior to World War II, the pathway to congressional attention for certain groups and specific types of crimes had already been created—criminal justice agencies, moral issues, drugs, white victims, alcohol—while the pathways for others had either *eroded* or had never had the opportunity to become established: black interests, race and class stratification, Klan and other white supremacy violence. As the interests of dominant groups were threatened—through people's increased mobility, and through the increasingly influential mass media with their attention to celebrities and their families—Congress responded by creating new laws and institutions. As these institutions gained strength, patterns of access were established that defined the crime problem in such a way as to privilege narrowly tailored groups focused on morality and to deemphasize broader victimization based on race or class status. These important developments that began in the early twentieth century have had lasting institutional consequences for understanding group representation in congressional crime control politics today.[81]

Three

CONTEMPORARY CRIME POLITICS
IN CONGRESS

The Violent Crime Control and Law Enforcement Act of 1994 authorized
the expenditure of $30.2 billion dollars, including $13.5 billion for law
enforcement, $9.9 billion for prison construction and $6.9 billion for
crime prevention. The measure also made 60 federal crimes eligible for
the death penalty and mandated life sentences for "three strikes" violent
felons.

    —Michael Flamm, *Law and Order: Street Crime, Civil Unrest and the
Crisis of Liberalism in the 1960s* (2005)

Chapter 2 argued that the emergence of crime on the
congressional agenda had its origins in a gradual and sometimes sudden process involving shifting national and state jurisdiction,
highly mobilized policy entrepreneurs, and emerging political institutions
that shaped the policy environment and contributed to smooth paths of
access for criminal justice agencies and narrow citizen groups. In particular, criminal justice agencies became central to national crime politics,
and issue activists who called attention to crimes threatening whites and
women (particularly as those groups intersected) had an easier time than
those drawing attention to crimes against blacks and other marginalized
populations. These early efforts led to the institutionalization and growth
of federal agencies whose missions expanded with the rise of new crimes,
new issues, and new organized groups.

This chapter draws on three data sources to assess the relationship
between institutional venues and political representation on crime and
justice issues in Congress from 1947 to 2002. The first dataset includes

all congressional hearings on crime topics during that period (n = 2903). The second consists of a sample of those hearings (n = 574) and analysis of the group witnesses represented therein (n = 5764). Third, I analyze all of the congressional hearings from 1991 to 1998 on six substantive crime topics: drugs, crime prevention and riots, juveniles, crimes against women and children, police/weapons, and the criminal code (n = 301 hearings, 2,385 witnesses).[1] In each analysis involving witnesses, I pay particular attention to the role of citizen groups, bureaucratic actors, and the nature of crime hearings. This chapter demonstrates that the emergence of the modern policymaking process in the late twentieth century, coupled with the social cleavages and racial stratification of the 1950s and 1960s social movements, provided a few opportunities for representation of urban crime victims but largely reinforced and solidified previous patterns of group access. These changes contributed to a policy environment in which highly mobilized groups, such as bureaucratic agencies of the criminal justice system and a few single-issue citizen groups, were able to translate their interests into relatively stable patterns of national political representation, crowding out less formally organized groups and those with a more diffuse focus. As a result, the policy environment for crime and justice concerns at the national level simplifies complex social processes that contribute to crime and violence; decouples crime and victimization from broader historic structural phenomena, including white supremacy and systematic racial hierarchy; and relies heavily on criminal justice experts in the problem definition stage of policy making. This process thus generates the kind of reflexive, internal bureaucratic goals for policy outcomes that disaggregate the activities of criminal justice agencies from broader social problems.[2] Somewhat paradoxically, while single-issue citizen groups proliferated and victims' "rights" gained momentum in the late twentieth century, the present crime policy environment brings together groups whose interests intersect more readily on punishing offenders than on reducing harm to victims or mitigating the factors that lead to victimization in the first place.

Crime and Congress in the Latter Twentieth Century

The post–World War II period witnessed dramatic growth in congressional attention to all kinds of social problems, including but not limited to, crime.[3] This is important, as the growing attention to crime can be seen in the context of an expanding national government that was pressed to address a wide a range of new issues. As chapter 2 showed, the primary obstacle to extensive congressional involvement in the criminal law was

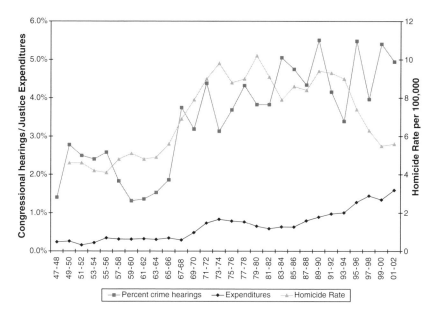

Figure 3.1. Congressional hearings, spending on crime, and homicide rates (per 100,000), by congressional years, 1947–2002

jurisdictional, but as federal and state boundaries shifted through the Civil War, the Great Depression, and World Wars I and II, Congress increased its attention to crime. Through the 1950s and 1960s, boundaries between federal, state, and local jurisdictions eroded even further, leaving ample opportunity for Congress to pursue a wide range of social issues, including crime.[4]

Even with the growth of congressional attention across issues, however, both attention to crime in Congress and spending on crime and justice grew as a proportion of attention to and spending on other issues. Figure 3.1 illustrates crime hearings and spending as a proportion of all hearings and spending, as well as the homicide rate (per 100,000).

In the Eightieth Congress, 1946–47, less than 1.5 percent of all congressional hearings were about crime. By the early twenty-first century, hearings on crime regularly made up roughly 5 percent of all congressional hearings.[5] Similarly, in 1947 the percent of the federal budget allocated for justice administration, including all law enforcement, court, and corrections functions, as well as aid to state and local governments, was less than one-fourth of 1 percent, but that percentage has grown steadily over the past half century, culminating in roughly $38 billion, or close to 2 percent (1.78 percent) of the federal budget, in 2004.[6]

Immediately following World War II, attention to crime and justice in Congress was still sporadic. In fact, as figure 3.1 shows, after a modest upsurge in attention to crime in the early 1950s (focused primarily on juvenile delinquency), crime virtually dropped off the congressional agenda for about five years between 1959 and 1964. This is consistent with the sporadic nature of crime and violence as a topic of inquiry in Congress described in chapter 2. Beginning in the mid-1960s, however, congressional attention to crime began a long, steady growth that continued into the early 1990s. The homicide rate was also rising in the early part of this time period, and the trend lines are highly correlated (.576, p < .00).[7] Even by 2002, however, long after homicide rates had leveled off, the number of congressional hearings on crime remained well above the late 1960s levels when crime rates were still rising and urban riots and political protests focused national attention on crime. Spending also continued an upward trend, with expenditures and the homicide rate highly correlated from 1947 until 1985 (.915, p < .00) and negatively correlated thereafter (-.792, p < .00). Figure 3.2 illustrates the growing public attention to crime by juxtaposing stories about crime in the *New York Times* with the homicide rate.[8] The trend lines for the homicide rate and the percent of stories in the *New York Times* are highly correlated (.89, p < .00), as are the trends for *Times* stories and congressional hearings (.73, p < .00).

While a number of scholars have aptly noted that rising crime rates do not in themselves explain growing attention to crime, the very high correlation between crime rates, media coverage of crime, and congressional attention is suggestive of some causal relationships (see chapter 2).[9] Historians and criminologists have demonstrated that a combination of

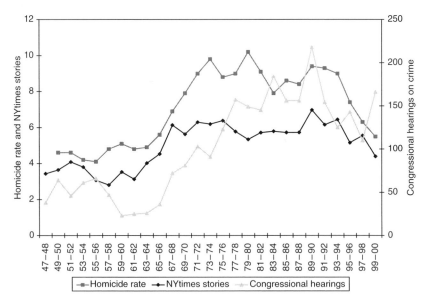

Figure 3.2. Homicide rates, *New York Times* and congressional hearings on crime, by congress. *Times* articles expressed as a percentage of all articles in the *Times*

factors, including the Great Migration of World War I, the Cold War, the declining economy of the late 1960s, and a shift in age demographics all contributed to an increase in crime rates that began in the late 1950s and gained strength through the 1960s.[10] Indeed, the relationship between rising crime rates, racial tensions, media coverage of crime, and congressional attention illustrates a by now familiar relationship in which a new social deviance (real or perceived), growing public anxiety (sometimes out of proportion to the actual events), substantial public or elite focus on the issue, and a spike in congressional attention coincide. And, as figures 3.1 and 3.2 illustrate, while attention to crime in Congress remains high, the massive increase of law and order concerns seems to have peaked— at least for now—around the early 1990s. This is consistent with other research on issue attention cycles that indicate a rise and decline of attention, even as institutional legacies remain.[11]

While attention to crime in Congress has grown steadily, the type of issues Congress considers has varied substantially over time. Between 1947 and 2002, Congress held 2,903 hearings on crime and justice topics.[12] Figure 3.3 illustrates the shifting issue terrain over the time period.

Several trends are noteworthy. First, here we see clearly how substantive crime issues trade time in the spotlight, illustrating Congress's fluid jurisdiction over crime. An upsurge in attention to juvenile delinquency

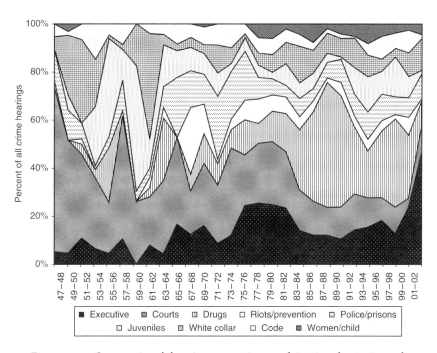

Figure 3.3. Congressional hearings on crime and justice, by topic and congressional years, 1947–2002

following World War II is illustrated by an increase in hearings and legislation aimed at reducing juvenile violence and delinquency, culminating in the Juvenile Delinquency and Youth Offenses Control Act of 1961.[13] By the early 1960s, however, juvenile delinquency had largely fallen off the agenda and was replaced by growing concerns about urban riots, police, and prisons.[14] By the 1980s, the topic du jour was illegal drugs, and by the 1990s, crimes against women and children began to occupy some congressional attention as well. Since the mid-1960s, the amount of time devoted to executive branch activities on crime and justice has also grown dramatically, while attention to courts has declined.

A second trend that is plainly visible in figure 3.3 is the trend toward stability of issue attention as crime settles into regular agenda status in Congress. Up until the mid-1960s, three topics dominated congressional attention to crime: courts, juveniles, and white-collar crime; other topics came and went from the agenda fairly quickly. For example, in the Eighty-fourth Congress, 1955–56, there were 15 hearings on illegal drugs. But this time period is bracketed by the previous eight years (1947–54), in which there were only four such hearings, and six subsequent years (1957–62), in which there were just two. Beginning in the mid-1960s, other issues, for example riots, policing, and drugs, began to emerge as well, and by the mid-1980s, the more dramatic ebbs and flows of topic areas had settled down. Between 1980 and 2000, every Congress had at least 20 hearings on drugs (with two exceptions: the 100th Congress, which had 81, and the 101st Congress, which had 101). By 1980, most congressional years also had between 10 and 20 hearings on juveniles a year (except for the 100th and the 101st Congresses, when drugs crowded almost everything else out).

Table 3.1 compares each topic across three time periods. The first time period (1947–66) reflects lower crime rates and the intermittent attention that characterized congressional attention to crime through most of the nation's history. The second time period (1967–80) is characterized by rapidly rising crime rates; increasing public, media, and elite attention to crime; and urban unrest, riots, and other forms of political agitation. This period also saw the establishment of the Law Enforcement Assistance Administration and the passage of the Omnibus Crime Control and Safe Streets Act of 1968, which contributed to the professionalization of law enforcement and courts at all levels of government.[15] This bill had significant implications for the development of more professionalized criminal justice agencies, particularly the police, and created new agencies, new funding opportunities, new crimes, and an institutional network of interlocking bill titles that would set the foundation for future congressional crime bills.[16]

The last time period (1981–2002) reflects the more stable policy environment that figure 3.3. illustrates. Crime rates level off, and much of the political protests and frenzied public attention to crime quiets down.[17]

TABLE 3.1. Number of Crime and Justice Hearings, per Topic and Time Period, 1947–2002

Topic	1947–1966	1967–1980	1981–2002	Change from 1st to 3rd period
Courts	159 (36.8%)	196 (25.3%)	218 (12.9%)	−23.9%
Drugs	27 (6.3%)	81 (10.4%)	511 (30.1%)	23.9%
Executive	28 (6.5%)	130 (16.8%)	292 (17.2%)	10.7%
Juveniles	75 (17.4%)	46 (5.9%)	125 (7.4%)	−10.0%
White-collar	65 (15.0%)	45 (5.8%)	161 (9.5%)	−5.5%
Women/children	2 (0.5%)	19 (2.4%)	74 (4.4%)	3.9%
Riots/crime prevention	4 (0.9%)	72 (9.3%)	76 (4.5%)	3.6%
Code	29 (6.7%)	53 (6.8%)	76 (4.5%)	−2.2%
Prisons	20 (4.6%)	43 (5.5%)	51 (3.0%)	−1.6%
Police/weapons	19 (4.4%)	72 (9.3%)	87 (5.1%)	0.7%
Other	4 (0.9%)	19 (2.4%)	24 (1.4%)	0.5%
Total	432	776	1,695	

Among the most dramatic changes is the decline in congressional attention to the courts. In the first time period, over a third (36.8 percent) of all congressional hearings discussed courts. Most of these hearings addressed jurisdiction, procedural, and staffing issues. Over the course of the next two time periods, attention to court concerns plummeted. This is particularly noteworthy, since the mid-1980s involved a major reorganization of the federal criminal code, with the formation of the U.S. Sentencing Commission and the promulgation of the Federal Sentencing Guidelines. But attention to other issues was growing at such a rate that even a spike in attention to courts during this time does little to alter the trend.

In contrast, the percent of hearings concerning executive branch agencies nearly tripled between the first two time periods. Some of this increase is attributable to the increasing oversight of the FBI Congress exercised in the late 1970s as it sought to investigate the FBI's counterintelligence programs. In addition, 25 hearings in 1978 and 1979 involved renewed investigation into the assassinations of Martin Luther King Jr. and John F. Kennedy. A significant portion of the growth of attention to executive agencies, however, simply has to do with the increasing centrality of the Justice Department to congressional crime politics. Congress holds executive branch hearings about budget reauthorizations for and oversight of the Drug Enforcement Agency (DEA), the FBI, the Law Enforcement Assistance Administration, the Bureau of Alcohol, Tobacco and Firearms, the Secret Service, the U.S. Marshals, and Customs, but it is also grappling with assassination investigations, surveillance technology, dispute resolution, witness protection, threats to members of Congress and the executive, data collection on serial killers, sharing of FBI criminal histories and records with state and local authorities, asset forfeiture, DNA identification systems, bioterrorism, and racial profiling. And this is just in relation to the functioning of the executive branch. Once the executive branch gained increased attention in the 1970s, the relative amount of attention it received remained fairly constant across the next 30 years.

Even more dramatic than the growth in attention to executive agencies is the increase in congressional attention to illegal drugs.[18] Occupying merely 6 percent of all hearings before 1967, the topic of drugs gradually gained attention in the 1970s and exploded onto the congressional agenda in the 1980s and 1990s, taking up almost one-third (511/1,695) of the hearings. In fact, in the last congressional year in the dataset, 2001–2, congressional hearings on drugs fell to 10 percent of all hearings for the first time since 1978. In the 15-year period from 1985 through 2000, drug hearings were more than a third of all congressional crime hearings (427/1,288), and from 1987–90 were almost half (182/374). Many of these hearings are about federal interdiction efforts in international drug trafficking, including efforts targeting Latin America, Southeast Asia, the Caribbean, the Middle East, and Africa, as well as the work of government agencies such as the Federal Aviation Administration, the Coast Guard, Customs, border authorities, the Treasury Department and, of course, the Department of Defense.[19] Reflecting the passage of the 1970 Comprehensive Drug Abuse Prevention and Control Act of 1970 and the Reagan Administration's prominent War on Drugs in the 1980s, drugs replaced white-collar crime and juveniles as the major interest of lawmakers in Congress in the 1970s and 1980s.[20] Together, juveniles and white-collar crime took roughly a third (32.4 percent) of the congressional agenda in the first 20 years after World War II. After 1968, these topics combined occupied only 15 percent (377/2,471) of all hearings.

Also worth noting is the increase in hearings on crimes against women and children. Though they make up a fraction of all hearings, they are almost entirely a more recent phenomenon. Other than two hearings on creating a federal crime for child abandonment held in 1949, no hearings on crimes against women and children were held in the first time period. In contrast, in the second time period, 19 hearings were held on this topic, primarily focused on domestic violence and crimes against children. By the 1980s and 1990s, Congress held 74 hearings on crimes against women and children, including sexual assault, rape, domestic and family violence, child abductions, parental kidnapping of children, child pornography, and stalking. These issues materialized on the congressional agenda with nine hearings in 1977–78 addressing sex crimes against children and domestic violence, and have remained on the agenda ever since.[21] The passage of the Violence Against Women Act, enacted as part of the Violent Crime Control and Law Enforcement Act of 1994, illustrates the significant attention to these issues in Congress.[22]

The second time period also reveals a spike in attention to riots and crime prevention, prisons, and police. This is consistent with the growth in incidence of and public attention to prison uprisings, urban riots, and conflicts between racial minorities and the police. However, as these events recede, these topics retreat to the back burner of congressional attention. Most of these topics remain largely unaltered between the first and third time periods, and the percentage of hearings on riots/crime prevention is cut in half after the spike in attention in the 1970s.[23]

The shifting of attention from one topic to another is a familiar pattern. Members of Congress do not seem to sustain attention to one *particular* crime policy issue permanently, though the duration of attention has lengthened. What is different about the past 30 years is that when one issue declines, another issue takes its place, ensuring a fairly steady level of attention to crime at the national level. This contrasts sharply with previous eras, when a single crime issue would capture the imagination of lawmakers, only to recede, at which point crime essentially fell off the national agenda entirely. The spike in attention to crime in the 1950s that appears in figure 3.1, for example, was due largely to a growing attention to juvenile crime. When this issue declined in prominence, the number of overall number of hearings dropped dramatically. In contrast, since the late 1960s, while some issues have waxed and waned, the *overall* level of attention to crime has not only been sustained but has grown.

What explains this? Several analyses offer clues. First, crime follows a pattern similar to that of other substantive issue areas that began to receive more attention in the wake of the social and political upheavals of the 1960s and 1970s.[24] Health care, education, social welfare, and other topics addressing social problems gained substantially more attention in the aftermath of the period's civil rights, women's, welfare rights, and consumer movements, as well as antiwar protests and awareness of drug use and political corruption. This is due, in part, to the rise of citizen interest groups, structural changes in congressional leadership, staffing, and internal rules, and social movements pressing for national government attention to substantive concerns. Given increasing crime rates in this context, it is not surprising that attention to crime remains, just as attention to a wide range of other social problems has found a more permanent place on the congressional agenda. As Baumgartner and Jones have noted (1993, 2002), high levels of attention to a given issue create institutional legacies that remain, long after issues fade from public view.

Second, the number of congressional hearings on crime in which a bill is under consideration (known as referral hearings) has declined dramatically between the two time periods, suggesting that more and more

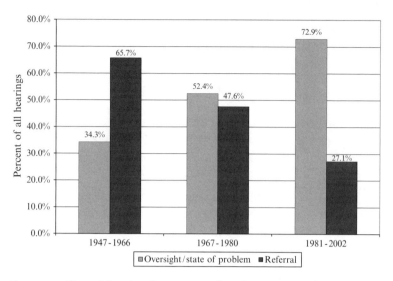

Figure 3.4. Type of hearing, by time period, and congressional years, 1947–2002

legislators find the crime issue worth talking about, even in the absence of specific legislation.[25] Figure 3.4 illustrates the percent of all crime hearings in each time period that are bill (referral) hearings. The three time periods reveal a gradual shift away from bill hearings, so that by the 1980s and 1990s, almost three-fourths (72.3 percent) of all crime hearings are nonbill ones. The first and last time periods are almost mirror images of each other, with referral hearings the dominant form of congressional crime hearing until 1966 (284/432) and oversight/general crime hearings dominating in the latter time period (1,235/1,695).[26]

Bill hearings involve consideration of a specific piece of legislation that has been proposed by a member of Congress. For example, a 1976 executive branch hearing in the Senate addressed a bill that would amend Title I (Law Enforcement Administration Agency) of the Omnibus Crime Control and Safe Streets Act of 1968 (S521–58). A 1992 hearing in the House of Representatives considered a bill that would prohibit payment of witness fees to prisoners (H521–8). And a 1996 juvenile justice hearing contemplated legislation that would amend the Higher Education Act of 1965 to require open campus security crime logs at institutions of higher learning (H321–19).

Nonreferral hearings, in contrast, in which no bill is at stake, involve oversight of government agencies or are general hearings on the scope of a specific problem. Oversight hearings involve congressional investigations into the day-to-day activities of criminal justice institutions, most typically the Department of Justice. These hearings can be general, as in a 1953 general review of the activities of the FBI, or they can be aimed at ferreting out specific problems, for example, a 1980 Senate hearing on alleged misconduct by agents of the Alcohol, Tobacco and Firearms agency.[27] These hearings also include consideration of general crime problems and issues in criminal justice. For example, a 1994 House hearing on drugs assessed the impact of the Administration's strategy to prevent drug smuggling (H401-75). A 1976 hearing considered proposals to apprehend, prosecute, and rehabilitate persons caught driving while intoxicated (H641-6), and a 1993 Senate hearing contemplated antistalking proposals to reduce harassment of women (S521-21). Notably, it is not just in the area of executive agency hearings that there has been a drop in referral hearings. Almost 90 percent of all hearings on illegal drugs (457/511), three-fourths of the hearings on riots and crime prevention (56/76), and over half of the hearings on crimes against women (42/74) between 1981 and 2002 were nonreferral hearings. This suggests that following the initial spike in attention to crime in the 1960s, new opportunities arose for organized interests as well as members of Congress to stake claims to fiscal and symbolic resources that the crime topic generates.

Such hearings themselves are not new. In fact, most of the hearings on crime and violence—including hearings on riots, labor disputes, and arson—between the Civil War and World War I were nonreferral hearings. What is noteworthy in the contemporary context is both the sheer *volume* of hearings that address no particular bill and the level at which these types of hearings have been *sustained* on the congressional agenda, migrating from issue to issue.

A Herfindahl index of congressional committee attention to crime illustrates the growing attractiveness of substantive crime issues to a wide range of members of Congress. A Herfindahl index is a measure of concentration popularized by economists interested in assessing market concentrations. The index here is based on the squared proportion of all hearings in a given congressional year and is used to assess whether crime hearings are broadly spread out across a range of congressional committees or are largely monopolistic (controlled by one or two committees). A decline in committee clarity represents increased interest in an issue area because it suggests that more members of Congress, beyond the traditional House and Senate judiciary committees, are taking an interest in crime.[28] Figure 3.5 illustrates the proliferation of crime hearings into a wide range of committees over the 55-year time period, as well as several major crime bills during that time.

Prior to 1966, 26 different committees held crime hearings, but the Senate and House Judiciary Committees held 68 percent of them (196/432). This is reflected in a high overall average clarity score of 32.1 and an even higher score in nonreferral hearings (56.0). In the next time

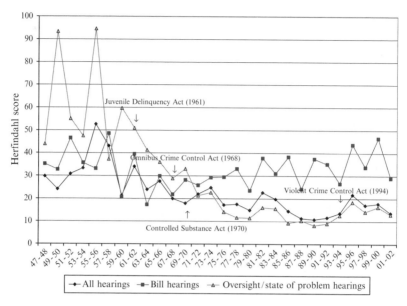

Figure 3.5. Committee clarity for congressional crime and justice hearings, 1947–2002

period, with heightened public awareness, rising crime rates, and growing attention to crime in Congress, 38 committees held crime and justice hearings, and the portion that were held in Senate and House judiciary committees dropped to 55 percent (424/766). The overall average clarity score dropped to 19.2, and the nonreferral score declined to 20.5. In the final time period, the hearings spanned 44 committees, and just barely 50 percent were in judiciary committees (841/1,695).[29] By this time, overall clarity is 15.9, and the clarity score for nonreferral hearings is a mere 13.0, a full 43-point drop from the first time period.

Clarity scores for referral hearings, in contrast, decline modestly during the second time period but rebound to essentially the same score by the latter period. This suggests that the burst of attention during the second time period created opportunities and incentive for new committees to take up crime legislation but the stabilization of the policy process reverted control to the traditional committees, primarily Senate and House judiciary committees. In fact, the portion of referral hearings held in these committees actually increased slightly between the post-World War II period (208/284, 73 percent) and the 1980s and 1990s (359/460, 78 percent).

Clearly, the bursts of attention to and spending on crime in the late 1960s and early 1970s generated institutional legacies that remain, and the passage of major crime bills during this time likely had an effect on legislators' interest in the topic. Government Reform and Oversight (House) and Government Affairs (Senate) Committees each held 7 to 8 percent of the hearings after 1966, and appropriations committees in both chambers each held about 2 to 3 percent of hearings. From there, the range of committees is huge, including the House Committees on Banking, Currency, and Housing; Education and Labor; Interstate and Foreign Commerce; Aging; Narcotics Abuse and Control; and the District of Columbia and the Senate Committees on Labor and Public Welfare, Foreign Relations, and Banking and Currency, among others, each of which has held at least 20 crime hearings since 1966.

This decline in overall committee clarity is consistent with other research findings indicating that issues with low levels of attention in Congress have few attentive legislators and groups but that when an issue becomes "hot" there is a frenzy for jurisdictional control, particularly in nonreferral hearings where committee jurisdiction is more fluid.[30] Members of Congress take an interest in new issues if they think they will serve their constituents' and or their reelection interests. In the crime case, as Murakawa (2005), Beckett (1997), Flamm (2005), and others have demonstrated, Democrats' initial linkage of rising crime rates with the unfulfilled project of racial equality quickly unraveled as Republicans and southern Democrats actively linked crime to black civil rights. Democrats and Republicans alike saw political opportunities in embracing a tougher law-and-order stance, culminating in President Clinton's 1994 crime bill, which was criticized by some Democrats as privileging police, courts, and corrections over preventive activities. As shown in chapter 2, crime as an opportunistic policy issue is not a new phenomenon. But as crime rates began to rise and public attention focused on the issue, and particularly as race riots and other racial tensions became prominent on the national agenda, a growing number of lawmakers saw addressing crime and violence as politically beneficial, either for symbolic position-taking or for the potential to wrest control over legislation from the traditional committees. The story is by now familiar: the victimization of blacks and the socioeconomic foundations of racial violence have been marginalized in the congressional policy environment.

But the committee clarity scores also illustrate that crime was becoming a topic of increasing interest to a wider range of members of Congress as early as 1960, even before the overt racialized politicization and the more dramatic and persistent spike in crime rates and public attention to crime. A closer examination of the homicide trends reveals a jump in homicides in the late 1950s, and the homicide rate and committee clarity scores are highly negatively correlated (-.66 p < .00, two-tailed).[31] Most of the early proliferation of hearings across committees in the 1950s, in fact, had to do with the attention to juvenile delinquency and organized crime mentioned earlier. The House Education and Labor Committee, for example, held five hearings on juvenile delinquency between 1957 and 1962. The Government Reform and Oversight Committee in the House (originally the Expenditures in Executive Departments Committee) and the Government Affairs Committee in the Senate (formerly the Expenditures in Executive Departments Committee) held 10 hearings between 1954 and 1962 on racketeering, gambling, and organized crime. In fact, many of the hearings that proliferated into new committees between the late 1950s and early 1960s reflected a globalizing economy and communication technology that made illegal activity more prevalent, dangerous, and fluid. The Senate Post Office Committee, for example, held a hearing on transporting firearms through the mail in 1958, and in 1954 the Merchant Marine and Fisheries Committee addressed the revocation of merchant marines permits to persons convicted of narcotics violations. Indeed, most of the crime bills passed during the 1950s and early 1960s addressed drugs, organized crime, and juveniles.[32] There were, of course, also increasing racial tensions that were reflected in civil disturbances and a revival of Klan activity, though hearings on these topics do not really emerge until the mid-1960s.

While it is tempting to see the increased attention to crime as purely a function of racial politics, growing congressional interest in crime included organized crime, gambling, racketeering, juveniles, and other concerns not obviously linked to the racial divisions of the time. New crimes, new contexts, and new institutions have long driven crime issues onto the national agenda. As crime rates began to rise and the national political process inexorably entered into the strife over white supremacy and equal protection, crime became a target for both advocates and opponents of civil rights, thus drawing more attention, more institutions, and more interests into the political process. We turn now to the nature, quantity, and quality of those interests.

Interest Groups and Crime and Justice in Congress

Table 3.2 reveals the general pattern of group representation across the entire 55-year time period. Most notably, witnesses from criminal justice agencies represent more than a third of the witnesses (2132/5,764) and appear at more than four out of five (478/574) congressional hearings on crime. This represents a plurality of witnesses across crime hearings, and no other type of witness comes close to this dominating presence. Government agencies also have a strong presence and include members of Congress, representatives from executive agencies such as the Treasury Department, the Department of Defense, and the Immigration and Naturalization Service, as well as state and local elected officials and agencies. It is worth noting that many of these witnesses represent agencies that are involved in the

TABLE 3.2. Witness Representation by Witness and by Hearing,
Congressional Crime Hearings, 1947–2002

Type of witness	Total witnesses at hearings	Hearings with at least one witness
Criminal justice agencies and organizations	2132 (37.0%)	478 (83.3%)
Government agencies	1301 (22.6%)	400 (69.7%)
Professional associations	872 (15.1%)	253 (44.1%)
Individuals	505 (9.0%)	164 (28.6%)
Citizen groups	407 (7.1%)	164 (28.6%)
Single-issue	240 (4.2%)	110 (19.2%)
Broad	125 (2.2%)	68 (11.8%)
Civil liberties	42 (0.7%)	34 (5.9%)
Business/labor	447 (7.8%)	137 (23.9%)
Other	87 (1.5%)	57 (9.9%)
Total	5,764 (100.0%)	574[a]

[a] Totals do not add to 547 because any given hearing may have representatives from multiple groups.

war on drugs in some capacity, as in a 1975 hearing on opium trafficking that included the senior advisor and coordinator for international narcotics matters in the State Department, or a 1993 hearing on border drug interdiction in which testimony from the assistant commissioner for border control with the Immigration and Naturalization Service was a participant.[33]

Professional associations combined, such as medical and educational organizations (e.g., the University of California, Cook County Hospital), religious institutions (the St. Louis Rabbinical Society), social service agencies (the National Council of Community Mental Health Centers), and legal associations (e.g., the American Bar Association) make up only 15 percent of witnesses, though they appear at close to half of the hearings (253/574). Individuals with no group affiliation, business and labor, and citizen groups all have comparable rates of participation, each with less than 10 percent of witnesses and appearing at about one-fourth of the hearings. This table also reveals that the citizen group category is populated with far more single-issue groups than broad ones.

Given the growth of citizens' groups over the past 40 years, including the emergence of victims' groups (e.g., the National Victims Assistance Organization) and organizations advocating or opposing specific criminal legislation (e.g., Families Against Mandatory Minimums and the Sentencing Project), it is striking that citizen groups of all kinds make up barely 1 in 14 witnesses. Table 3.3 breaks down the witnesses over time, across the three time periods utilized in the previous section.

Here it becomes clear that the presence of criminal justice agencies has a long history. In the immediate postwar period, police, prosecutors,

TABLE 3.3. Witnesses at Congressional Hearings on Crime and Justice, 1947–2002

| Type of witness | Total witnesses* | | | |
	1947–1967	1968–1980	1981–2002	Total
Criminal justice	353 (28.4%)	587 (35.0%)	1192 (41.9%)	2132
Government	236 (19.0%)	418 (24.9%)	647 (22.7%)	1301
Professional	155 (12.5%)	304 (18.1%)	413 (14.5%)	872
Citizen	55 (4.4%)	152 (9.1%)	200 (7.0%)	407
Individuals	254 (20.5%)	75 (4.5%)	189 (6.6%)	518
Business/labor	166 (13.4%)	115 (6.9%)	166 (5.8%)	447
Other	22 (1.8%)	26 (1.6%)	39 (1.4%)	87
Total	1,241	1,677	2,846	5,764

| | Hearings with at least one witness | | | |
	1947–1967	1968–1980	1981–2002	Total
Criminal justice	68 (73.9%)	122 (85.3%)	288 (85.0%)	478
Government	65 (70.7%)	103 (72.0%)	232 (68.4%)	400
Professional	38 (41.3%)	68 (47.6%)	147 (43.4%)	253
Citizen	18 (19.6%)	46 (32.2%)	100 (29.5%)	164
Individuals	33 (35.9%)	40 (28.0%)	91 (26.8%)	164
Business/labor	31 (33.7%)	40 (28.0%)	66 (19.5%)	137
Other	16 (17.4%)	20 (14.0%)	21 (6.2%)	57
Total	92	143	339	574

*Chi-squared (12 $d.f.$) = 398.18 (p < .000).

judges, and corrections officers already made up more than one-fourth of the witnesses and appeared at nearly three-fourths of the hearings. Some of this is due to the number of referral hearings addressing specific criminal justice institutions and oversight of new programs. But even hearings on substantive crime topics and state-of-the-problem hearings involved a good many criminal justice interests. For example, a 1948 hearing on labor riots in Kalamazoo, Michigan, involved 27 business and union representatives but also 10 local police officers, the attorney general of Michigan, and the assistant city attorney of Kalamazoo.[34] Organized crime hearings also frequently included a large number of law enforcement officers; a 1950 hearing on organized crime in interstate commerce included seven local sheriffs and police officers, as well as the Florida attorney general.[35] By the third time period, criminal justice agencies supply more then two of every five witnesses and appear in a staggering 85 percent of all hearings.

Prosecutors and police have been particularly successful in expanding their presence (table 3.4).

They have solidified their presence in the policy process, virtually doubling from the first time period to the last. Indeed, law enforcement

TABLE 3.4. Criminal Justice Agency and Citizen Group Witnesses at Congressional Crime and Justice Hearings, 1947–2002

| Type | Total witnesses* | | | |
	1947–1967	1968–1980	1981–2002	Total
Prosecutors	65 (5.25%)	148 (8.8%)	282 (9.9%)	495
Law enforcement	110 (8.9%)	202 (12.0%)	580 (20.4%)	892
Other criminal justice	178 (14.3%)	237 (14.4%)	330 (11.6%)	745
Citizen Single-issue	22 (1.8%)	85 (5.1%)	133 (4.7%)	240
Citizen Broad	27 (2.2%)	54 (3.2%)	44 (1.5%)	125
Citizen Civil liberties	6 (0.5%)	13 (0.8%)	23 (0.8%)	42
Total	1,241	1,677	2,846	

| | Hearings with at least one witness | | | |
	1947–1967	1968–1980	1981–2002	Total
Prosecutors	35 (38.0%)	66 (46.2%)	147 (43.4%)	248
Law enforcement	26 (28.4%)	63 (44.1%)	176 (51.9%)	265
Other criminal justice	51 (55.4%)	67 (46.9%)	130 (38.4%)	248
Citizen Single-issue	10 (10.9%)	26 (18.2%)	74 (21.8%)	110
Citizen Broad	12 (13.0%)	28 (19.6%)	28 (8.3%)	68
Citizen Civil liberties	4 (4.3%)	12 (8.4%)	18 (5.3%)	34

*Chi-squared (4 $d.f.$) = 121.86 ($p < .000$).

representation has *more* than doubled, and now appears at just over one-half (176/574) of all hearings. In fact, police officers, sheriffs, federal law enforcement agencies, and their organizational interests now supply roughly 30 percent of the witnesses in hearings on illegal drugs, and roughly 10 percent of the witnesses in hearings on white-collar crime, riots/crime prevention, and juveniles.

Before 1967, prosecutors dominated the executive branch topic (18 of 41 witnesses), but outside of these hearings, prosecutors did not make up more than 5 percent of all witnesses in any other topic. In contrast, by the 1980s and 1990s, they had such a small presence in only three categories: prisons, juveniles, and police. Figure 3.6 illustrates how prosecutors have actually shifted their attention from procedural and police/prison hearings to substantive crime topics (drugs, riots, white-collar crime, etc.). In the first time period, prosecutors were intermittent as witnesses and usually confined to procedural concerns. During the second time period, however, prosecutors spread out across topics, and by the 1980s and 1990s their presence shifted from procedural to substantive crime concerns.

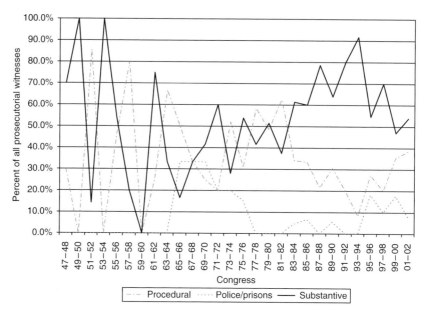

Figure 3.6. Prosecutorial witnesses at crime and justice hearings, by topic, 1947–2002

Other criminal justice personnel—judges, corrections officers—were even more of a presence in the first time period than police and prosecutors, making up more than 1 in 5 of the witnesses in hearings regarding the executive branch, the courts, the prisons, and the criminal code. By the 1980s and 1990s, other criminal justice personnel make up a smaller portion of criminal justice witnesses overall, but have proliferated in new areas, including juveniles; women and children; and riots and crime prevention (not shown).

Clearly, criminal justice agencies have greatly expanded their presence at crime and justice hearings. Prosecutors, law enforcement officers, corrections and probation officers, judges, and other criminal justice personnel are not simply routine participants in the policy process—they form the backbone of national crime policy making. And legislators are not simply hearing from an isolated police officer or prosecutor: more than one-fourth of the entire sample of hearings (156/574—not shown) include a minimum of five criminal justice witnesses. Even in committees whose jurisdiction and missions would suggest a broader focus, such as the House Education and Labor Committee or the Senate Labor and Public Welfare Committee, criminal justice agencies make up more than one- fourth of the witnesses. Members of Congress, then, are exposed to a bulwark of strong, sustained, routine witnesses representing the concerns, perspectives, and interests of criminal justice agencies.

In addition, other government representatives have a strong presence. These witnesses are often elected officials from local, state, or national government, but they also represent government agencies such as the Department of Labor, crime prevention bureaus, and branches of the military.

Citizen Groups: Gaining Strength but Losing Breadth

In stark contrast to the steady and broad-ranging growth of representatives of criminal justice agencies, citizen groups exhibit a different pattern. Though they make up a small portion of all witnesses, citizen groups have increased their presence over time. However, this has occurred primarily through the volume of hearings in which they are represented and is almost entirely due to the proliferation of *single-issue* citizen groups *across* issue areas. The number of hearings in which single-issue groups appeared doubled, from only 1 in 10 in the first time period to 1 in 5 by the 1980s and 1990s (see table 3.4). Between 1947 and 1966, single-issue citizen groups appeared in only five of the ten topic categories (drugs, courts, juveniles, police, and the criminal code), and a third (7/22) of all these single-issue group witnesses represented advocates or opponents of gun regulation. Later, however, in the 1980s and 1990s, single-issue citizen groups occupied at least a small place at *all* categories of hearings. While hearings on police and weapons still attract a high percentage of the single-issue citizen witnesses (12/22 police and weapon hearings include a single-issue group witness), these types of groups are also appearing in growing numbers at hearings on women and children (13/20), the criminal code (5/20), and crime prevention and riots (3/11). While the overall numbers remain below 20 percent in most cases, almost two-thirds of the hearings on crimes against women and children include single-issue citizen groups, for example Women Against Rape, Citizens Against Physical and Sexual Abuse, the National Center for Victims of Crime, and the Pennsylvania Coalition Against Domestic Violence (PCADV).

Despite their proliferation, single-issue citizen groups in the 1980s and 1990s fell into some fairly predictable categories. An astonishing 66 percent of all single-issue citizen group witnesses appearing in the most recent time period (88/133) came from just three types of groups: gun advocates and opponents; groups representing women and child victims; and the ACLU. In contrast, a paltry 7 percent of single-issue citizen group witnesses (9/133) clearly represented minority citizens. For example, each of the following groups appeared just once: Black and White Men Together, the Coalition of Ex-Offenders Against Community Violence, the National Black Police Officer Association, the National Alliance Against Racist and Political Repression, and Concerned Minorities in Criminal Justice.

In stark contrast to single-issue groups, after a burst of activity in the volatile 1968–80 period, broad citizen groups representing urban minorities and the poor have actually lost ground relative to the earliest time period. By the 1990s, they made up a barely visible 1.5 percent of all witnesses and showed up at just 8 percent of all hearings. In fact, the only time broad citizen groups made up an even modestly formidable presence was during the second time period, when crime rates were rising and riots, urban strife, civil rights, and community activism were high on the national agenda. At that time, a broad citizen group witness appeared at nearly one in five hearings (though they were still only 3 percent of all witnesses). In the earliest time period, few groups representing urban or minority interests appeared. The NAACP appeared at two separate 1950s hearings on limiting habeas corpus appeals in the federal courts, and the Urban League also appeared twice, at 1954 and 1959 hearings on juvenile delinquency.[36] Between 1967 and 1980, however, the NAACP appeared at six hearings on corrections, capital punishment, juvenile delinquency prevention, and gun control.[37] In addition, a number of other groups organized around black, Latino, and poor people's interests appeared during this period, as follows. The Leadership Conference for Civil Rights appeared at a hearing on federal jury selection.[38] Operation PUSH appeared at a hearing on domestic violence and federal court standing.[39] New Detroit Inc., a coalition of civil rights organizations, appeared at two separate hearings on federal aid to urban high-crime areas in 1973.[40] The National Center for Urban and Ethnic Affairs appeared at a 1978 hearing on violence.[41] El Pueblo Unido, La Casa de Puerto Rico, and United Puerto Ricans of Greater Miami all appeared at hearings on citizen standing in federal court (first two) and the national legal services corporation.[42] The National Federation of Settlements and Neighborhood Centers, a national nonprofit organization with neighborhood-based member agencies aimed at improving quality of life in neighborhoods throughout the country, appeared at a 1974 juvenile delinquency hearing on runaways.[43] And the National Urban League, the Chicago Urban League, and the Urban League of Greater Miami appeared on hearings on community anticrime assistance, legal services corporations, and gun control.[44]

By the 1980s and 1990s, however, the NAACP was the only one of these groups that remained active, with appearances at five hearings on policing, habeas corpus, church arsons, and the Justice Department's civil rights enforcement.[45] Two new groups, the Congress for Racial Equality and the National Black United Front, each appeared at two hearings on policing and gun control.[46] But by this time, these types of groups were virtually invisible, making up just 1.5 percent of witnesses. Sustaining a regular, national presence on crime issues proved to be a heavier load for some groups than others.

Thus, to the extent that citizen groups have proliferated in the post-1960s era, they have done so only modestly in terms of sheer numbers but more impressively in terms of the volume of hearings in which they assert a presence. However, it has been almost exclusively the single-issue groups' presence that has increased, particularly those representing citizens concerned about guns, crimes against women and children, and civil liberties. The mobilization capacity of criminal justice agencies and single-issue groups seem to have crowded out broader citizen organizations from a sustained presence in national crime policy making. The highly politicized nature of national crime politics in the 1960s and 1970s afforded the latter some opportunity to have a presence in Congress, but once the issue declined in salience and institutional routines were established, these groups virtually disappeared. The fluid congressional jurisdiction on crime once again illustrates the limited ability of citizen groups representing more marginalized interests (the urban poor, in this case) to remain active on the congressional agenda.

The Declining Significance of Individual Witnesses and Business Interests

Another substantial change across the time periods involves individual witnesses and witnesses from business or labor groups, both of whose level of representation has declined precipitously. Individual citizens—victims of crime, family members of victims, or citizens with no particular group affiliation—were 20.5 percent of all witnesses prior to 1966, but since then they have virtually disappeared (5.8 percent). The portion of hearings in which these witnesses appear has also declined. This is particularly interesting, since individual witnesses often represent victims or their families. Despite growing attention to issues involving clear victims, for example crimes against women and children or gun crimes, the number of individuals with no particular group affiliation testifying in Congress has dropped dramatically. To some extent, this probably reflects the growth of a legislative process that requires intensive fundraising, specialized legislation, robust lobbying communities, and more formal channels of access to members of Congress.[47] It is also probably a function of the increasing professionalization of victims, now represented by interest groups and government agencies at a level unheard of 40 years ago.[48] Nonetheless, the decline in appearances by regular citizens offering testimony about their experiences with criminal victimization, the justice system, or some collateral consequence thereof without a preexisting policy frame and preferred solution has largely been removed from the national policy process.

Representation from business groups, a small but solid portion of witnesses in the earlier time period (12.4 percent), was cut in half by the later period (6.2 percent). The decline of business group witnesses reflects the decrease in attention to white-collar crime between the two time periods. Over a third of the business and labor witnesses in the first time period (64/179) testified at hearings on white-collar crime. Business and labor groups also attended far fewer hearings on juvenile crime in the 1980s and 1990s than they did in the earlier time period. This space has been filled in by professional associations, primarily educational and legal groups such as the Juvenile Law Center of Philadelphia and the National Association of Secondary School Principals.[49]

Professional groups have changed little, both in terms of their overall presence and the number of hearings in which they appear. We will look more closely at these groups in the next section.

Institutions and Interests

Several aspects of the development of crime as a national policy issue described in chapter 2 are visible in the contemporary context. First, the nature of congressional jurisdiction over crime creates a context in which legislative attention waxes and wanes and is responsive both to underlying social conditions and policy entrepreneurs. Congressional attention to substantive crime issues has a long history, and the contemporary version of these concerns—drugs, riots, crimes against women and children—reflects the changing structure of national politics as much as any new discovery of the crime issue. What is different about the contemporary era is not that crime is an agenda item but that as specific crime issues continue to wax and wane, overall attention to crime remains elevated; this was not the case in previous eras, when the decline of attention to one or two issues signaled a reduction in congressional attention to crime in general. This is consistent with the process whereby bursts of attention to issues generate institutional legacies (recall the Herfindahl index of committee proliferation, the solidification of criminal justice interests and the proliferation of single-issue groups) that remain long after public, elite, and media attention have turned elsewhere. Since the 1960s, several crime issues have risen to prominence— most notably drugs, executive branch activities, and crimes against women and children—but history suggests that there is nothing permanent about these issues. Indeed, it is possible that the drug issue is already giving way to terrorism, national security concerns, and cybercrime. Crime as an agenda item, however, like other major social policies issues such as health care, education, environmental concerns, and social welfare, seems unlikely to depart from the congressional docket entirely anytime soon.

Second, the attention these issues receive contributes to a policy environment in which criminal justice agencies grow in number and single-issue groups find members of Congress receptive to their concerns. The portions of both criminal justice witnesses and single-issue citizen witnesses are significantly correlated with the Herfindahl index of nonreferral hearings.[50] Like the issues themselves, specific single-issue groups come and go, but there is a long history of these types of groups agitating for their policy preferences, and their intersection with criminal justice agency interests also has deep roots (recall the Society for the Suppression of Vice and the Post Office). And some groups have more staying power than others. The ACLU first appears in the sample at a 1955 hearing on limiting the right of persons convicted in state court to use habeas corpus to appeal to federal court. Over the next 47 years, the ACLU appears in 34 separate crime hearings. The NRA first appears in the sample in 1960 at a hearing on excise taxes on the manufacturing of weapons.[51] State and national rifle associations then appear at 18 hearings in the sample over the next 40 years.

From these beginnings, a feedback process has generated a kind of symbiotic environment in which the groups already at the table can generate problem definitions and policy solutions in ways that reinforce their organizational missions. Drug hearings represent an excellent illustration of this. Since the Harrison Narcotics Tax Act of 1914, the illegal drug problem has long been tackled as an enforcement problem. Indeed, mental health experts lamented the policing approach to drug use and abuse as early as the 1920.[52] But at the time, no level of government, least of all the national one, had the capacity to conduct extensive investigations, arrests, or incapacitations of drug users and dealers. With the growth of the national policy process, new crime legislation, and the professionalization of policing and prosecutors, opportunities for these professionals to intersect with the policy process have grown. As a result, criminal justice agencies make up almost half of the witnesses at all drug hearings. Similarly, as women's groups have brought issues of violence against women and children into the national spotlight, they have developed a place for themselves in the policy process that includes a high percentage of single-issue groups focused on serving victims.

Baumgartner and Jones (1993) note the positive feedback process that perpetuates existing institutional arrangements, making it difficult for outsiders to work their way in. Opportunities for broad citizen groups to break into this highly organized, resource-rich environment are few. Indeed, recall that the representation of broad citizen groups actually increased during the second time period. This suggests that the increased attention to crime provided a momentary opportunity for groups of all types to reach the national policymaking table. However, a relatively narrow type of citizen group is most likely to sustain a long-term, regular presence on the national agenda, and broad citizen groups—particularly those concerned with minorities and the poor—have fewer opportunities to maintain a presence in this policy environment.

Finally, one of the implicit themes of chapter 2 is that national crime politics lends itself to participation by single-issue citizen groups more than broad ones. There are several reasons for this. First, the cyclic nature of congressional attention to crime recognizes one or two major substantive crime issues at a time, creating a policy context in which groups focused on that single issue are likely to find a receptive audience and generate additional policy contexts in which to appear. In contrast, citizen groups with broad and diffuse interests have more difficulty meshing their goals into such a context. Second, while the congressional crime agenda has expanded, it has done so in a piecemeal way, without clear boundaries and limitations, thus creating opportunities for mobilized groups or members of Congress to draw attention to specific issues when it has been politically strategic to do so. In other words, given the enormous range of issues Congress addresses in each legislative session, there are few substantive crime issues that it is bound by jurisdiction and law to confront. Thus, groups with a lot of resources and/or a focus on a single but high-profile crime issue have a distinct advantage in this policy environment. Finally, because of crime's increasing strategic significance to members of Congress, it makes sense that the most appealing ways of addressing crime would focus on single, high-profile issues that can call attention to lawmaking, taking a stand against crime, and any federal fiscal benefits to be spread around. No doubt the increasing professionalization, specialization, and intensified lobbying atmosphere also make single-issue groups—with their streamlined policy goals and information—attractive to lawmakers. Even before the modern era of national crime politics, however, as chapter 2 showed, single crime issues (prostitution, kidnapping, drugs, and alcohol) cropped up on the congressional agenda with more ease than issues of concern to groups with more diffuse interests, such as white violence against blacks in the context of racial stratification or the public health crisis of drug and alcohol addiction.

The smoother path for single-issue groups has some important consequences for crime politics. Some crime problems fit neatly into single-issue organizations. Opponents or advocates of gun control—the NRA or Handgun Control, Inc. for example—have unequivocal, singular policy messages that can fit into straightforward policy goals. Even the names of some groups, for example Families Against Mandatory Minimums and the Coalition for Battered Women, suggest a singular focus. These groups tend to place a great deal of their resources into specific problem definitions, policy frames, and legislative solutions.

Urban crime presents different problems. Citizens most deeply affected by drug violence, gang activity, assault, theft, homicides, guns, and juvenile crime frequently have a range of other quality-of-life concerns as well that are difficult to isolate from day-to-day crime victimization. While groups like the Urban League, for example, do occasionally appear on the national scene, there are far fewer groups representing broad community concerns than those focusing narrowly on one set of crime problems. The absence of broader groups or their proxies and the dominance of criminal justice agencies often blends well with the interests of single-issue groups interested in enhancing criminal sanctions or increasing police activity. As a result, the policy process emphasizes the internal goals of criminal justice agencies, which serve as a proxy for the goals of actually significantly reducing crime victimization.

Contemporary Crime and Justice Hearings

This section examines substantive crime hearings in the 1990s—drugs, crimes against women and children, juvenile crime, riots and crime prevention, policing, and the criminal code—and describes the issue niches that have developed and have further isolated broad citizen groups (n = 309 hearings and 2,385 witnesses). These hearing topics potentially provide tremendous opportunities for the appearance of urban crime victims, advocates for young offenders, and other citizen groups with broad concerns about quality of life, criminogenic conditions, victimization, offender reentry, among others. Yet as table 3.5 illustrates, all citizen groups combined represent barely 8 percent of the witnesses (5.8 percent for single-issue and 2.2 percent for broad groups).[53]

Several patterns are noticeable across issues. First, the hearings where we might expect to find citizen groups representing urban crime victims—drugs, riots and crime prevention, and policing, for example—not only have the fewest of these groups but are also heavily dominated by criminal justice agencies. In fact, nearly half of all the witnesses at these hearings represent criminal justice agencies (578/1,249), and the overwhelming majority of these witnesses are from law enforcement (391/578—not shown). These groups are frequently reporting on their successes and making requests for additional resources. In 1996, for example, the House of Representatives Subcommittee on National Security, International Relations and Criminal Justice of the Committee on Government Reform and Oversight held a hearing on illegal drugs in San Luis Obispo, California, entitled "Report from the Front Line: The Drug Battle in California." One of the primary witnesses represented the DEA, and his remarks were aimed primarily at detailing the successful efforts of his agency in tackling drug cartels of Central and South America. He spent some time discussing the agency's efforts and concluded:

> Counterdrug operations during the 1990s successfully dismantled massive conversion labs in Bolivia and Peru, forcing the traffickers to abandon these large operations in favor of small, more mobile

TABLE 3.5. Witnesses at Select Congressional Hearings. 1991–1998

Type of witness	Drugs		Juveniles		Police		Crime code		Riots/crime prevention		Women		Total	
Criminal justice	354	45.2%	193	30.6%	135	52.9%	82	38.0%	89	42.4%	63	21.6%	916	38.4%
Government	210	26.8%	98	15.6%	21	8.2%	33	15.3%	30	14.3%	62	21.3%	454	19.0%
Individuals	55	7.0%	58	9.2%	42	16.5%	29	13.4%	25	11.9%	62	21.3%	271	11.4%
Social service	21	2.7%	97	15.4%	2	0.8%	0	0.0%	5	2.4%	30	10.3%	155	6.5%
Single issue	27	3.4%	26	4.1%	18	7.1%	17	7.9%	22	10.5%	28	9.6%	138	5.8%
Education	15	1.9%	61	9.7%	8	3.1%	5	2.3%	6	2.9%	4	1.4%	99	4.2%
Law	3	0.4%	24	3.8%	5	2.0%	29	13.4%	11	5.2%	14	4.8%	86	3.6%
Business	37	4.7%	3	0.5%	3	1.2%	12	5.6%	6	2.9%	3	1.0%	64	2.7%
Research	26	3.3%	17	2.7%	1	0.4%	1	0.5%	8	3.8%	4	1.4%	57	2.4%
Broad citizen	9	1.1%	17	2.7%	7	2.7%	6	2.8%	3	1.4%	10	3.4%	52	2.2%
Medical	10	1.3%	16	2.5%	7	2.7%	1	0.5%	3	1.4%	6	2.1%	43	1.8%
Religious	4	0.5%	13	2.1%	6	2.4%	0	0.0%	1	0.5%	2	0.7%	26	1.1%
Other	12	1.5%	7	1.1%	0	0.0%	1	0.5%	1	0.5%	3	1.0%	24	1.0%
Total	783		630		255		216		210		291		2385	

laboratories in remote locations. Also, law enforcement efforts took aim at the air transportation bridge, which was a trafficker's preferred method of transporting cocaine base from the mountainous jungles of Bolivia and Peru to the cartel operations in Columbia. This resulted in the traffickers having to abandon their air routes and resort to riskier transportation over land and water.[54]

This claim of successfully disrupting major drug organizations is fairly typical of the presentations criminal justice agencies make to Congress when they give testimony about the success of police or prosecutorial efforts and additional necessary resources required to continue to fulfill their missions. This is logical and perfectly consistent with bureaucratic agency interaction with the legislative branch of government.[55] What it does, however, is draw public conversation about crime away from actual measures of harm and toward self-referential outcome measures that may have little bearing on the experiences of people most likely to be victimized by crime. Indeed, the relative sparsity of individual witnesses in these hearings suggests that despite the increased attention to substantive crimes and the emergence of victims' groups on the national scene, the number of individual victims of routine street crime that Congress actually hears from is certainly no higher than it was in the 1940s and 1950s and is probably significantly lower. Instead, Congress hears extensively from criminal justice agencies detailing new and more sophisticated ways to intercept offenders. Important and worthy policy goals to be sure, but hardly approaching the broad spectrum of interests and perspectives to be heard.

While rates of broad citizen group representation for all these topics are low, the topics of policing and riots/crime prevention do show average or slightly higher than average levels of single-issue citizen group representation. In the policing category, this is due almost entirely to gun advocates and opponents. Fourteen of the eighteen single-issue citizen groups at police hearings were gun advocates or opponents (10 to 4 in favor of opponents). Of the 22 witnesses representing single-issue and civil liberties groups in the riots/crime prevention category, five were pro- or antigun groups yet again, and another five were groups representing battered women, victims of sexual assault, or child murder victims. Two witnesses were from the ACLU. Thus, more than half of the witnesses in these categories represented groups that are highly organized and have a programmatic focus that either ignores urban minority interests altogether or emphasizes legal responses to criminal justice system injustices (the ACLU).[56] Of the ten remaining single-issue groups in the riots/crime prevention category, three are strong supporters of law enforcement: Citizens for Law and Order, the Law Enforcement Alliance, and MADD.[57] An additional two are victims' rights groups (the National Organization for Victim Assistance and the National Victims Constitutional Amendment Network). Three groups represent minority concerns, though only one of them is specifically aimed at urban minorities: Positive Anti-Crime Thrust (the programmatic arm of the Afro-American Patrolman's League), the Anti-Defamation League of B'nai B'rith, and the National Network Against Anti-Asian Violence. The remaining two are consumer and conservation groups. Even groups from the social service professions are hardly represented in drug, police, and riots/crime prevention hearings. The most substantial type of interest group witness, outside of government and single-issue groups, is the legal profession, which makes up 5 percent of witnesses in riot/crime prevention hearings.

A second point revealed in table 3.5 is the more pluralistic nature of hearings on juveniles and crimes against women and children. At hearings on juveniles, 30 percent of witnesses are criminal justice agencies. Each of the other types of witness—government agencies and social service and education groups and individuals—takes up about 10 percent or more of the whole. In hearings on crimes against women and children, groups are spread out fairly evenly across five categories: criminal justice, government, individuals, single-issue, and social service. In fact, a Herfindahl index of concentration of witnesses across the group categories in figure 3.7 reveals that the crimes against women and children has the lowest score, 16.2, indicating that witnesses are most spread out among different groups in this category. Note that hearings on policing, drugs, and riots/crime prevention have the highest scores—in part a reflection of the high concentration of witnesses from criminal justice agencies, but also because of the more narrow range of other groups represented in general.

Individual witnesses also play the most substantial role in hearings on crimes against women and children, matching the representation of criminal justice agencies almost exactly. While individuals were not always identified in the witness lists, when they were, they frequently represented victims, their family members, or their advocates. One in five witnesses (62/291) at hearings on crimes against women and children was an individual. In contrast, at drugs, police, riots/crime prevention, and juvenile hearings, less than 1 in 10 (180/1,878) witnesses is an individual with no group affiliation.

The array of witnesses at hearings on crimes against women and children is notable in another respect. By far, these hearings have the fewest representatives from criminal justice agencies. The absence of these groups is filled in by social service agencies, single-issue citizen groups, and individuals. The single-issue groups are typified by anti–violence against women groups such as the National Network to End Domestic Violence,

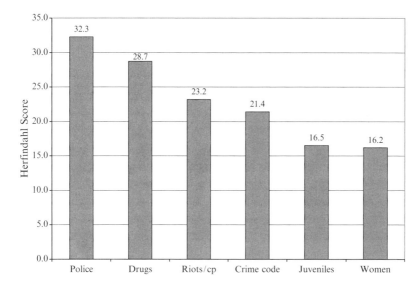

Figure 3.7. Herfindahl concentration scores for group type, select hearings on crime and justice, 1991–1998

the Jacob Wetterling Fund, the Schuylkill Women in Crisis, the National Woman Abuse Project, the Nevada Network Against Domestic Violence, the D.C. Coalition Against Domestic Violence, and child advocacy groups like National Child Support Advocacy Coalition and Wisconsin Fathers for Equal Justice. Nearly 60 percent of the social service groups are shelters and crisis support groups (17/29), whose missions and goals generally dovetail with the aforementioned single-issue groups.

Repeat Players

The vast majority of nongovernmental interest groups are one-shotters, appearing at a congressional hearing only once in the dataset. But a few groups have much higher rates of participation. Table 3.6 lists all of the citizen and professional groups *with more than two* appearances and the total number of hearings in which they appear. Only 11 citizen groups appear more than twice across the 301 hearings and 2,385 witnesses, and almost two-thirds (seven) are single-issue groups.

Groups representing advocates and opponents of gun control; women, children, and family interests; and civil liberties appear most often. Handgun Control, Inc. is the single most common interest group, with 14 appearances in nine separate hearings over the eight years. The NRA has only six appearances, but they are in six separate hearings (in other words, Handgun Control, Inc. witnesses are more likely to come with a

TABLE 3.6. Citizen and Professional Groups Represented at More than Two Congressional Crime Hearings, 1991–1998

	Total hearings	Total appearances	Type
Citizen groups			
Handgun Control, Inc.	9	14	Single-issue
National Organization for Women	6	8	Broad citizen
NRA	6	6	Single-issue
ACLU	5	7	Single-issue
Coalition for Juvenile Justice	4	5	Single-issue
Family Research Council	4	4	Broad citizen
NAACP	4	4	Broad citizen
Safe Streets Coalition	4	4	Broad citizen
Community Anti-Drug Coalition	3	4	Single-issue
Citizens for Law and Order	3	3	Single-issue
National Organization for Victim Assistance	3	3	Single-issue
Professional groups			
Boys and Girls Club	12	13	Social service
American Bar Association	7	8	Legal
Rand Corporation	6	8	Research/policy
National Association of Criminal Defense Lawyers	5	6	Legal
Cato Institute	5	5	Research/policy
University of Utah School of Law	5	5	Legal
American Psychological Association	4	4	Social service
New Citizenship Project	4	4	Research/policy
University of Maryland	4	4	Educational
American Bankers Association	4	4	Business
SEARCH	3	4	Research/policy
House of Ruth	3	3	Social service
National Network of Runaway and Youth Services	3	3	Social service
YWCA	3	3	Social service
Brookings Institute	3	3	Research/policy
Heritage Foundation	3	3	Research/policy
Milton S. Eisenhower Foundation	3	3	Research/policy
National Council on Crime and Delinquency	3	3	Research/policy
Ten Point Coalition	3	3	Religious
Public Defender Service	3	3	Legal
Rutgers University	3	3	Educational

friend). The National Organization for Women has eight appearances in six hearings and the ACLU has 7 in 5 hearings. In fact, 40 percent (77/191) of all the citizen group witnesses represent citizens concerned with guns, women and children, and civil liberties. Put differently, 119 *different* citizen groups appeared at the 301 hearings in the 1990s, of which nearly half (56) represented citizens mobilized around gun rights and gun control, drugs, and crimes against women and children. A mere 6 percent of citizen witnesses (12/190) can arguably be said to represent urban black interests: the NAACP, Unity in the Community, the Black Community Crusade for Children, Communities/Mothers Against Gangs, and the Martin Luther King Jr. Memorial Society. Safe Streets Coalition, which appears four times in four separate hearings, is a collection of local community organizations and local government and other professionals interested in community safety and development . . . from Canada!

While a high percentage of citizen group witnesses are drawn from a small, select group of highly mobilized groups, professional associations are less concentrated. Only 4 percent of the professional groups appear more than twice (21/554), but the pattern is worth noting. Seventeen of the twenty-one groups with more than two appearances are from legal, social service, or research-and-policy organizations. What distinguishes these groups from other professional organizations such as medical, educational, religious, and business groups? First, legal, social service, and research-and-policy groups all stand to benefit from significantly government largesse in the area of crime control, and their policy interests intersect with a wider range of crime issues. In addition, compared to teachers and preachers, these groups have substantial professional resources. And while the medical community would have an obvious stake in the drug debates, we have already seen that the congressional drug policy has long favored criminal justice frames, an approach that leaves little room for public health problem definitions. As table 3.5 illustrates, these groups tend to specialize; juvenile crime attracts educational and social service groups; legal groups are attracted to the criminal code and juveniles; and 80 percent of social service groups (107/155) appear at juvenile or women/child hearings.

Conclusion

The incremental and then rapid appearance of crime on the national agenda generated policy environments that were particularly hospitable to some groups more than others. One of the most interesting findings in this chapter is the growth, persistence, and ubiquity of criminal justice agencies throughout the second half of the twentieth century and particularly in the latter two decades. The growth of these institutions has roots in the increased attention to crime in the early part of the twentieth century, but criminal justice agencies began a professionalization, bureaucratization, and organization process around midcentury that has also been a factor in their solid presence in the policy process today. The social movements of the 1960s contributed to some of this reform by drawing attention to racist police behavior, prison conditions, and abuses of prosecutorial authority, though the history of police reform dates back to the turn of the century.[58] Prison litigation also strengthened the organizational capacity of criminal justice agencies. This process accelerated the professionalization process by "providing a new and important forum for the ideas of national correctional leaders who had long advocated reform."[59] The growth of these agencies has been substantial. Total employment in criminal justice, including local, state, and national employees of police, judicial, and corrections agencies, has gone from 54.7 to over 80 employees per 10,000 persons since 1980.[60]

The prominence of these groups says something about the nature of crime policy making in Congress. Criminal justice agencies proliferate across issues, time, committees, bills, and oversight and state-of-the-problem hearings. Clearly, these witnesses represent not just agencies reporting on their activities but also perceived *experts*, detailing to Congress their perspectives, policy goals, and agency needs. The fact that prosecutors have nearly doubled their presence at hearings while spending by Congress on courts has declined in relation to other areas of criminal justice spending suggests that prosecutors are not simply testifying about how they are spending taxpayer money but also are being called to serve as policy experts. Their expertise is, however, deeply intertwined with their agencies' needs and their professional experience. The tendency of criminal justice agencies to measure success by reference to internal agency goals (arrests, prosecutions, incapacitations, etc.) offers some empirical confirmation of what Jonathon Simon and Malcolm Feeley have referred to as the increasing self-referential nature of criminal justice policy. In this formulation, program goals seem less attenuated to solving objective social problems and more tethered to accomplishing agency priorities.[61] Indeed, the growth of criminal justice professionals—in part a response to the substantial growth in attention to crime rates and racially biased or otherwise unfair criminal justice practices—has contributed to an understanding of crime and justice that is deeply rooted in individualistic, offender-focused, and punishment-centered frameworks. The history of crime on the national agenda described in chapter 2 suggests that the evolution of the national policy process and dramatic changes in crime rates and legal institutions that took place over the course of the twentieth century created ample opportunities and incentives for elected officials to use crime, violence, and punishment as readily available modes of governance that have few political costs.

The prominence of criminal justice agencies no doubt reflects the hard work of law enforcement and prosecutors, many of whom have lost their lives trying to keep the illegal drug markets, for example, from infecting more and more communities. But these accomplishments themselves are not evidence of policy effectiveness and tell us little about the day-to-day harm their actions mitigate or exacerbate. Indeed, as we shall see in chapters 5 and 6, they provide little comfort to those facing serious crime on a regular basis and would hardly qualify as responsive to these groups' concerns.

A second important finding is the balkanization of interests, as the crime issue settles into a stable policy process in the wake of the gradual and then sudden attention to crime through the twentieth century. Issue entrepreneurs are nothing new in crime policy. Anthony Comstock is the classic example; the NAACP's behind-the-scenes efforts to take advantage of returning World War I veterans to craft antilynching legislation is another. What is distinctive about the past 30 years, however, is the infrastructure that has developed for these groups, creating opportunities for legislation, funding, the setting of problem definitions, and the crafting of policy goals. But this infrastructure is not porous and fluid, providing opportunities for any group that comes along. To the contrary, it has long been responsive to highly organized, singularly focused groups who have mobilized around high-profile crime victims such as women and children, preference-intense single issues such as guns and civil liberties, and bread-and-butter economic concerns such as auto theft and fraud. Since members of Congress are under no obligation to address run-of-the-mill crimes, they are most interested in crime issues that will have some appeal to their constituents or can be used to obtain fiscal resources. The most prevalent citizen groups, by far, represent citizens concerned with guns, crimes against women and children, drugs, and civil liberties. These are serious issues, but they can hardly be said to be representative of the broad range of citizen interests on crime and justice issues in the United States. Just how unrepresentative they are is the subject of chapters 5 and 6. For now, I note the relatively narrow niche that citizen groups have been able to carve out.

Indeed, though I have emphasized the proliferation of single-issue groups across issues, it is worth repeating that all citizens' groups combined still make up a surprisingly small percentage of witnesses at congressional crime hearings. And this is true not only where we might expect it—in agency oversight hearings, for example—but also in nonbill hearings on substantive crime topics around which there is a great deal of citizen mobilization and agitation, from differing points of view. That the total representation from citizen groups in national crime hearings makes up a meager 7 or 8 percent of witnesses is astonishing.

Professional groups offer a similarly narrow picture as single-issue citizen groups, with legal, social service, and research-and-policy groups emerging as the most successful in national crime politics. Again, given the broad range of policy options for addressing crime, the limited presence of educational, medical, and religious groups is glaring. Thus, some groups are very effectively mobilized—hypermobilized in fact—while others remain on the periphery. As chapter 4 will demonstrate, the NRA has been particularly adept at shifting agendas and maneuvering across legislative venues. Such flexibility and mobility is no doubt enhanced by, if not essentially related to, their formal, highly organized structure.

A third observation is the long-standing decoupling of crime from broader concerns about race and class stratification. Recall from chapter 3 that the hearings on antilynching legislation were explicitly decoupled from race and class concerns, both by opponents of the legislation and— by some accounts—by its primary supporter, the NAACP. While lynchings are no longer a routine concern of black Americans, the stunningly skewed nature of crime victimization persists. Chapter 1 provided some details about the nonrandom distribution of crime victimization. Black teenage males, for example, are eight times more likely to be murder victims than white teenage boys. Yet few groups represent their interests in Congress. Legislation to collect data on hate crimes was passed in 1990, but such legislation can reinforce the disconnect between race and class inequality and crime victimization because it takes an individualistic, volitional approach to crime rather than a more structural view that connects racial hierarchy and class exclusion to the incidence of crime and its victims.[62] Indeed, the dominance of criminal justice agencies, single-issue groups, and legal, research, and social service organizations reveals a distinctive lack of voice from groups representing broader concerns that might include the dynamics of race and class stratification, such as broad citizen groups, religious organizations, and educational groups. Since the highly politicized issues of urban riots, policing, and crime prevention receded from the national spotlight in the 1970s, the thin wedge that broad citizen groups concerned with race and class stratification inserted into the policy process has largely disappeared.

In one sense, this is not surprising, given the cavernous gap between the day-to-day lives of citizens most likely to face serious crime on a regular basis—minorities and the poor, particularly as those groups intersect— and the legislators elected to serve in Congress. But it is striking that even during the period of high-intensity focus on urban crime, riots, policing, and crime prevention (1967–80), while these groups appeared in nearly 1 in 5 hearings, their total numbers barely registered, making up only

3 percent of all witnesses. This chapter demonstrates the consistency of this gap and the fact that the opportunities for citizen groups to participate regularly in national crime policy is generally limited to the groups with high levels of organizational capacity and/or singular attention to specific issues or crimes. That this has become increasingly true reflects the specialized, fragmented nature of congressional policy making in the wake of the massive social movements, governmental growth, and upheavals of the latter twentieth century.

Of course, the limited presence of these groups does not mean that national crime policy does not have racial dimensions. On the contrary, as others have demonstrated, the volatile 1960s and 1970s generated a specific context for policy making that—in the long run—further disadvantaged black interests in a process in which they were already marginalized. Numerous scholars have shown how the demand for order has come loudest from those most resolutely set against black demands—reactionary southern Democratic and Republican senators and representatives in Congress.[63] The blatant racist remarks of members of the southern delegation in the 1960s are almost identical to the claims made by opponents of antilynching legislation in the early 1900s, who were pledged to a system of racial supremacy that included widespread acceptance of violence against blacks and extralegal responses to black insurgency. But it is clear that both Democrats and Republicans helped maintain crime on the national agenda, with Republicans increasingly equating civil rights with black lawlessness and northern Democrats trying to link urban strife to the need for a more robust civil rights agenda.[64] In the end, the Democratic party lost that fight, lost the South, and would lose seven of the next ten presidential elections. While the environment for national crime policy is no longer infused with the overt racism of 40 years ago, the legacy of the earlier fights remains, with limited opportunities for connecting crime to larger structural conditions and with punishment the default orientation of national crime policy.

My purpose here is not to downplay the deeply rooted racial context in which crime was politicized in the 1960s. Rather, it has been to illustrate how the scaffolding of the national policymaking process on crime grew in size and scope as a perfect storm of rising crime rates, increased congressional attention to social movements, growing government involvement in addressing social problems, and the black civil rights movement took shape in the 1960s. In fact, as the remaining chapters demonstrate, the absence of black interests and the poor from this process reflects a deeper, more profoundly structural problem than old-fashioned racism at work here. Rooted in the nature of federalism is a process that makes it difficult for poorly resourced groups to sustain a presence in national crime policy debates—groups representing crime victims or those exposed to the collateral damage of criminal justice policy. In addition, as subsequent chapters will also illustrate, the racial overtones of crime, violence, victimization and justice are magnified in a political system in which the decision-makers at the national level have strong incentives to respond to powerful political, economic and professional interests. In contrast, the disincentives for broadening the scope of conflict to include the deep link between racial hierarchy and existing social outcomes are legion. The next chapter investigates this process at the state level.

Four

INTEREST GROUPS AND CRIME POLITICS AT THE STATE LEVEL

The fact of the matter is, you know, this is a system geared towards
responding to lobbyists who make PAC contributions, lobbyists who
take people out to dinners.... I used to joke with [staff member] here
that some of the advocacy groups that we represent that are lower
income—we would be better off raising money and letting them take
some of these folks out to Tavern on the Hill than to [have them] come
in here and be protesters du jour. That would actually probably have a
better impact, assuming some of them would be willing to go...and it is
a sad commentary but I don't think Pennsylvania is any different than
anywhere else, including the Congressional level.
                          —Democratic senator, Pennsylvania General Assembly

In May 1989, the Pennsylvania House of Representatives
held a public hearing in Philadelphia's City Hall on proposed
antidrug legislation; 21 witnesses were called to offer their perspectives on
drug addiction, drug dealing, and the devastating impact of the illegal drug
market. Half of these witnesses came from citizen organizations, and many
represented broad citizen groups, including the Southwest Germantown
Block Group, the Ivy Hill Upsal Neighbors, and Kensington Action Now.[1]

What is striking about this hearing is not that it offers a glimpse of
state crime policy process in action but that it is utterly anomalous. Seven
different broad citizen organizations were represented at this hearing; an
exhaustive analysis of over 300 hearings on crime and justice in Pennsylvania over 40 years reveals that such representation is highly unusual.
In fact, almost half of the hearings on crime and justice in the state

legislature between 1964 and 2004 and examined here involved no citizen group representation whatsoever, and broad groups are vanishingly rare. In contrast, the vast majority of the hearings include a representative from a criminal justice agency, and nearly half include prosecutors in some form or another. In striking similarity to the paths of access in Congress, the common pattern is a dominance of criminal justice agencies and a smattering of groups representing professional and single-issue citizen interests. When citizen groups do appear, they specialize in the crime issue du jour—guns, sex offenses, crimes against children, or the death penalty. This picture of Pennsylvania legislative crime hearings is confirmed by extensive interviews with state legislators, whose contact with citizen organizations is limited to a handful of high-profile, single-issue, and civil liberties groups such as the ACLU, MADD, and several statewide women's organizations, namely the (PCADV) and the PCAR. The absence of groups representing broader community interests, particularly those citizens who face serious crime on a daily basis, is glaring.

This chapter draws on six data sources in order to understand the range of groups that participate in the construction and maintenance of crime policy and the criminal law in Pennsylvania.[2] First, I look at 479 legislative hearings over 40 years, paying attention to their topics and types. Second, I analyze 2,497 witnesses at 309 Pennsylvania House and Senate Judiciary Committee hearings across the same time period (1965–2004).[3] These events represent a wide range of crime and justice hearings conducted by the Judiciary Committees of both chambers of the General Assembly and provide a rich dataset of active groups to systematically analyze.[4] Third, I supplement the hearings data with extensive in-person interviews with 12 state representatives from the General Assembly's Judiciary Committees (five Republicans and seven Democrats) in which we discussed the groups that members of the Committee hear from most when crime issues arise. Finally, I review several major public hearings in order to gain an understanding of the testimony of the different groups.

Two smaller sources round out the data. The Judiciary Committee of the House of Representatives maintains an "interested parties list" for the purpose of providing information on Committee activity to groups that have expressed an interest in Committee business. Lastly, I analyze lobby registration rolls from the 1997 state lobby list first collected and analyzed by Virginia Gray and David Lowry. On their own, these two lists are problematic for my purposes because they may underrepresent citizen groups and miss other important actors, such as criminal justice agencies or less formal professional associations. However, they do provide a nice complement to the other data, providing an opportunity to compare the formal lobbying community to the universe of groups that contact legislators through hearings or other means.

The first section of the chapter gives a brief overview of state legislative development in the second half of the twentieth century and of the growth of crime issues on state agendas. From there, the chapter provides a descriptive analysis of the scope of group participation in legislative hearings over a 40-year period. The final section provides a more detailed discussion of the nature of legislative crime debates in Pennsylvania and the groups that are the most frequent participants.

The Professionalization of State Legislatures

As with Congress, the post–World War II period brought major changes to state legislatures. Interest group systems became more pluralistic, and new groups, organizations, and institutional interests arose, including groups representing citizens who had not traditionally been represented in state politics, such as women, the disabled, children, crime victims, good governance groups, and the poor.[5] In the latter half of the twentieth century, legislatures in all 50 states became increasingly professionalized through the raising of salaries, the improving of physical facilities and infrastructure, staff increases, and additional sessions.[6] Professionalization is typically measured by the number of days in a legislative session and the level of legislative salaries. As such, it offers a window into the "expertise, seriousness and effort" of a legislative process.[7] At least a third of the states have developed fairly high levels of professionalism over the past 50 years, and in many states, service in the legislature has become a political career, something that was unheard-of at the turn of the twentieth century.[8] The professionalization process has been accelerated in part by increasing legislative demands.[9] It is likely that the professionalization process has also generated new institutional arrangements and policy domains that have served as a feedback loop, putting pressure on legislatures to further expand and professionalize.[10]

In Pennsylvania, several measures of professionalism indicate distinct changes between 1960 and 1980.[11] In 1960, for example, nearly one-fourth of the legislators in the House served for four years or less. By the 1980s, less than 10 percent served for that short a time, and nearly half of the legislators had served 15 years or more.[12] The trend in both Houses of the Pennsylvania General Assembly has been toward greater careerism, including longer tenure in office and high rates of reelection. In addition, fewer state legislators today have previously held elected office, suggesting a more personalized, individualized electoral process than one in which candidates were selected and cultivated by political parties for long-term political careers. While Pennsylvania consistently ranks among the top 10 percent of legislatures in terms of professionalism, another 10 or 12 states rank similarly.[13]

Lobby registration rules in Pennsylvania require groups that influence public policy and spend over a minimum amount of money to register and report their expenditures.[14] Groups are defined fairly narrowly, however, so many grassroots organizations, amateur lobbyists, and government officials who engage in pressure group politics are not required to report their activities. Several studies of interest group activity in Pennsylvania have revealed a wide range of groups participating, though a narrow set of groups occupies the registered lobby list. The most influential groups tend to be highly organized and specialized, for example, business, insurance, medical, and banking interests. Notably, the Pennsylvania Trial Lawyers' Association ranks high in terms of effectiveness, as is evidenced by its status as a registered lobbyist, its visible and active political action committee, the fact that many of its members share the same background with legislators (many of whom are lawyers) and that legislators mention it as an effective lobby.[15]

Crime on State Legislative Agendas

Much of the research on state crime policy has come from legal scholars eager to understand how the criminal law is constructed.[16] This body of literature notes the importance of criminal justice actors in the state policy process. Prosecutors—and those representing their interests—appear to play a particularly important role. Indeed, referring to prosecutors as principle actors, one study suggested that the process of developing the criminal law in Illinois in the 1960s was "dominated by white, middle-class, prosecution-oriented lawyers."[17] There are a number of reasons why we might expect prosecutors to occupy a central role in the state criminal law and policy process. The ability of prosecutors to leverage plea bargains through the threat of additional charges, mandatory minimums, and longer sentences is widely recognized by legal scholars and openly embraced by prosecutors.[18] Thus, prosecutors have a strong incentive to participate regularly in the creation or modification of criminal law because regulations that are favorable to prosecutors' interests—that is, rules that provide prosecutors with more discretionary authority in relation to defense attorneys and their clients and even judges—make it easier to obtain convictions. And convictions are a central goal of prosecutorial authority.[19] In addition, state legislators and prosecutors may have overlapping interests that smooth the path toward legislative access. As law professor Bill Stuntz notes, "Prosecutors are better off when criminal law is broad then when it is narrow. Legislators are better off when prosecutors are better off. The potential for alliance is strong and obvious."[20] Other studies have confirmed the significance of criminal justice actors in the state criminal justice process, as well as the fact that they frequently represent a unified set of interests.[21]

A related and important point that emerges from the literature on state crime policy is that some groups are more likely to be repeat players than others, and most empirical studies on state crime policy have consistently found that agents of the criminal justice system (prosecutors, police, corrections) and high-profile national interest groups (e.g. the NRA, the ACLU) are likely to be among the more regular participants. John P. Heinz and his colleagues (1969) identified three types of groups: ad hoc, recurrent, and principle. Principle and recurrent players included prosecutors' associations, law enforcement, and the ACLU. In a study of the Three Strikes You're Out legislation in California, Franklin E. Zimring and his colleagues similarly found that the California Corrections Peace Officers' Association and the NRA were active participants.[22] There is also some evidence that the private prison industry—Corrections Corporation of America and Wackenhut—has a presence in state legislatures.[23]

Missing from this literature is a more systematic account of citizen groups—specifically groups representing victims, those at high risk of victimization, and criminal defendants. While the criminal justice policy process at the state level has the potential to attract a wide range of advocacy groups—including traditional groups such as the ACLU and the NRA but also newer groups such as the Drug Policy Alliance, the Sentencing Project, Families Against Mandatory Minimums, Common Sense for Drug Policy—most of the literature does not indicate a strong or regular presence of these groups. Citizens' groups do make their way into specific policy discussions, as victims' rights groups did in the Three Strikes legislation in California, but it is unclear how frequently these groups participate in the absence of particular legislation that directly affects their interests.[24] In the Heinz study (1969), community organizations were only ad hoc participants in the process. This literature suggests that some disaggregating of groups is necessary, distinguishing between routine groups, intermittent ones, and those that appear only rarely.

On the heels of the professionalization of the state legislative process, state legislative activism on crime issues increased substantially in the last quarter of the twentieth century. Herb Jacob has demonstrated that states actively and increasingly modified and expanded the criminal law over a period of 30 years from 1948 to 1978. "The net scope of the law in terms of the specificity of offenses did not change much over the period. But the number of people who might fall into the orbit of the criminal law increased substantially."[25] Of the five dimensions of the criminal law Jacob studied—volume, scope, criminalization, sanctions, and procedures—all but one (scope) grew substantially during the 30-year time period under study. Jacob attributes these changes primarily to rising crime rates and increasing fear during that time period, but he also notes that the decentralized nature of the American polity made for interesting distinctions in policy responses across jurisdictions.

For example, Jacob (1984) discusses the various groups that participated in the expansion of the criminal law during this time period and suggests that while issue entrepreneurs were rare, that did not preclude group action from influencing legislative activity. Jacob observes, in particular, the presence of groups closely affected by the legal system, such as the National Conference of Commissioners on Uniform State Law, the ACLU, the defense bar, and the growing mobilization of national organizations of public officials, such as district attorneys. Berk, Brackman, and Lesser (1977), in their study of changes to the California penal code, noted the importance of the law enforcement lobby (specifically the California Peace Officers' Association) and the less organized but nonetheless visible civil liberties lobby (primarily the ACLU and the Friends Committee on Legislation). In addition, the researchers argued that established law enforcement lobbies had a clear stake in the growth of criminal justice bureaucracies and that legislators "widely indulged in horse-trading [with these groups] to enhance their own political influence and organizational interests."[26]

State legislatures began extending the reach of the criminal law after World War II, and this trend continued well into the 1990s. Similar to the growth of the congressional crime agenda described in chapter 2, crime issues have come onto state legislative agendas in fits and starts through most of the twentieth century and have only recently—even more recently than in Congress—become a more routinized part of state agendas. A number of factors pushed accelerated crime agendas in state legislatures, including rising crime rates, social movements eager to draw attention to urban violence or violence against women, an increasingly professionalized criminal justice system, and the growing strength of attorneys general and other public prosecutors.[27] The net result was the growth of mandatory sentences and an increase in criminal penalties—a general widening of the net of the criminal law.[28] Most states began by expanding criminal penalties in the 1970s, exemplified by New York state's 1973 Rockefeller Drug Laws, which created the harshest penalties in the nation for various narcotics offenses and placed limits on plea bargaining.[29] These laws set the stage for other states to adopt mandatory minimums, and today every state in the Union has some form of mandatory minimum sentences. In addition, a resurgence in death penalty statutes following the Supreme Court's ruling in *Gregg v. Georgia* in 1976 contributed to a growing effort to put law-and-order issues on state legislative agendas.[30]

But other forms of criminal law changed as well, in particular, alterations to existing criminal codes that subjected a wider range of citizens to criminal penalties and increased the likelihood of incarceration and/or the length of sentence (Jacob 1984). New gun regulations in the 1970s, for example, increased the number of people potentially out of compliance with the law by increasing requirements for obtaining permits. In addition, as an outgrowth of the criminal process reforms, sentencing guidelines began to proliferate that, for the most part, ratcheted up criminal penalties and the length of time actually served by inmates.[31] By the 1980s, the harsh drug penalties Congress had passed began to generate "copycat" legislation in the states, which both increased criminal penalties and encouraged prosecutors and judges to give drug cases greater priority.[32] Finally, in the 1990s, a flurry of new criminal statutes concerning recidivism and sex offenses were passed, including Three Strikes You're Out, the sex offender notification known as Megan's Law, Amber Alert, and juvenile waivers. Between 1992 to 1995, all but 10 states had modified their statutes to make it easier to prosecute juveniles in adult court and 24 states had passed Three Strikes laws, and by 2000, all 50 states had a form of Megan's Law.[33] Following the lead of Washington and California and the movement to reduce recidivism in the mid-1990s, Pennsylvania passed a Three Strikes You're Out law in 1995, as well as a Megan's Law in the same year.[34]

As state legislatures evolved, so did variation in each state's political organization, centralization of decision making, and extent of civic participation, all contributing to different policy environments and outcomes in crime control.[35] These variations help shape not only the extent of citizen group participation but also the nature and quality of that participation.[36] Given the large number of local power centers in Pennsylvania and its long history of civic engagement, Pennsylvania crime politics is highly participatory, since it provides a relatively open process for groups in terms of both its narrow lobby reporting requirements and its multiple municipalities.

Of course, no single state case study is ideal, and Pennsylvania is no exception. While representative of many states in its legislative professionalism, diversity, major urban cores, suburban and rural populations, crime rates, and political partisanship, Pennsylvania also has some unique features.[37] For example, Pennsylvania ranks seventh in the amount of home rule authority it has devolved to local governments and has one of the highest numbers of local municipalities in the country.[38] This has implications for what types of groups access which legislative venues and may result in overstatement of the limited role of citizen groups in state politics in relation to other states. On the other hand, Pennsylvania's fairly narrow lobby registration rules allow access to a wide range of groups, and research suggests that the rules do not get in the way of many groups interested in participating.[39] In addition, Pennsylvania is now considered a swing state and ranks pretty much in the middle of all states in terms of policy liberalism and partisanship. The policy environment is not heavily skewed toward one type of group over another, so organizations of all types can find at least some legislators sympathetic to their interest. Finally, a number of other large states with extensive criminal justice systems, inmate populations, and urban centers occupied by racial minorities and poor citizens also have highly professionalized legislatures, including California, New York, New Jersey, Ohio, Michigan, and Illinois.[40] Thus, while the Pennsylvania context may illustrate higher than average rates of professional lobbying by very organized groups and a higher number of groups active at the local level, the *range* of groups is likely to fall within boundaries similar to those of other similarly situated states. In addition, there is growing evidence that the findings I present in the next three chapters, demonstrating differences in interest group participation across state and local venues, are comparable to findings in in other states and localities.[41]

Pennsylvania Legislative Crime Politics

As with congressional hearings, legislative hearings in Pennsylvania are hardly democratic affairs. Groups are either on or off the legislative radar. When they are on it, they sometimes receive an invitation to a public hearing. Notification of hearings is published through the chief clerk's office in local newspapers and posted on the General Assembly's website. In addition, some committee members maintain "interested parties lists" and notify the listed groups and individuals by mail whenever a hearing is held on issues of interest to them. Public hearings and informational meetings are generally well-coordinated affairs consisting of scheduled speakers and/or organized panels of participants. As one legislative aide noted when asked whether hearings are a method through which legislators learn new information, "No, not at all. By the time they come in, we already know what they are going to say."[42] Because of this, as noted in chapter 3, hearings represent a particularly valuable opportunity to identify the range of groups that legislators regard as important participants—key players—in the policy process. To be sure, they represent a winnowing of all the groups, since there are many reasons why organized interests may not appear at hearings, for example, they are unknown to legislators, they represent viewpoints the legislators do not wish to hear about, or they are insufficiently organized to appear at state legislative hearings. The interviews were designed to ferret out the groups that legislators may hear from but do not typically attend hearings.

I have also divided the hearings dataset into two time periods, 1965–1980 and 1981–2004, which reflect several of the aforementioned changes. For example, by the early 1980s many state legislatures were significantly more professionalized than at any other time in history, and states had already begun to pay increasing attention to crime issues. In addition, by 1980, the dust had settled on the more overt politicization of law and order that had emerged out of the 1960s social movements, and the presence of new citizen groups and highly mobilized professional associations was well established.[43] The second time period saw a dramatic growth in incarceration rates while crime rates were simultaneously leveling off. In Pennsylvania, incarceration rates jumped from 68 per 100,000 residents in 1980 to 329 in 2004.[44] During the same period, the average incarceration rate across all the states increased from 130 per 100,000 to 432. Thus, the two time periods offer an opportunity to compare a policy environment that is relatively quiescent to one that has had time to generate institutionalized patterns of access.

While the topic of legislative hearings on crime as well as the array of interested parties have shifted during the 40 years under study, some fundamental aspects remain consistent throughout. Table 4.1 illustrates the topic of legislative crime hearings in Pennsylvania and the number of hearings associated with each.

TABLE 4.1. Public and Informational Hearings in Pennsylvania General Assembly, 1965–2004

Topic	1965–1980	1981–2004	Total	Percentage change between time periods
Criminal justice administrative issues (courts, prisons, police)	56 (50.0%)	132 (36.0%)	188	−14.0
Urban crime and violence	23 (20.5%)	37 (10.1%)	60	−10.4
Crimes against women and children	5 (4.5%)	48 (13.1%)	53	+8.6
Other crimes[a]	12 (10.7%)	64 (17.4%)	76	+6.7
Criminal procedure, prison, and sentencing issues	15 (13.4%)	67 (18.3%)	82	+4.9
Death penalty	0 (0.0%)	7 (1.9%)	7	+1.9
Other/unknown	1 (0.9%)	12 (3.3%)	13	+2.4
Average number of hearings per year	7.5	15.3	11.9	+7.8
Total	112	367	479	

[a] Organized crime, hate crimes, arson, drunk driving, general criminal code.

Of the 479 hearings on crime and justice identified for the 40-year time period, over three-fourths (367/479) occurred in the second time period.[45] While it is likely that some hearings were lost in the archiving process, the growth of crime on the Pennsylvania legislative agenda during this period is consistent with other research that has found that crime and justice became increasingly salient in state legislatures during the 1980s and 1990s.[46] Among the most dramatic changes in hearing topics was the shift away from urban crime and violence and toward crimes against women and children. While hearings on crimes against women and children were a rarity in the earlier time period, with only five hearings during the 15 years, they grew to 48 hearings between the 1980s and 2000s. This is consistent with research on the growth of women's groups interested in placing violence against women and family violence on legislative agendas in the 1970s and 1980s.[47] It is also consistent with the congressional data presented in chapter 4 demonstrating a growth of attention to crimes against women and children beginning in the late 1970s. Hearings on urban violence, such as juveniles, guns, and homicide, in contrast, have been cut in half—oddly incongruent with the dramatic growth in incarceration rates of racial minorities, who come primarily from Pennsylvania's inner cities.

Hearings on other substantive crime topics, for example organized crime, the criminal code generally, hate crimes, arson, and drunk driving, have also increased, from 1 of every 10 hearings (12/112) to almost 1 in 6 (64/367). The other topic with modest growth has been criminal procedure questions, for example the insanity defense, plea bargaining, wiretapping, prison conditions (riots and overcrowding), and sentencing issues, such as mandatory minimums. Finally, administrative issues of the criminal courts, prisons, executive agencies, and police occupied a consistent and large share of hearings through both time periods but diminished dramatically in the second period. Administrative topics accounted for half of all crime hearings. In the 15 years from 1965 to 1980 but in the second time period accounted for just over one-third. This is an important finding for several reasons. First, if criminal justice agencies are routine players in the policy process even as the share of hearings directly related to their agencies declines, this is indicative of a proliferation and diffusion of expert testimony and input at the problem-definition and problem-solving stage of the policy process. To the extent that criminal justice agencies play this part, they have become institutionalized players in a process that may be difficult for outsiders to penetrate. Second, the fact that administrative issues have less of a share of the legislative agenda today than they did immediately following the dramatic increase in crime rates and the politicization of crime on the national agenda suggests that crime is a legislative agenda that persists not simply because of the necessary oversight of criminal justice institutions but because, similar to the congressional context, new issues and interests continue to arise.

Group Participation

Who are legislators hearing from at these hearings? Taking an aggregate look, table 4.2 reveals the breakdown of all 309 legislative crime hearings and 2,497 witnesses in the sample dataset from the period 1965–2004.[48] Several dramatic differences among the types of groups represented are immediately obvious.

Organizations and groups that have a professional stake in policy outcomes represent the primary source of testimony before the state assembly (57.8 percent); in particular, representatives of criminal justice agencies are ubiquitous. Police, prosecutors, corrections officers, judges and other criminal justice personnel make up the plurality of witnesses, with 2 of every 5 witnesses (nearly 40 percent) representing a criminal justice agency or organization. In addition, a representative from one of these agencies or organizations appeared at almost 9 out of 10 hearings. Prosecutors alone appeared at 43 percent of all hearings (134/309, not shown). The next largest group type is professional associations—including religious, medical, educational, legal, social service, and business groups—but representatives from all of these groups combined make up less than half as many witnesses as those from criminal justice agencies. Citizen groups of all kinds represent only 14 percent of all witnesses, only slightly more than the number of ordinary individual citizens who testify before the General Assembly. In fact, while professional organizations and citizen groups appeared at just over half of all hearings, the witnesses from both groups combined are outnumbered by the witnesses from criminal justice organizations.

TABLE 4.2. Witness Representation by Hearings and by Witnesses, Pennsylvania Legislature Crime Hearings, 1965–2004

Type of witness	Total witnesses at all hearings	Hearings with at least one witness
Criminal justice agencies and organizations	977 (39.1%)	264 (85.4%)
Professional associations	466 (18.7%)	170 (55.0%)
Citizen groups	349 (14.0%)	163 (52.7%)
Individuals	261 (10.4%)	89 (28.8%)
Government agencies	220 (8.8%)	113 (36.5%)
Business and labor	169 (6.8%)	68 (22.0%)
Other/unknown	55 (2.2%)	44 (14.2%)
Total	2,497 (100.0%)	309 (100%)

TABLE 4.3. Citizen Groups at Pennsylvania Legislative Crime Hearings, 1965–2004

Type of group	Number and percentage of citizen group witnesses	As percentage of all witnesses	Hearings with at least one witness
Single issue	196 (56.1%)	7.8%	110 (35.6%)
Civil liberties	79 (23.2%)	3.2%	70 (22.7%)
Broad	74 (21.2%)	3.0%	45 (14.6%)
Total	349 (100%)	2,497 (14.0%)	

Though witnesses from citizen groups appeared at slightly more than half of all hearings, it was single-issue citizen groups and civil liberties groups that were largely responsible for this level of representation (see table 4.3). They appeared at more than a third of hearings, whereas broad citizen groups were represented at only 15 percent of the crime hearings in the dataset and made up a tiny fraction of all witnesses (3 percent). Broad groups were outrepresented in this regard by business and labor groups as well, which represented only 6 percent of the total witnesses but appeared in 22 percent of the hearings, as well as by individuals, who represented only 1 in 10 witnesses and appeared at almost a third of all hearings. One the whole, the presence of citizen groups in general is considerably smaller than that of criminal justice agencies, and broad citizen groups are rare.

These data are highly consistent with responses from legislators during the interviews. All 12 respondents mentioned criminal justice agencies in response to the open-ended question "What are some of the groups you hear from on crime issues?"[49] Each respondent spent considerable time discussing criminal justice agencies, in particular the Pennsylvania District Attorneys Association and law enforcement agencies (sheriffs, state police, fraternal orders of police). One aide to a Republican Senator noted:

The District Attorneys Association is very outspoken on the side, as you would guess, of the law enforcement and the prosecution and specifically, the legislative unit for the Philadelphia District Attorney's office acts as the legislative arm of the state District Attorneys Association. So...[in] almost every issue they are involved....[And on] law enforcement issues...chiefs of police get involved, state police, government agencies, we hear from them or the Department of Corrections, or Probation and Parole, those are all agencies that we hear from, or groups that we hear from.[50]

Another Democratic senator, when specifically asked "Do you hear from district attorneys?" replied: "Yes, all the time...the District Attorneys

TABLE 4.4. Groups Mentioned Most Frequently by Respondents

Name	Respondents who mentioned
Pennsylvania District Attorneys Association	12 (100%)
ACLU	10 (83.3%)
Treatment providers	10 (83.3%)
PCAR	8 (66.7%)
Fraternal Order of Police	7 (58.3%)
MADD	7 (58.3%)
Pennsylvania Chiefs of Police	7 (58.3%)
Pennsylvania Prison Society	5 (41.7%)
PCADV	5 (41.7%)
Department of Corrections	5 (41.7%)
Board of Probation and Parole	4 (33.0%)
NRA	4 (33.0%)
Association of Retarded Citizens	3 (25.0%)
National Conference of State Legislators	2 (16.7%)
ACORN	2 (16.7%)
NAACP	2 (16.7%)
Pennsylvania Coalition to Abolish the Death Penalty	2 (16.7%)

Association, and my local DA…chiefs of police too. I mean we have local chiefs-of-police associations, statewide…the State Police Association."[51] Finally, an African American lawmaker representing parts of Philadelphia noted: "You hear from the lobbyists most regularly—DAs Association. The lobbyists that work all the time, like law enforcement, DA, ACLU. The only group *the people* seem to have is the ACLU."[52] Single-issue groups' prominence over broader citizen organizations was also borne out in the interviews. Not a single respondent mentioned a broad citizen group without a specific prompt ("Do you ever hear from citizen groups that have a broader focus, such as neighborhood associations, the Urban League, the NAACP?"). Even when prompted, only two actual organizations were mentioned by name (Kensington Welfare Rights and ACORN).[53] In contrast, as table 4.4 illustrates, all of the respondents mentioned single-issue and civil liberties groups; the most frequently mentioned groups were the PCADV, the ACLU, and MADD.[54] Respondents' discussion of government agencies and professional association revolved primarily around social service and treatment providers. Virtually no one mentioned business or labor groups.

Changes over Time

Comparing group representation over time provides an opportunity to see how patterns of access have been established over the course of crime

TABLE 4.5. Witness Representation by Witness and by Hearing, Pennsylvania Legislature Crime Hearings, 1964–2004

Type of witness	Witnesses represented at crime and justice hearings			Number of hearings with a witness from each category	
	1964–1980	1981–2004	Total	1964–1980	1981–2004
Criminal justice agencies and organizations	228 (41.5%)	749 (38.5%)	977	52 (88.1%)	212 (84.8%)
Professional associations	83 (15.1%)	375 (19.3%)	466	41 (69.5%)	128 (51.2%)
Citizen organizations	58 (10.5%)	292 (15.0%)	74	23 (39.0%)	140 (56.0%)
Individuals	67 (12.2%)	194 (10.0%)	261	27 (45.8%)	62 (24.8%)
Government agencies	62 (11.3%)	158 (8.1%)	220	28 (47.5%)	85 (34.0%)
Business and labor	37 (6.7%)	131 (6.7%)	169	11 (18.6%)	57 (22.8%)
Other/Unknown	15 (2.7%)	48 (2.5%)	55	10 (16.9%)	35 (14.0%)
Total witnesses/ hearings	550	1947	2,497	59	249

and justice emerging as a major policy area for state legislatures. Table 4.5 illustrates subtle but important shifts.

The sheer volume of witnesses from criminal justice agencies—police, prosecutors, prison officials, probation and parole boards, and judges—in both time periods is remarkable. Witnesses from criminal justice agencies and organizations represent the plurality of witnesses at crime and justice hearings in both time periods, and while their share of total witnesses has declined slightly, they have hardly diminished their strong presence, appearing at well over 80 percent of all hearings in both time periods. Both professional associations and citizen organizations have slightly increased their share of the witness lists, though the proportion of hearings in which a professional witness testified declined substantially from nearly two-thirds of all hearings in the earlier period to just over half in the later. This suggests that professional groups are increasingly consolidating their witness testimony to a specific range of legislation even as they are strengthening their presence as witnesses. In fact, most professional organizations specialize in hearings that are directly related to their interests. For example, of the witnesses from religious organizations, more than 2 in 5 testified at death penalty hearings. Similarly, over half of the medical witnesses and over 40 percent of social service agencies testified at hearings on illegal drugs or on prostitution and sex crimes. Almost half of the legal group witnesses testified at death penalty, criminal code, or court procedure hearings. Of the 170 hearings with at least one witness

TABLE 4.6. Number and Percentage of Citizen Group Witnesses, by Type

Type	All citizen group witnesses		Hearings in which citizen groups appeared	
	1964–1980	1981–2004	1964–1980	1981–2004
Single-issue	24 (4.4%)	165 (8.5%)	12 (20.3%)	98 (39.2%)
Civil liberties/ victims	11 (2.0%)	75 (3.8%)	10 (16.9%)	60 (24.0%)
Broad citizen	23 (4.2%)	52 (2.7%)	14 (23.7%)	32 (12.8%)

from any professional group, 111 (65 percent) had only one type of professional group represented, suggesting that professional groups infrequently share legislative terrain with other professional groups.

In the later period, citizen group witnesses increased their total share of the witnesses (from 10.5 percent to 15.0 percent) but, more dramatically, appeared at more than half of all hearings (56.0 percent) compared to just over a third (39.0 percent) of hearings in the earlier time period. Government agencies appeared at fewer hearings and made up a slightly smaller percentage of witnesses in the later period.

The growth in citizen groups at hearings is due almost entirely to the emerging presence of single-issue groups and civil liberties organizations, at a larger number of crime and justice hearings, as table 4.6 illustrates.

These groups have been present more and more often at hearings and in greater and greater overall numbers, while broad groups, which appeared at almost 1 out of every 4 hearings in the earlier time period, appeared at only 1 in 8 after 1981. Similarly, all citizen groups combined represented a very small portion of witnesses in the earlier time period (in fact, civil liberties groups were the smallest), but in the later period the single-issue and civil liberties groups strengthened their share of witnesses, while broad groups declined even further to a mere 2.7 percent of all witnesses. Thus on the one hand, crime hearings appear to have opened to citizen organizations over time, with criminal justice agencies and professional organizations slightly decreasing some of their share of representation and giving ground to more citizens' groups. On the other hand, the type of citizen group that has proliferated is exclusively single-issue and civil libertarian in nature, and criminal justice agencies still remain a routine part of the policymaking landscape.

Several other analyses nicely illustrate this point. I use a Herfindahl index to measure the concentration of group types in the legislative hearings in the dataset (see chapter 3 for details on the index). A decline in group concentration indicates increased plurality of representation. A perfect monopoly—all witnesses from the same group type in a year—

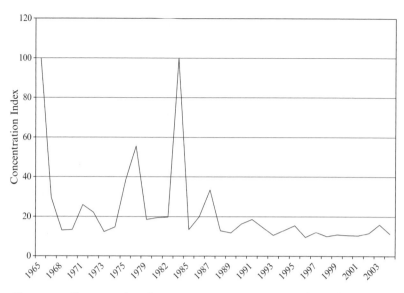

Figure 4.1. Concentration of group representation at Pennsylvania legislative crime hearings, 1965–2004

would represent a score of 100.[55] Dramatic declines in the index over a period of time, from 55 to 20 for example, indicate that witnesses are spread across a wider range of groups.[56]

Figure 4.1 illustrates the Herfindahl index for the full spectrum of possible groups (16 types).

The Herfindahl index indicates that group representation becomes less monopolistic as we move through the time period. In other words, groups become increasingly spread out across hearings over time. The data presented earlier indicate, however, that it is an increase in single-issue groups in both quantity of witnesses and volume of hearings that largely explains this shift and that it has come at the expense of broad organizations.[57] Mean differences across the two time periods are significant (see appendix 2).

Table 4.7 also demonstrates the concentration of representation in the hands of single-issue citizen groups and a few professional associations.

Looking only at hearings between 1990 and 2004 (n = 200), only one broad citizen group, the Alliance for the Mentally Ill, appeared at more than two hearings in the sample. As confirmed by the interviews, the major citizen groups were women's antiviolence groups and, dwarfing them all, the ACLU. Gun rights groups and gun control advocates, along with MADD, also make it into the top 10. As noted earlier, the Pennsylvania Prison Society stands out as the primary citizen group advocating specifically for more humane prison conditions and alternatives to incarceration.

TABLE 4.7. Citizen and Professional Groups Represented at More than Two Pennsylvania Legislative Hearings, 1990–2004

	Total Hearings	Total Appearances	Type
Citizen groups			
ACLU	52	58	Single-issue
Pennsylvania Prison Society	20	23	Single-issue
PCAR	17	19	Single-issue
PCADV	13	22	Single-issue
Alliance for the Mentally Ill	8	11	Broad citizen
Anti-Defamation League	4	4	Single-issue
MADD	4	6	Single-issue
Pennsylvanians for Modern Courts	4	5	Single-issue
NRA	3	3	Single-issue
Pennsylvanians Against Handgun Violence	3	4	Single-issue
Professional groups			
Defender Association of Philadelphia	11	12	Legal
Pennsylvania Association of Criminal Defense Lawyers	11	12	Legal
AFSCME	10	11	Labor
Pennsylvania Bar Association	9	9	Legal
Philadelphia County Bar Association	9	11	Legal
Pennsylvania Psychological Society/Association	6	6	Medical
Pennsylvania State University	6	6	Educational
Pennsylvania Trial Lawyers Association	6	7	Legal
Pennsylvania Medical Society	5	8	Medical
AFL-CIO	5	6	Labor
Philadelphia Defenders Association/Public Defender's Office	4	4	Legal
Joseph J. Peters Institute, Philadelphia	4	4	Social service
Pennsylvania Catholic Conference	3	3	Religious
Duquesne University School of Law	3	3	Legal
Women's Law Project	3	3	Legal
Drug and Alcohol Service Providers Organization of PA	3	3	Social service
Motion Picture Association of America	3	3	Business

Notable in the professional associations category is the dominance of legal groups, who made up almost half (8) of the 17 groups that appeared at more than two hearings. No other type of group came close to this dominating presence; the social service, medical, and labor categories each supplied only two groups that appeared at more than two hearings. Thus, while the range of groups has increased, the concentration of testimony at legislative hearings has narrowed, providing a regular forum for a few, highly organized groups while others appear infrequently (social services), sporadically (educational and religious), or almost never (broad citizen).

Interested Parties and Lobbyists

Table 4.8 summarizes the Pennsylvania House Judiciary Committee "interested parties list" and the lists that Gray and Lowery (1996) compiled of lobby registration rolls from all 50 states and gathered in the category entitled "law."

Not surprisingly, citizen groups are virtually absent from the lobby lists and make up just 13 percent of the House "interested parties." All of the citizen groups on the 50-state lobby list are single-issue groups, and only 3 of the 13 citizen groups on the interested parties list are broad (a mere 2.8 percent). Most of the single-issue citizen groups on the "interested parties" list have little connection to crime, though there are the usual suspects: the NRA, the PCAR, and the Pennsylvania Prison Society. The three broad groups are the Pennsylvania Family Institute, Common Cause, and the Center for Lesbian and Gay Civil rights. In addition, consistent with the findings from legislative hearings and interviews, criminal justice agencies represent a substantial portion of both the "interested parties"

TABLE 4.8. "Interested Parties" (2002) and Lobbyists (1997)

	PA House Judiciary Committee "interested parties list"	PA lobbyists[a]	Lobbyists across 50 states[b]
Business/lobbyists	47 (43.9%)	20 (66.7%)	355 (45.5%)
Criminal justice	20 (18.9%)	4 (13.3%)	177 (22.7%)
Law	6 (5.6%)	6 (20.0%)	233 (29.9%)
Single-issue (citizen)	12 (11.2%)	0 (0.0%)	4 (0.5%)
Other professional	13 (12.1%)	0 (0.0%)	2 (0.2%)
Government	6 (5.6%)	0 (0.0%)	0 (0.0%)
Broad citizen	3 (2.8%)	0 (0.0%)	0 (0.0%)
Total	107	30	780

[a] From Gray and Lowry 1996.
[b] From Gray and Lowry 1996.

and the lobbyists. They make up almost a fifth of the "interested parties," though a smaller portion of the lobbyists in Pennsylvania. Across all 50 states, however, criminal justice groups make up close to one-fourth of all the lobbyists in the law category, and in 28 states (56 percent) criminal justice agencies make up 25 percent or more of the lobbyists on legal issues (not shown).[58]

These data confirm the central findings presented in this section: criminal justice actors have been and continue to be ubiquitous across a wide range of Pennsylvania crime policy topics and have relatively unfettered access to legislators. From legislative hearings to lobbying to informal personal contacts with legislators, the presence of prosecutors, law enforcement officials, judges, corrections officials, probation and parole departments, and crime commissions signals their privileged position in state policy making on crime and justice. In contrast, citizen organizations are far less common, with only a few single-issue highly mobilized groups accessing legislators through all of these means. Broad groups are rarely represented before the Pennsylvania legislature in any forum. They have no lobbyists, and they make up a tiny fraction of the "interested parties," a minuscule portion of witnesses at hearings, and an almost imperceptible percentage of personal contacts with legislators. Professional groups—medical, religious, educational, legal, business—are fairly active, but they have become increasingly specialized, zeroing in primarily on those issues that are of direct importance to their membership, which arise on an irregular ad hoc basis, with legal and social service agencies being the most active.

"Frequent Fliers," Specialization, and the Routinization of Crime Politics

The interviews with state representatives shed light on the interaction of different groups and the nature of institutionalized patterns of access in the legislative process. Of the unsolicited groups that figured prominently in interview discussions, all respondents mentioned the District Attorneys Association, 10 respondents also mentioned the ACLU, and 8 mentioned the PCAR, the PCADV, and/or Women Organized Against Rape (see table 4.4). The hearings and "interested parties" data illustrate the dominance of these groups as well. Of the 275 witnesses from single-issue, civil libertarian, and victims' groups in the hearings dataset, 58 percent (160) come from just five organizations: the ACLU (77); the PCAR, the PCADV, and Women Organized Against Rape (47); and the Pennsylvania Prison Society (36). One respondent termed these groups, along with the Pennsylvania and Philadelphia District Attorneys Associations, "frequent fliers."[59] The Pennsylvania District Attorneys Association is also a registered lobbyist in Pennsylvania, and the Philadelphia District Attorney's Office, along with the PCAR and the Pennsylvania Prison Society, are all on the House Judiciary Committee's "interested parties" list.[60] Clearly these groups have a smooth path of access to legislators on crime issues. As one respondent noted:

> At the beginning of the session over a course of three weeks we held half-day informational meetings where every interest group that are our "frequent fliers," as we call them, we invited them in to basically share their legislative priorities for the new session. We basically said, "talk about anything you want to…just tell us what issues interest you." Frequent fliers are PCAR, PCDAV, Mother's Against Drunk Driving, the DA's Association, the state agencies.[61]

In contrast, broad citizen groups arose during the interviews only after a specific prompt. For example, one senator, who had served as a local city councilman, was asked, "Do you hear from community organizations?" He responded:

> I don't see [them]. I see it all happening, all the angst and frustration, at the local level. But I don't see it coming out, to express itself as much [in the state legislature]. This is an insular process here…as a local official I would go out of my way to seek out public input through public hearings, discussion, legislation, holding up bills for public citizen comment…you don't have that here in Harrisburg.[62]

A Democratic senator from Pittsburgh also lamented the difficulty he has in getting urban broad groups to Harrisburg, as noted in the epigraph to this chapter.

Each of these groups is highly organized, with a formal policy agenda and extensive staff. A brief description of each group follows.

The Pennsylvania District Attorneys Association

This association was formed in 1912 "for the purpose of providing uniformity and efficiency in the discharge of duties and functions of Pennsylvania's 67 District Attorneys and their assistants." Today, the association has about a thousand members, who include current and former district attorneys and their assistants, and is located just 8 miles from the capitol building in Harrisburg. The Association is highly active in the legislative arena:

The Association periodically mails to all District Attorneys' offices notice of recently enacted or moving legislation of importance to District Attorneys. Through the Association's statewide telephone network, District Attorneys are also contacted by members of the Executive Committee to actively participate in legislative efforts which will impact on the prosecution of criminal cases, victim rights and public safety. Periodic trips have been made to Harrisburg to meet with Pennsylvania senators and representatives to address State legislative issues, and also to Washington, D.C. to address relevant federal issues.[63]

The Association's legislative lobbying is ubiquitous. According to one respondent in the House,

> The DA's Association has an excellent relationship with the judiciary committees in both the House and Senate but also with PCAR and PCADV. So there are open lines of communication. So typically PCADV and/or PCAR will have some type of an idea and if they realize it is going to come within the purview of the DA's office, before they even look at introducing the legislation they'll get everybody to the table and have like a break-out session of "Let's just work this out" so that when we . . . let's just get all on the same page. Work out our respective kinks so that we can actually present a model piece of legislation for them to run with.[64]

Another respondent indicated that legislators work closely with the Association on crime policy.

> The DA's Association, they have an agenda, a legislative agenda that's set by their membership. . . . The DA's staff, generally, their position on issues is closely aligned with our caucus' position on issues. So I don't have a problem saying, "Hey guys, I need your help. I need a memo on such and such." And they'll find someone out there amongst their membership who did last on that issue who can throw something together really quickly, whereas I would have to do all of the research and start fresh. So, they're a great tool to us. Now, because I go to them to help with stuff, they sometimes have a clue as to what we are going to do more so, in advance of others. But again, that's generally because they're on the same side with us.[65]

These comments parallel legal scholars' investigations into the development of criminal law and criminal justice policy at the state level. That there is correspondence between the interests of lawmakers and the interests of prosecutors finds empirical support in these data.

The PCAR

This organization was founded in 1975 to

> challenge public attitudes, raise public awareness, and effect criti-
> cal changes in public policy, protocols and responses to sexual
> violence.... PCAR takes positions regarding public policy affecting
> sexual violence victims and rape crisis centers. As an organization
> dedicated to providing services to and advocating for the rights of
> sexual violence victims, PCAR informs the public; the professional
> community; criminal justice, medical and legal systems personnel;
> government officials; and legislators as to its views that affect the
> goals of the organization.[66]

Both the PCAR and PCADV are central to the criminal law in Pennsylvania. One respondent outlined the legislative process when issues involving abuse of women or children arise:

> The informational meeting before that we brought in the Coalition
> Against Rape and the Coalition Against Domestic Violence and
> asked that they update us on their legislative agenda, and where
> things were.... The chairman happens to be roommates with the
> Speaker, so they talked and thought it would be good for our caucus
> to do some type of family, women, children pieces of legislations.
> So I've been working with PCADV and PCAR to develop that leg-
> islation, have them come back before the committee for domestic
> violence month, so as part of that kickoff we wanted more some of
> the bills and to announce that we are working with them to address
> some other issues that weren't quite ready. So, we brought them
> back and they basically told the committee everything that had hap-
> pened since they were last here in January and where things stood.
> And the next week we were able to move some of that legislation.[67]

The ACLU

The Pennsylvania ACLU has 11 chapters throughout the state and follows the national chapter in promoting advocacy, education, and litigation to preserve and promote civil liberties, including the freedom of
speech, the right to privacy, reproductive freedom, and equal treatment
under the law.[68] In 2005–6, for example, the Pennsylvania ACLU supported improved police-community relations; opposed the death penalty,
argued against surveillance cameras in municipalities; opposed stringent
sex offender registration laws as ineffective; worked on issues such as
improving legal defense for indigent offenders and better access to court

interpreters and providing better health care for geriatric prisoners; and conducted public education forums on felon disenfranchisement. The ACLU has also supported the creation of an "innocence commission," which would review cases of wrongful conviction and exoneration in order to make recommendations to the legislature for changes in policy and procedure.

The Pennsylvania Prison Society

Since its founding in 1787, this group has been an advocate for prisoners and their families. Its mission is to promote humane prison conditions and reduce the use of incarceration as a response to criminal behavior. The society conducts extensive advocacy in the Pennsylvania legislature, supporting bills to abolish the death penalty, promote mental health and drug courts, establish intermediate punishments, and provide compensation for wrongful convictions. As part of its mission, the Society supports restorative justice programs, which seek to involve offenders, victims, families, and communities in establishing accountability and healing. The Society also offers programs that target the special needs of women and elderly prisoners and that address issues for people reentering communities and the workforce after having been in prison.[69]

Each of these groups has formidable missions and represents a substantial portion of the public. They can even all be said to represent specific public interest goals, as each has an interest in reducing criminal victimization. However, taken collectively, they can be seen as operating in two separate policy worlds, with prosecutors and advocates for women victims pressing for stronger enforcement of crimes against women and civil libertarians and prison reformers lobbying for more accountability and attention to the treatment of criminal defendants.

How Repeat Players and Broad Citizen Organizations Differ

One of the major themes in the interviews—also clear in the types of group present at most hearings—was that groups with regular access to legislators were highly organized and coordinated and had specific sets of policy priorities. Citizens' groups with more diffuse interests are less likely to have specific policy proposals, which puts them at a serious disadvantage in the state legislative process. One legislative staffer expressed open hostility toward groups whose concerns are more diffuse, using as an example groups that approach the legislature about racial profiling:

Even amongst those type groups, there are the groups that have the "Here's what we want you to do, here's the words . . . " and then there are the people that just bitch generally about an issue. "I don't have a solution, I don't even know what the problem is, just cops keep pulling over black people." . . . I mean, I guess I could try and come up with a definition of racial profiling and say it's a misdemeanor in the third degree to racially profile. . . . And that was something I just came up with here sitting with you. Those groups have never even suggested something as simple as that. They don't ever have a solution, they just say "the cops are going in and making stops." We have groups that come in here and have no idea how the legislative process works, or anything like that. . . . I've been successful in getting some of them to work with me through a session. But the more legitimate groups start over the next session where we left off the session before, the less legitimate groups, they go back to square one because there's a new session and they come back with the same legislation we started with two years ago.[70]

What is noteworthy here is that citizens facing crime victimization and contact with police on a regular basis are, almost by definition, demobilized in the terms that appear to be required for participation in the state legislative process. Broad citizen groups bring to legislators a set of problems with depth and breadth that have few simple policy solutions. The convergence of citizen organizations interested in quality-of-life concerns and a legislative process that seems most amenable to policy-oriented groups results in a highly restrictive venue for these broader groups.

Hearing transcripts reveal that criminal justice agencies, for example, spend a great deal of time discussing budgetary priorities and staffing and equipment needs, as well as providing legislators with data. These are concrete, tangible priorities. For example, the first 95 pages of a 185-page transcript of the May 19, 1989, hearing in Philadelphia on antidrug legislation are taken up by just two witnesses—the attorney general and the Philadelphia district attorney, who lay out their organizations' priorities and detail prior accomplishments. In general, bureaucratic agencies of the criminal justice system support legislation that they believe will help them do their job and oppose legislation that they think will hinder it.[71]

In contrast, the broad groups represented at the same hearing raised substantially different issues that were more diffuse and were decoupled from specific policy proposals but tightly connected to other quality-of-life concerns. A representative from Kensington Action Now testified:

Kensington Action Now is a coalition of groups, block groups, neighborhood groups, and business associations and we work together to empower community members and advocate for change. Our service area includes a section of Kensington which is a neighborhood in eastern north Philadelphia that was formerly known as the industrial heart of Philadelphia and the workplace of the world....Drug abuse is one of the most serious problems confronting our community. It is directly related to some of our other more serious problems, such as crime and joblessness. To date, government programs have failed to solve the drug problem, and we believe that now is the time for the community which lives with the drug problem 24 hours a day to receive the necessary resources so we can win over the hearts and minds of our youth, our neighbors, our community leaders. Our community is plagued by violent gangs whose existence is directly related to drug profiteering and drug abuse.[72]

A member of the Bucks County Tenants Association said:

We all agree that we need adequate enforcement, but enforcement alone is not the total answer. When the TV lights go out after the Bucks County District Attorney's press conference on the latest drug busts, the nightmares of drugs and death still remain. We don't have the luxury to go to our nicely trimmed lawns or colonial homes. Our tenant families must return to their apartments in complexes where drugs are not a press conference but a 24 hour a day, 7 day a week matter of life and death.[73]

The testimony of a community organization at the drug hearing in Philadelphia mentioned at the beginning of this chapter also illustrates some of the key differences between the resources of repeat players and those of broad citizen organizations. In response to comments earlier in the hearing by then Attorney General Ernie Preate about the need for greater resources for prosecutors, police, and prisons, a representative from the Regional Council of Neighborhood Organizations made the following observation:

It's hard to be sympathetic to people who come in here, such as the Attorney General's office, and I think what they're doing is absolutely fantastic, don't misunderstand me. But it's hard to be sympathetic to them when they say that they are underfunded. Let me tell you about underfunding. Let me tell you about need. We're not on a line item of anybody's budget. We give our time free, we search for a home or a church where we can have a community meeting...we have no staff. We frequently can't afford a telephone. We don't even have a typewriter sometimes. That's underfunding. That's real underfunding. And we're told that this has to be a team effort, and I feel like a disabled member of the team, and I'm not quite sure what I can do if only the generals and the colonels are receiving the funding and not us, the troops in the trenches.[74]

When groups do offer policy solutions, they are often inconsistent with agency priorities or practices (this will be discussed further in chapter 6). The same witness went on to make an appeal for distributing some of the asset forfeiture funds seized by drug enforcement agents back into the communities from which they were seized.[75]

> We believe that this money [asset forfeiture] belongs to us. It was stolen from us, whether it was used by our people or not. It was stolen from us, and we want that money back, and it's quite a serious thing. We need it. We can't go after the banks, which we're not shy to do, and accuse them of redlining, when the biggest redliners in the entire country are the drug dealers. Nothing is being reinvested in the communities. What's happening is that our neighborhoods and our communities and our towns are being crushed to death by these problems, and all of us feel helpless.

The comments were echoed by a representative from Ivy Hill/Upsal Neighbors in Philadelphia:

> The authorities are netting a windfall of seizures from the drug busts taking place with ever greater regularity. It's as though the government is levying a sort of tax against the dealers, allowing the dealers to just go on. It's nothing to the dealers, they make so much money. This money is coming from our community and virtually none of it is coming back. Community organizations like ours are the keystones of the solution of the drug menace. We are on the front lines. We have everything to lose and everything to gain. Without our eyes and ears, the police will never be able to solve the problem.[76]

Broad citizen groups also display a pragmatic streak, demonstrating a willingness to support whatever policy proposals are likely to work. At a December 1997 hearing on expanding night courts in Philadelphia and hiring additional magistrate judges, one witness from the Somerton Civic Association noted:

> I think whatever form we follow here, whatever format we follow, whether it be the Minor Judiciary or we use attorneys, the bottom line is we need safety in the Northeast....I wasn't really for the magistrates, but at this point if this I what's going to help, if this is going to deter crime, so be it...whatever it takes, I'm asking that this [House Bill 1897] be passed.[77]

What is particularly interesting about these comments is their contrast with the focused remarks made by criminal justice agencies. At the same hearing, for example, Ernie Preate and Philadelphia district attorney Ron Castille spoke about their own successful efforts against drug crime and the ongoing need to increase policing, build more prisons, create more mandatory minimum sentences, and make other changes to the criminal law that would increase punishment. There was a good deal of mutual admiration going around—prosecutors praising legislators, police administrators praising rank-and-file officers, legislators praising both prosecutors and law enforcement.

The marginalization of citizen organizations and the centrality of "frequent fliers" in the policy process is evident in the following exchange between the chair of the House Judiciary Committee and a community organizer at the drug hearing held in Philadelphia. After making some opening remarks, a member of the Regional Council of Neighborhood Organizations began to introduce the half dozen community organization members who had accompanied him so that they could each present a short testimony. As he began introducing the first person, the chair of the committee interrupted him, and the following exchange ensued:

> REP. CALTAGIRONE: Are they going to read their statements or do you want just want to have that submitted into the record and then . . .
>
> KAKALEC: Some have statements and some don't. They're very brief. Does that answer . . . ?
>
> REP. CALTAGIRONE: Well, there's a district attorney that has to get back to Montgomery County that has a case that he has to prosecute. He basically is going to be supporting your position on this. If we could just have him come up, stay where you're at, and have District Attorney Marino—
>
> KAKALEC: Why don't we do as many as we can, all right?
>
> REP. CALTAGIRONE: Okay. If the district attorney would like to come up, make your statement—
>
> KAKALEC: Please, we have been very patient all morning—
>
> REP. CALTAGIRONE: I know you have.
>
> D.A. MARINO: I don't want to interrupt.
>
> WOMAN IN AUDIENCE: The people are always last.
>
> REP. CALTAGIRONE: No, no, no. We're going to stick here. I'll be here with you to the very end, believe me. As long as they stay here, the people will.
>
> KAKALEC: Well, they have to get back to work as well. We have a real conflict. We were scheduled between 9:30 and 12:00. I think it's only fair.

D.A. MARINO: I have no problem with that. I can come back, if you would like.

REP. CALTAGIRONE: All right. If you would make yourself available to come up to Harrisburg, then we'll probably have some additional hearings on some of this over the summer months.

It is difficult to imagine that if some members of the broad citizen organizations present at the hearing that day had been unable to give their testimony due to time constraints, the House committee would have reconvened in Philadelphia "over the summer months" to ensure that they had the opportunity to do so. In fact, several interviewees noted the difficulties of being farther removed from day-to-day crime problems. A Democratic senator said:

> The more you get away from where it [crime] begins, the more you're talking more about [just] a bad guy that has committed a crime. . . . What are we going to do? Without knowing or caring whether he has a family, who's supporting him, what ties he has to the community or she has to the community. And you don't care how he got there. It's too bad, it's too late.[78]

And a Democratic House representative said:

> Local officials are living in those communities, they're confronted by community leaders who can't make it to Harrisburg, saying, "If we did this, clean up this neighborhood . . ." It's more real and pragmatic and more visceral at the local level. Those local officials don't leave their place of work and go off somewhere else. They're there all the time.[79]

Group Representation across Crime Issues

The presence of criminal justice agencies and single-issue groups in conjunction with the absence of community groups representing broad interests signals an even deeper, more profound disparity in representation at legislative hearings on crime than might be initially obvious. As we have seen, within citizen groups, some populations are better represented than others, and the most prominent single-issue groups sometimes have more in common with prosecutors and law enforcement than with other citizen groups. Groups representing the urban poor and racial minorities in general, and black victims or black citizens at risk of drug and crime victimization in particular, are almost entirely absent from state legislative hearings on crime. Given the impact of crime and violence on urban neighborhoods, we might expect to see groups representing the interests of residents of those neighborhoods or groups serving as proxies for those citizens. But groups such as the NAACP, the Urban League, the Black Legislative Caucuses, the Industrial Areas Foundation, the Regional Council of Neighborhood Organizations, and smaller neighborhood organizations that might represent those interests are rarely heard from. In their place are highly mobilized, single-issue groups representing primarily women and children.

A closer examination of several hearings brings this issue to light. A December 1999 hearing on racial profiling included verbal testimony from three prosecutors, six police officers, a law professor, and a representative from the ACLU. Written testimony was submitted by the black legislative caucus and a Philadelphia black clergyman. An August 2001 hearing on the same topic took the testimony of four police officers, a judge, two academics (Temple University and Pennsylvania State University), the ACLU, and the NAACP. Of the 22 witnesses across these two hearings, only three (14 percent) represented citizen organizations of any kind (the ACLU twice and the NAACP once) and three represented African American constituents broadly (the NAACP, the Pennsylvania legislative black caucus, and a representative from the Black Clergy of Philadelphia). In contrast, almost two-thirds (14/22) of those testifying represented the perspective of the criminal justice system (primarily the police [11/22]). Finally, in all of the many full transcript hearings read for this analysis, the testimony of the criminal justice agencies opened the hearings, and broad citizen group members were always last, coming after more formally organized groups such as the ACLU or NAACP.

Guns, Violence, and Juvenile Crime

Similarly, across four hearings, between 1985 and 1994, on the topic of violence and juveniles, 21 of the 43 witnesses (48.8 percent) were from criminal justice agencies (including five law enforcement and six juvenile court/probation representatives), 10 (23.2 percent) represented educational, social service, or legal support for juveniles, 9 (21 percent) were from citizen organizations, and 3 (7.0 percent) represented other government agencies or individuals. Not a single citizen group represented citizens facing serious juvenile or gang violence. Only two of the groups, Philadelphia Citizens for Children and Youth and the Philadelphia Anti-Drug/Anti-Violence Network, had missions that clearly targeted families and children in high-risk neighborhoods. The remaining citizen groups were civil libertarian or single-issue (ACLU, Pennsylvanians Against Handgun Violence, the Philadelphia Anti-Graffiti Network) or organizations without a direct connection to gang and juvenile violence (the

Pennsylvania League of Women Voters and the National Council of Jewish Women). African Americans, who not only are subjected to substantially higher rates of violence by juveniles than their white counterparts but also experience specific connections to individual juveniles who are caught in the throes of gang activity, were largely unrepresented.

In fact, an analysis of all hearings from 1986 forward that addressed urban crime issues (guns, police, juveniles/gangs, and drugs) revealed that 40 percent of all the witnesses were criminal justice agents (131/324) and only 15 percent (50/324) represented citizen organizations. More important, only 11 witnesses represented broad citizen organizations, and eight of those were at one hearing in Philadelphia in 1989 described at the beginning of this chapter.

Searches in the full dataset of 40 years of hearings for the following terms revealed distressingly little representation of urban minority interests: "black/African American," six mentions; "black lawyers' association," four; "black clergy," one; "Pennsylvania Legislative Black Caucus," one. The black lawyers' associations were present at hearings discussing the merit selection process for judges that addressed the need for more women and minority candidates. One representative of Philadelphia black clergy attended a hearing on the death penalty and another on racial profiling, and the Black Caucus witness testified at the racial profiling hearing.

"NAACP" and "Urban League"showed up three times: the NAACP at a hearing on hate crimes and at one on racial profiling, the Urban League at one —on hate crimes. "Community" turned up four community organizations. One appeared at an antidrug hearing and the other at a judicial selection/appointment hearing, and two appeared at hearings on prison overcrowding. Three additional community organizations were religious in nature (Episcopal community services). The remaining groups with "community" in their names were treatment providers or community-based government and social service program providers.

"Neighborhood" turned up four neighborhood organizations that appeared once each—at two drug hearings, a hearing on judicial procedure, and a hearing on motor vehicle theft prevention. "Gangs" brought up five witnesses from an antigang group that appeared at the 1973 hearings on gang violence in Philadelphia. "Race" brought up one race relations council that appeared at a hearing on municipal police training.

A series of six hearings in 1973 on gang violence featured 71 witnesses, only one of whom was from a citizen organization. Interestingly, however, that organization was a community group—the Neighbors of the Hill and Sedgwick Playground Advisory Group—more striking, 17 of the witnesses were gang members.[80] Of all the witnesses from criminal justice agencies at that hearing, none were from specialized juvenile agencies. At hearings on juvenile violence and gangs in the more recent time period, there is a glaring absence of groups representing actual citizens who face the threat of violence or who are themselves caught up in gang activity.

Women, Children, and Sex Crimes

Hearings on rape and domestic abuse reveal a very different pattern of access. A 1991 hearing on domestic violence included five witnesses, two of whom represented the PCADV (the other three were law enforcement officers). In fact, seven hearings in the dataset between 1991 and 2004 discussed domestic violence issues, and a stunning 19 of the 44 witnesses (41 percent) across the seven hearings were from just two organizations, PCADV and PCAR. In fact, of all witnesses at all the hearings on rape and domestic violence in the dataset (excluding hearings on treatment of sex offenders) since 1985 (20 hearings), almost a third were from citizen organizations (48/166). Fully 64.5 percent (31/48) of the citizen group witnesses were from just three organizations: the PCAR, the PCADV, or Women Organized Against Rape. In addition, these groups appeared at 75 percent (15/20) of all the hearings. Overall, comparing hearings on urban violence (police, juveniles, drugs, guns) to hearings on violence against women and children, the former have a much stronger criminal justice presence (41 percent of all witnesses) than the latter (24 percent) and about 1 in 5 witnesses at hearings on violence against women and children was from a citizen group, compared to only 1 in 8 at hearings on urban crime.

In the 2007 legislative session alone, 32 bills and resolutions were introduced into the General Assembly involving domestic violence in some form. The bills addressed, among other topics, release of criminal histories for the Domestic Violence Fatality Review Board, methods for identifying victims of domestic violence at health-care facilities, establishing leaves of absence from employment for domestic violence victims, and the establishment of October as Domestic Violence Awareness Month.[81] The PCADV has supported the passage of a Domestic Violence Fatality Review Board that would "bring together key persons, offices and systems in a collaborative, focused-examination of the circumstances surrounding domestic violence-related homicides and suicides with the goal of identifying gaps in systems, missed opportunities for intervention and barriers to safety."[82] In 2006, the General Assembly passed Senate Bill 944, which refined the state's sex offender laws and provided additional penalties for failing to register under sex offender registration laws and for failing to identify and report child abuse.

One can clearly see from the data that citizen advocacy for women victims has more political salience in the state legislature than advocacy

for black victims generally, particularly black males. Indeed, Marie Gottschalk argues that many women's antiviolence groups developed in conjunction with state-supported programs, for example California's Office
of Criminal Justice Planning, suggesting that the link between women's
antiviolence organizations and state bureaucracies has a long history.[83]
In addition, the early antirape movement was often charged with being
focused primarily on white women's framing of sexual violence and being
insensitive to a wide range of violence against minority women, as well
as the history of the rape charge against black males being used a tool of
white supremacy.[84] Certainly the major women's advocacy groups that
are active in Pennsylvania now are highly attentive to victimization of
low-income women and minority women. But that nonetheless leaves
a distorted policy environment that favors access for women victims, in
comparison to the day-to-day victimization of minority men and youth,
whose victimization rates are staggering. In addition, because these
highly mobilized women's groups emphasize *sexual* and *domestic* violence
(at least that is what legislators are hearing about most), this process also
obscures the serious, nonsexual victimization of women and children,
along with other forms of violence that are not domestic in nature in
areas of high crime.

Conclusion

In the Pennsylvania General Assembly, criminal justice agencies and a
few prominent single-issue citizen groups dominate crime and justice
hearings in much the same way as in Congress. While there is some
variation across the datasets, all of the data sources support this conclusion. The ubiquity of prosecutors and law enforcement and single-issue
groups focused on women, children, and civil liberties leaves a glaring
hole in policy debates about crime, one that omits the interests of the poor
and urban minorities, many of whom face serious crime on a regular
basis. The most visible groups with alternative policy approaches are the
Pennsylvania Prison Society and the ACLU, which advocate for alternatives to incarceration, humane prison conditions, and more democratic
forms of policing and social control. While these groups are very active
and have clear lines of access and communication with lawmakers, they
remain primarily focused on the problem of what to do with offenders.
Together, these groups represent the dominant voices opposing the death
penalty and mandatory sentencing, promoting better prison conditions,
and advocating for the rights of criminal defendants. Of the 31 hearings
in which the Pennsylvania Prison Society appeared, the ACLU had a
witness in 9.[85]

Despite its strong presence, the ACLU presents some problems as a group representing the broad interests of citizens facing crime victimization. The ACLU is primarily focused on relatively narrow, individualistic aspects of the criminal process, for example the death penalty, surveillance, and policing, that are quite far afield from the concerns voiced in the few comments we observed coming from broad citizen organizations in Philadelphia. To be sure, the ACLU's agenda is broad, and it appears to be the strongest, most consistent alternative voice challenging the dominant law-and-order frames offered by criminal justice agencies. However, the focus on the rights of the accused, coupled with legal strategies that must necessarily emphasize specific instances of individual harm, risks further perpetuating a policy frame that obscures the more diffuse quality-of-life focus of urban citizen groups. As a result, the presence of the ACLU may serve, in fact, to reinforce the individualized nature of this policy domain. Police, prosecutors, and the ACLU can tangle in predictable ways about individual rights and established criminal justice practices while remaining in the individualized framework of law-and-order politics where bad guys are punished and the policy focus continues to be on high-profile, single-issue causes.

While citizen group presence is less frequent than that of criminal justice agents, some groups are represented significantly more than others and have substantially increased their representation over the past 40 years. In particular, single-issue groups have a much stronger presence than broad citizen organizations, and to the extent that citizen groups generally have nudged criminal justice agencies and professional groups out of the way, it has been single-issue groups and the ACLU that have done so. The imbalance between single-issue and broad citizen organizations appears to be even greater in Pennsylvania than in Congress. Within citizen groups, those representing women and children are much more effectively mobilized in Pennsylvania state crime politics than those representing urban minorities. This contributes to a policy domain for crime control in which victimization is dominated by groups that represent traditionally "worthy" victims—for example, white females—in contrast to people victimized by crime who are themselves involved in criminal enterprises or who are connected to criminal activity by virtue of living in dangerous neighborhoods or perhaps because of their race or ethnicity (see the discussion of antilynching legislation in chapter 2). This observation is not intended to denigrate the successes of the women's movement in drawing much-needed attention to the victimization of women and children, but it does call attention to the continued absence of citizens whose day–to–day lives are threatened not only by violence but by living conditions that go largely undiscussed in crime policy debates. This policy environment, with its emphasis on white women and children and the relative absence of black victims, may perpetuate punitive outcomes in the justice system by de-coupling victimization from underlying socio-economic conditions. Studies of crime policies that involve high levels of participation by single-issue groups focused on women and children victims, have cited particularly punitive policy outcomes, for example.[86] In other words, thinking in the abstract about people who appear to live in otherwise safe environments and are victimized by random violence may contribute to the push for highly punitive sanctions *throughout* the justice system. The effect is to ratchet up penalties for those most likely to come in contact with the justice system, minority males, even when their offenses have nothing to do with the initial victimizations that generated increased penalties.

When attention does turn to the problems of urban minority crime victims, legislators in Pennsylvania seem to have a great deal of difficulty actually hearing from any. In fact, the major groups that legislators turn to when these issues arise are criminal justice agents, in particular police and prosecutors. This depoliticizes the legislative process because it provides police and prosecutors with the opportunity to offer up a set of problem definitions and policy solutions that go largely unchallenged, save for the ubiquitous presence of the ACLU. Thus, when citizen groups are present, they are primarily single-issue citizen groups who often have more in common with professional organizations or even criminal justice agencies that share their areas of specialization than with other citizen groups. The PCADV and PCAR are as likely as not to be on the same side of any criminal justice issue as prosecutors, and both have a stake in increased punishment and higher levels of policing. Even when groups with alternative frameworks do appear, such as the ACLU, the policy environment is more likely to resemble the distributional politics of "a little something for everyone" than the conflictual politics that seeks to reframe problem definitions and policy solutions.

The result is that state legislative policy debates on crime are frequently characterized by networks of groups whose policy preferences are either not particularly opposed to one another or fall into predictable and manageable debates. The process is also largely distributive: groups with established policy programs compete for a pot of resources. While criminal justice agencies cross issues and types of hearings, professional associations specialize, zeroing in on issues of greatest significance. This is facilitated by a policy venue in which legislators are called on to make ever finer distinctions in the criminal code and can hardly be expected to familiarize themselves with each and every policy proposal that is placed before them. Professional associations and single-issue citizen groups thus provide opportunities for lawmakers to narrow policy frames and take on and prioritize manageable legislative projects. Legislative debates about issues that are of great and immediate concern to urban minorities—for example drugs, guns, violence, and juveniles—are infrequently and when they do happen, they are depoliticized, with little major conflict over policy frames. These hearings are dominated by police and prosecutors and include few citizen organizations of any kind, let alone the grassroots community groups that confront and address these problems daily and lobby local legislators for policy innovations. On a regular basis, there are crime-fighting state agents but only a tiny number of broad citizen organizations that bring to the policy table a set of policy frames informed by day-to-day experiences with violence. This is confirmed by the limited contact legislators have with these types of groups and their clear connection to hypermobilized, highly specialized organizations whose interests are professional or are single-issue focused. The process is then reinforced by the institutional context in which police, prosecutors, and other criminal justice actors are regular players across a range of issues, such that when groups show up that have a policy frame or agenda consistent with that context, they are likely to fit neatly into the policy process. In contrast, when groups appear that conflict with these agencies and established single-issue groups or, more likely, are simply operating on a completely different plane, they are less likely to become consistent players. Thus, well-worn paths of access help construct institutional context in which group representation takes place, and in this respect, the Pennsylvania state legislative environment for crime policy seems to be even more monopolistic than the congressional one.

Five

CRIME, LAW, AND GROUP POLITICS
IN TWO URBAN LOCALES

We deal with everything from barking dogs to a shoot-out.
—Legislative aide, Philadelphia City Council

The 2000 public hearing in Philadelphia on the proposed gun ordinance discussed in chapter 1 was not the first, or the last, time Philadelphia tried to address gun violence through local legislation. In fact, several of the same citizen organizations that testified at the 2000 hearing were on hand again for another round in 2004, when the city council tried once again to enact regulation, aimed this time at reducing straw and multiple gun purchases. A straw purchase is the process whereby the gun purchaser uses someone else to undergo the background check and buy the gun for him or her. Straw purchases are considered a significant problem in the proliferation of guns in the inner-city. Ex-Offenders for Community Empowerment, a locally based organization that includes former inmates and has worked extensively on the gun problem, testified at both hearings, as did a local women's group, Mothers in Charge, and Pennsylvanians Against Handgun Violence. In a one-year period from mid-2006 to mid-2007, council members introduced a total of 10 bills that targeted gun violence.[1]

My analysis of interest group representation in the local crime policy process is based on examination of 500 witnesses at 45 city council public safety committee hearings over a seven-year period and interviews with 17 local city council members in two urban locales.[2] In addition, I reviewed dozens of city council hearing transcripts and identified groups through the Internal Revenue Service's Cumulative List of Organizations, newspaper coverage, the Internet, and archival research.[3] I begin with a discussion of the need to reconsider political mobilization and interest group activity through the lens of politicized urban neighborhoods. The scholarly emphasis on formal organization, resource mobilization, and policy strategies often obscures the active political engagement of low-income residents on a full range of quality-of-life issues, from garbage collection, graffiti, vandalism, and billboard advertisements to aggressive drug dealing, hate crimes, sex assaults, and gun violence.[4] The nature and quality of the administration of justice—through prisons, courts, and police—are also frequently the subject of political mobilization by groups that are not typically a part of policy research. Rethinking political mobilization in this way requires empirical investigation that can measure a wide range of participation.

I then offer a brief history of political mobilization in my two urban sites—Philadelphia and Pittsburgh—highlighting the various forms of citizen participation in these local settings and the salience of crime on urban citizen groups' agendas. From there, I explore the range of groups participating in urban crime policy debates in these locales and make several important observations about the nature of crime politics at the local level. First, participants discuss a surprisingly broad range of issues, despite the limited number of crime and justice issues over which local municipalities have direct control. Second, a wide range of groups participate in the legislative process, including a dizzying array of broad citizen groups. Third, many of the groups participating in local crime politics operate below the radar of traditional measures of interest group involvement, employing a variety of insider and outsider strategies in order to be heard. Indeed, some of them appear at city council hearings but are unidentifiable through any other means.

Fourth, the participation of prosecutors and other representatives of the criminal justice system tends to be largely reactive, responding when groups pose direct challenges or when policymakers initiate contact. This is consistent with research on policing that indicates that the primary focus of day-to-day policing is reactive and incident-based. Such work tends to keep police organizations occupied, and it appears that they have little incentive to regularly advocate their positions to local policymakers. When they do appear, they appear to be responding to city council members who seek their support or input on various proposed legislation. Similarly, like the police, prosecutors appear now and then, but their presence is muted. The gap created by the absence of these groups whose presence is so powerful in state and national venues is filled actively and vociferously by citizen groups, particularly the broad ones. Finally, while other groups, such as social service agencies, other professional associations, and government agencies, appear more sporadically—often when issues directly affect their interests—they also appear more frequently at general hearings on substantive crime concerns, such as gun violence.

Local Political Mobilization in Perspective

In his extraordinary work *City Trenches*, Ira Katznelson noted that formally organized, dynamic interest group activity is largely absent from local politics. Indeed, cities are relatively quiescent in comparison to the hypermobilization of formally organized groups in state and national politics. As the previous three chapters demonstrated, interest group activity in Pennsylvania and Congress operates in venues that expanded gradually and in sudden bursts throughout the twentieth century. This process of expansion in the policy process has had profound implications for how problems are defined and policy making is conducted. The formal, organized nature of interest group activity in these arenas must be understood, in part, as an outgrowth of the nature of the political enterprise at those levels. State and national officials typically represent thousands of citizens, have offices in locations geographically removed from those citizens (sometimes across long distances), and are engaged in a policy process that is busy and complex, requiring a high level of specialization, formality, and detail. In crime control, police, prosecutors, and other criminal justice agencies are a formidable presence. They regularly participate in virtually every crime issue that arises on these legislative agendas. Single-issue citizen groups, often working with lobbyists, stake out terrain and occupy a consistent presence in those arenas that matter most. Sometimes these group interests converge, as when prosecutors and women's groups seek longer sentences for sex offenders. And business and professional organizations appear regularly when legislation threatens or enhances their interests

I argue that the local political environment is also the product of decades of political processes, external shocks (such as the riots of the 1960s and rising crime rates), social movements, and legislation (local home rule charters, for example). Often messy, informal, contentious, and broad, with a wide range of citizens groups representing diverse citizen interests, local politics has the potential to draw in a wide range of groups.[5] These groups are sometimes formal and multilayered, with representatives in local, state, and national levels of government, for example, civil rights organizations and labor unions. But frequently they are less formally organized and more local in character. Of course, the precise relationship between different groups and any given locale is a question for additional research and one that varies by region and locale, but few studies of urban politics reveal a political process that is devoid of active citizen groups. Indeed, decades of research on urban politics have demonstrated the persistence of political agitation from a wide range of groups.[6] In particular, the civil rights movement and other political activities of the 1960s opened up opportunities for blacks to develop autonomous political activity in urban areas.[7]

Nonetheless, there has been little systematic research on the range of groups—both formal and informal—that mobilize to affect change in urban politics in specific policy areas. Interest group scholars increasingly recognize the problematic nature of the assumption that measuring formally organized groups provides a valid indication of the underlying array of interests.[8] To observe citizen groups making up a growing segment of the interest group community says little about how representative of broader societal interests those groups are.[9] Changing from an ad hoc group of citizens that share a common concern into a formally organized group with funding and a staff to get onto the state or national policy scene not only involves the mobilization of resources but also, as Schattschneider has so poignantly noted, is an act of political bias, because "organization itself is a mobilization of bias."[10] It is not at all clear that more formally organized groups are more representative of citizen interests—in fact, as Fiorina (1999) has noted, successful single-issue groups may sometimes represent those citizens with the most extreme views, not necessarily the most widely shared. Indeed, it is clear that government policy itself plays a shaping role in the capacity of groups to mobilize, sustain themselves, and reach the specific legislative agendas they seek.[11]

Most research on local crime politics suggests that attention to crime at this level is both episodic and recurring.[12] On the one hand, crime is a routine part of the urban political landscape, and as a valence issue, local politicians find it easy to denounce.[13] In the simplest sense, there is really only one side of the issue to be on. Crime is often a powerful local electoral issue, particularly when high-profile cases emerge, and though it does not form the backbone of day-to-day urban politics, as fiscal concerns do, it is nonetheless a recurring theme.[14]

On the other hand, the crime issue becomes significantly more complicated where the rubber meets the road. When "political rhetoric turns into policy discussions," a wide range of perspectives emerge on this seemingly intractable issue.[15] While everyone is against crime, urban crime politics are rife with struggles over issues such as where and how police ought to patrol, accountability for police behavior, what criminal behaviors deserve the most attention, how to balance crime attack strategies with civil liberties, and how best to address the underlying causes of crime, to name just a few. In addition, local officials are limited in their ability to respond to crime. While they have clear authority over local police, and while local prosecutors are typically elected, city officials have little control over the day-to-day operations of these agencies. Similarly, the police learn of only a fraction of crimes; they are largely reactive, responding to crime after it happens. This means that there are some powerful disincentives for lawmakers to maintain crime on the local legislative agenda on a permanent basis. In contrast, groups facing serious crime have substantial incentive to ensure that legislators are paying attention to the issue.

A second theme that runs through the research on local crime politics is that the scope of groups involved is broad.[16] While police agencies are often regular players, a wide range of citizen organizations also participate in both formal and ad hoc ways.[17] In some cities with old-style machine politics, business, police, and political elites have been intertwined to a virtually impenetrable degree. But today, as a result of police reforms and professionalization, corruption scandals, and the civil rights movement (to name just a few of the dramatic changes in urban governance over the past century), most large cities tend to be more pluralistic.[18] Either way, the general consensus of those who study local crime politics is that a wide range of groups—citizens, law enforcement, businesses, nonprofits—participate in the local policy environment.

A third consistent theme is the long history of criminal justice institutions as tools used by elites for the maintenance of racial inequality, directed most harshly, though not exclusively, at African Americans.[19] This is particularly true for relations with local police departments. "Black Americans," one African American police officer has noted, "find that the most prominent reminder of his [sic] second-class citizenship are the police."[20] In addition, contemporary incidents of racial minorities—for example, Rodney King and Abner Louima—becoming victims of white law enforcement officers' abuse of power continue to fuel frustration and tensions between urban racial and ethnic minorities and the police departments that serve them.[21] Blacks consistently express less confidence than whites in the criminal justice system, significantly less confidence in the police, more fear that the police will arrest them unfairly, and substantially less certainty that the police treat all racial groups fairly.[22] Even when socioeconomic status and encounters with police are held constant—which themselves help account for attitudes toward the criminal justice system—race is a significant factor in citizen attitudes toward criminal justice institutions and actors.[23]

There is also considerable evidence that black political mobilization in resistance to a particular local crime policy can halt it or bring a change in its implementation strategies. For example, Heinz and colleagues describe the fight over armored personnel vehicles in Philadelphia, which the mayor requested and many civil rights and community groups opposed. They "protested so loudly about 'tanks' in the streets of Philadelphia that [Mayor] Tate had to retreat with a veto."[24] Additional examples include black resistance to national anticrime programs in the 1970s and 1990s that were insufficiently attentive to their needs and black community group pressure on local police for greater responsiveness to their interests.[25]

In short, local crime politics includes a mix of legislative disincentives, few regular institutionalized interests, a range of citizen groups who have an enormous stake in finding effective policy solutions, and ongoing racial tensions.[26] There is little systematic data, however, about the full range and type of groups that participate across a wide range of crime control issues. Thus, a more complete assessment of group participation looks not only at highly mobilized groups that sustain themselves across policy issues and across time but also at those groups, associations, and connections that appear before local legislatures and local lawmakers to press their claims. This chapter details such groups in Philadelphia and Pittsburgh, without regard to their level of organization, staying power, resource capacity, or informal nature.

Issues and Interests in Two Urban Locales

Both Philadelphia and Pittsburgh, like many other urban areas in the United States, have long histories of citizen mobilization around a wide range of social and political problems, including labor, poverty, housing, and crime.[27] They also share a number of features as urban political venues, including entrenched political machines, massive restructuring of the political process in the twentieth century, and major shifts in demographics.[28] Philadelphia's history of civic activism predates the Revolutionary War, when civic elites mobilized the citizenry in support of the insurrection against Great Britain. Subsequently, Philadelphia's diverse racial and ethnic composition made for a variety of clashing and pluralistic political encounters between Irish immigrants, Jews, Italians, and blacks. Frustration with the Republican political machine that dominated Philadelphia politics from the late nineteenth century through the 1930s led to grassroots efforts to end the long-standing graft and patronage that locked many Philadelphians out of local politics. Among the most successful efforts was the creation of the Charter Advisory Committee, which drafted a new home rule charter for the city, providing for a civil servant system and a stronger mayor and eliminating some of the opportunities for corruption that had kept it flourishing.[29] The Charter Advisory Committee consisted of over 500 diverse civic leaders. This was probably the most significant political development in Philadelphia in the twentieth century, and it opened up opportunities to participate in the political process for groups that had been locked out.[30]

Philadelphia's black leadership was also active in organizing around local political, social, and economic conditions. In fact, the mobilization of the black vote was crucial to upending the Republican machine, with the election of reform mayor Joseph Clark in 1952. The election of Clark and the revisions to the home rule charter had direct implications for blacks in Philadelphia, as a strict merit system for city employment opened up a wide range of job opportunities.[31] In addition, the city's newly created Commission on Human Relations handled employment discrimination cases and focused its energies on ensuring that black applicants had a fair shot at jobs that had traditionally been closed to them.[32] By the early 1960s, blacks made up 39 percent of the municipal workforce.[33] After the heady days of liberal reform, when the city began to relapse into politics as usual, some black political organizers continued to back the new Democratic organization that operated in many ways as narrowly as had the old Republican guard. Rather than risk losing the support of the Democratic machine, these leaders avoided wading into the racially divisive issues of the time.

In contrast, the Black Political Unity Movement sought to organize a broad cross-section of Philadelphia activists that cut across ideological, class, and religious lines. While successes were rare, the more aggressive activists were able to gain some victories in the schools and antipoverty programs. The larger challenge was the way the ward system controlled the black vote. The Democratic leadership, while willing to promote black leadership in some respects, maintained tight control over the local ward leaders, even in heavily black neighborhoods.[34] Nonetheless, black political mobilization continued to challenge the Democratic machine's control. Led by Reverend Leon Sullivan, the well-known pastor of Philadelphia's largest black Baptist church, a coalition of ministers organized to fight employment discrimination in the 1950s.[35] Other local black activists, including Cecil Moore, organized protests targeting particular Philadelphia companies whose hiring practices disadvantaged blacks. In 1970, an organization called the Black Political Forum was created to "make the black community's political representatives more responsive to the community's needs and more accountable to their constituents."[36] Blacks sometimes voted with astonishing unity. When Mayor Frank Rizzo, who was widely criticized for his indifference to black interests and his support for a aggressive police action in black neighborhoods, proposed amending the city charter to permit him to run for a third consecutive term in 1978, 70 percent of eligible black voters came to the polls, and 96 percent of them voted to reject the proposed change.[37]

Following World War II, corruption concerns had remained the primary crime focus, and it was this issue that had contributed to the demise of the 64-year Republican rule in the city. Crime fell off the agenda for a while after the new regime was established, but in the 1960s, rising crime rates, the politicization of civil rights, and race riots brought it back in full. The issue was fraught with race and class overtones. The race for district attorney in 1965, for example, featured a television advertisement clearly aimed at preying on racial prejudice and fear of crime by portraying a white woman walking down a deserted street followed by a "faceless street-prowling monster bent on rape."[38]

One of the biggest changes to Philadelphia politics, aside from the home rule charter changes in the 1950s, came from demographic shifts. Between 1950 and 1970, the percentage of blacks in Philadelphia's population nearly doubled.[39] In addition, like many other urban areas at the time, the city was becoming increasingly segregated by race. Despite these changes, black political mobilization in Philadelphia remains high. In the 2007 mayoral race, four of the five candidates were African American, and the winner, Michael Nutter, was an African American former city council member who represented the diverse Fourth District.

Political Mobilization in the Steel City

Pittsburgh's civic activism is even more deeply rooted in the local political process than Philadelphia's.[40] Its revolt against machine politics began closer to the turn of the twentieth century, and its political system developed in a way much more conducive to citizen organizations.[41] The local political machine shifted from Republican to Democrat around the New Deal, gradually bringing Pittsburgh's black population with it as the new leaders brought jobs, economic programs, and other advancement opportunities.[42] Around midcentury, civic and business elites like Richard Mellon helped create neighborhood institutions and revitalize Pittsburgh's ailing neighborhoods.[43] Like Philadelphia, several important African American leaders helped create lasting civic institutions and generate political activity among black residents, including Homer Brown, who was one of the first black elected officials in the state legislature and spent much of his career building black political strength in Pittsburgh.[44]

More recently, as the result of a series of complaints by African American residents that city council hearings were insufficiently attentive to citizens' needs, public hearings now begin with an open forum, allowing individuals and group representatives to speak for several minutes on any issue of concern to them. This makes for some interesting hearings in which a wide range of citizens and citizen organizations advocate for their interests. One city council meeting, for example, included public commentary by local peace organizations urging the city to adopt a resolution opposing the war in Iraq, followed by a local community development group asking for funding to improve the city's playing fields, followed by a local member of an ultimate Frisbee league advocating for more attention to the city's parks and recreation areas.

There are important differences between these two cities in terms of how citizen mobilization has developed and its relationship to the urban regime governing each city. In particular, Pittsburgh has an exclusively district system for electing council members while Philadelphia has 10 district members and 7 at-large members.[45] But for the purpose of this study, the combined data from these two sites provides ample opportunity to understand the range of groups participating in local legislative activity on crime. Both cities have long histories of civic activism, as is true of a wide range of urban landscapes across the nation, and combine mayoral/council governing structures that provide opportunities for citizen activism.

Crime Control Politics in the Two Cities

One of the most striking aspects of local crime debates in this analysis is the wide range of issues that are actually discussed by organized groups, ad hoc coalitions, individual citizens, and legislators. While local city councils have a relatively limited capacity to enact crime legislation or direct the activities of criminal justice agencies—relative to state and national legislatures—this does not appear to stop them from contemplating a full menu of crime control policies and procedures. In one sense, they have little choice. A wide range of groups and individuals bring up everything from "barking dogs to shoot-outs," as one legislative aide noted. In fact, my review of dozens of public hearings reveals a kind of overlapping web of issues as they arise on the local legislative agenda. When specific issues such as drug dealing, gang violence, graffiti, and vandalism arise, the same hearings or conversations are likely to include concerns about abandoned housing, supervision of youth, economic development, and a sense of disempowerment.

Table 5.1 illustrates the topics raised and the number of witnesses present at the 45 public hearings over nine years that dealt with crime issues in Philadelphia and Pittsburgh.

In addition to the topics addressed in formal city council hearings, a wide range of other issues are raised through less formal contact with legislators, for example, attendance at community meetings, phone calls, e-mails, and ad hoc rallies and vigils. During the interviews, city council members discussed graffiti, truancy, loitering, vandalism, gun violence, gangs, drug dealing, substance abuse, sexual assault, police conduct, mandatory sentencing, safety in schools, homicide, community policing,

TABLE 5.1. Crime Topics Discussed at City Council Public Safety Committee Public Hearings, Philadephia and Pittsburgh, 1997–2006

Hearing topic	Type of issue	Number	Witnesses
Guns, violence, terrorism	Gun regulations, homicide, high levels of violence, terrorism task force	11	118
Criminal code	Spray painting, vandalism, abandoned cars, park safety, surveillance cameras, prostitution	10	119
Domestic violence, sexual assault	Prosecution of sex crimes, coordinated response to domestic violence, protection-from-abuse orders	7	69
Prisons	Prison conditions, community notification of escapes, prisoner reentry issues	7	91
Policing, fire	Oversight of police and firefighter actions, community policing, civilian review	4	61
Drugs		3	18
School safety		2	22
Budget hearing		1	2
Total		45	500

Additional issues raised during interviews: Graffiti, truancy, loitering, vandalism, gangs, drug dealing, substance abuse, police conduct, mandatory sentencing, safety in schools, community policing, escaped prisoners, jail conditions, noisy teenagers, abandoned buildings, prostitution, and hate crimes.

escaped prisoners, jail conditions, noisy teenagers, abandoned buildings, prostitution, and hate crimes. There are few areas that are wholly left to state and national legislative agendas.[46] While some of these issues are raised by citizen groups who are then left hanging in the wake of the local legislatures' inability to address their concerns in a concrete manner, few of the legislators who were interviewed seemed willing to abandon whole categories of the crime policy arena to other levels of government.

At times, many of these issues are intertwined with others, as when gun violence, gangs, drug dealing, and homicide converge into tragic events. But even on the misdemeanor end of the policy spectrum, these issues commingle, as when citizen groups express concern that abandoned buildings might turn into magnets for prostitution, truancy, and drug sales; a local university raises the number of incoming students who then crowd into surrounding apartments, bringing noise, theft, and vandalism problems; or residents of low-income neighborhoods complain about the excessive presence of billboards advertising liquor.[47] Even more complex is that many of these issues are discussed in conjunction with a wide range of other social problems like housing, employment, education, overcrowding, and substance abuse. One legislative aide to a city council member in Philadelphia noted:

There's definitely a correlation between criminal justice issues or crime issues and also housing...quality of life, they're all kind of intertwined. [For example,] if you have a house that that becomes vacant on the block and then depending on where that house is located, you may have people who either live in the community or frequent the community who may either be selling drugs or may be involved in drug sales, and they may use that vacant house as a stash area. Then it may end up being a location where the actual activities are being done.[48]

The Contours of Group Participation

Both the interviews and the hearings revealed an enormous range of groups that are regularly active in local crime politics. These groups represent citizens and professionals from a broad cross-section of the urban landscape. Table 5.2 shows the range and extent of group participation through local hearings and through contacting local legislators (as reported by the legislators interviewed).

Though the ratio of citizen groups to criminal justice agencies varies between the two datasets (hearing attendance and legislator contact), in both sets, citizen groups are the plurality of witnesses. They were mentioned by all of the respondents and appeared at two out of three city council hearings. They also made up one-fourth of all witnesses at the hearings. In addition, other groups—government agencies, professional organizations, and businesses—lagged far behind citizen groups in both datasets. Only a fraction of the respondents interviewed mentioned criminal justice agencies, while all of them mentioned citizen groups. Table 5.3 illustrates these mentions.

Taking a closer look at citizen groups (table 5.2), though there is some variation across datasets, the patterns are the same. Notably, broad citizen groups occupied about the same share of witnesses at local legislative hearings as all criminal justice agencies combined (16 and 17 percent, respectively). This is a striking change from the state and national levels, where criminal justice agencies outnumber broad citizen groups by a factor as high as 17 to 1 (see table 3.2). By most measures listed in table 5.2, broad citizen groups were the dominant type of citizen group, making up two-thirds of the citizen witnesses and over half of the groups mentioned by legislators, and appearing at the same number of hearings as single-issue groups—a stark contrast to other venues, where single-issue groups typically outnumbered broad groups by at least 2 to 1 (see tables 3.2 and 4.3).

TABLE 5.2. Group Witnesses: Hearings and Interviews

Type of group	Interviews (total number of mentions)	Hearings	
		Total witnesses	Hearings with at least one witness
Citizen groups	107 (70.4%)	128 (25.6%)	30 (66.7%)
Broad	87 (57.2%)	80 (16.0%)	22 (49.0%)
Single-issue	18 (11.8%)	41 (8.2%)	22 (49.0%)
Civil liberty (ACLU)	2 (1.3%)	7 (1.4%)	5 (11.0%)
Individuals[a]	—	88 (17.6%)	21 (46.6%)
Criminal justice agencies	11 (7.2%)	86 (17.2%)	37 (82.1%)
Government agencies	1 (0.7%)	86 (17.2%)	34 (75.5%)
Professional organizations	16 (10.5%)	81 (16.2%)	27 (60.0%)
Business	14 (9.2%)	23 (4.6%)	14 (30.1%)
Other, unknown		8 (1.6%)	6 (13.3%)
Total	101 (100%)	500 (100.0%)	40 (100.0%)

[a]Individuals are left out of the interviews column, because, while legislators did discuss the fact that individuals (not necessarily affiliated with a group) frequently contacted their offices, it is difficult to determine how often such contacts occur compared to those made by groups whose names were mentioned specifically.

TABLE 5.3. Select Groups Mentioned by Local Respondents

Group	Number and percentage of respondents naming each group type
Broad citizen (e.g., Men United for a Better Philadelphia)	17 (100%)
Community associations (e.g., Shady Side Action Coalition)	12 (70.6%)
Churches (e.g., black ministers, St. Augustine's Parish)	9 (52.9%)
Fraternal Order of Police	6 (35.3%)
NAACP	4 (23.5%)
Service providers	3 (17.6%)
Local police	2 (11.8%)
ACORN	2 (11.8%)
ACLU	2 (11.8%)
Victims' services	1 (5.9%)
Treatment programs	1 (5.9%)
Juvenile Justice Commission	1 (5.9%)
Judges	1 (5.9%)

Table 5.4 lists all of the citizen organizations mentioned by the city council staff members, as well as organizations that were represented as witnesses at council hearings on crime. Clearly, the vast majority of these groups represent urban minorities, the urban poor, and working-class citizens. This no doubt reflects the disproportionate impact of crime and criminal justice institutions on these groups.

TABLE 5.4. Citizen Groups Represented in Local Legislative Crime Debates, 1997–2006

	Appearance
Broad groups	
ACORN	Interviews
Ad hoc youth advocacy	Hearings
African-American Heritage Coalition	Hearings
Alliance Organizing Project	Hearings
Philadelphia Anti-Drug/Anti-Violence Network	Hearings
Avenue Organization Corporation	Interviews
Banksville Civic Association	Interviews
Belmont Improvement Association	Hearings
Bloomfield Citizen's Council	Interviews
Bloomfield Neighborhood Association	Interviews
Brentwood Civic Group	Hearings
Philadelphia Citizens for Children and Youth	Hearings
Center for Family Excellence	Hearings
Center for Family Values	Interviews
Center for Lesbian and Gay Rights	Hearings and interviews
Concerned Black Citizens of Pittsburgh	Hearings
Concerned Citizens for the Preservation of Philadelphia	Hearings
Concerned Parents Inc.	Hearings
Congreso de Latinos Unidos	Hearings
East Carnegie Community Council	Interviews
East Falls Community Council	Interviews
East Falls Development Corp	Interviews
East Liberty Concerned Citizens Corporation	Interviews
East Mt. Airy Neighbors Association	Interviews
Eastern Philadelphia Organizing Project	Hearings
Enfield Civic Assoc.	Hearings
Esplen Community Council	Interviews
Families Are Victims Too	Hearings
Father's Day Rally Committee	Hearings
Fairywood Community Council	Interviews
Fishtown Neighbors/Civic Association	Interviews
Friends of Elmwood Park	Hearings
Garfield Community Council	Interviews
Bloomfield-Garfield Development Corporation	Interviews
Garfield Neighborhood Association	Interviews
Gay/lesbian advocacy	Interviews
Happy Hollow Advisory Council	Hearings

Heritage Community Economic Development Corporation	Hearings
Holmesburg Civic Association	Hearings
Homeward/Brushton Council	Interviews
Impact Services, Inc.	Hearings
Institute for the Study of Civic Values	Hearings
Kensington Action Council	Interviews
Logan Improvement Association	Interviews
Lutheran Settlement House	Hearings
Manayunk Neighborhood Council	Interviews
Men United for a Better Philadelphia	Hearings and interviews
Morningside Area Community Council	Interviews
Mothers in Charge	Hearings
Mothers United Through Tragedy	Hearings
Mt. Airy USA	Interviews
Mt. Washington Community Development Corporation	Hearings and interviews
NAACP	Interviews
National Council for Urban Peace and Justice	Hearings
Neighborhood Development Leadership Conference	Interviews
North Philadelphia Council	Interviews
North Point Breeze Planning and Development	Interviews
Northern Liberties Neighborhood Association	Interviews
Northside Neighborhood Organization	Interviews
Oakland Planning Development Corporation	Interviews
Oakland Community Council	Interviews
Oakwood Civic Association	Interviews
Old City Civic Association	Interviews
Out Front	Interviews
Parents Against Violence	Hearings
Parents' organizations	Interviews
Philadelphia Citizens for Children and Youth	Hearings
Philadelphia Direct Action Group	Hearings
Philadelphia Alliance for Community Improvement	Hearings
Physicians for Social Responsibility	Hearings
Point Breeze Community Development Coalition	Hearings
Project Home	Interviews
Public Safety Councils	Interviews
Queen Village Neighbors Association	Interviews
R2K Network	Hearings
Rittenhouse Square Community Association	Interviews
Roxborough Civic Association	Interviews
Safe Streets Group	Interviews
Shady Side Community Council	Interviews
Shady Side Action Coalition	Interviews
Sheraden Community Council	Interviews
Smart Program	Hearings
Society Hill Civic Association	Interviews
Southside Community Council	Interviews
SPCA	Hearings
Squirrel Hill Urban Coalition	Interviews
Stop the Violence	Interviews
Strawberry Mansion Community Concerns	Hearings

(*Continued*)

TABLE 5.4. *(Continued)*

	Appearance
Strawberry Mansion Neighborhood Action Center	Hearings
Sunny Hill Organization	Interviews
Thomas Merton Center	Hearings
Town Watch	Hearings and interviews
Tree of Hope	Interviews
Urban League	Interviews
Veterans for Peace	Hearings
Washington Square Civic Association	Interviews
West End Elliot Citizens Council	Interviews
West Pittsburgh Partnership	Interviews
Windgap Chartiers Civic Association	Interviews
Wister Neighborhood Council	Interviews
Ex-Offenders Incorporated	Hearings and Interviews
Youth Education for Safety	Hearings

Single-issue groups

ACLU	Hearings
ACT UP	Hearings
ADL	Hearings
Brady Campaign	Hearings
Cease Fire PA	Hearings
Ceasefire NJ	Hearings
Citizens for Police Accountability	Hearings
Community Town Watch	Hearings
Hallwatch.org	Interviews
Lawrenceville Block Watch	Interviews
Million Mom March	Hearings
Morrisville Block Watch	Interviews
Mothers of Murder Victims	Interviews
National Association of African-Americans for Positive Imagery	Hearings
Peace, Not Guns	Hearings
PA Against Handgun Violence	Hearings
PA Prison Society	Hearings
Philadelphia County Coalition of Prison Health Care	Hearings
Philadelphia Safe and Sound	Hearings
Police Advisory Councils	Interviews
Police Civilian Review Board	Hearings and interviews
Prisoner Health Advocacy Project	Hearings
Prisoner's rights	Interviews
Society Created to Reduce Urban Blight	Hearings
Friends of Tacony Creek Park	Hearings
Troy Hill Block Watch	Interviews
Women Against Abuse	Hearings
Women Organized Against Rape	Hearings and interviews
Women in Transition	Hearings
Center for Victims of Violent Crime	Hearings

A total of 131 *different* citizen groups, consisting of 102 broad groups and 29 single-issue groups, participated in crime policy discussions either through legislative hearings or by contacting their legislators directly in the two urban areas during the seven-year period. During the same period (1997–2002), only 22 different broad citizen groups appeared in the Pennsylvania legislature, compared with 46 single-issue groups, across more than twice as many hearings. As noted in chapter 3, only 28 broad citizen groups appeared in Congress during the 1990s over the course of nearly 300 hearings. In sharp contrast, community councils, neighborhood organizations, civic associations, and community development groups are highly visible to local legislators. They make up close to half (58/131) of the citizen groups appearing at hearings or named in interviews. Single-issue groups, primarily representing those concerned with policing, guns, sexual assault, homicide, and prisons, are also visible, but broad citizen groups outnumber single-issue citizen groups by more than 3 to 1.

The presence of these citizens in the local crime policy process is so normalized that every member of the city council and their staff who was interviewed talked about citizen organizations as regular, consistent, and important participants in local crime politics, and discussion of broad citizen groups dominated these interviews, in contrast to the ones with state legislators. Citizen group involvement comes in the form of both regular, day-to-day involvement with established organizations and sporadic contact with ad hoc groups that form in the wake of a particularly disturbing crime. One former city council member from Pittsburgh put it this way: "Residents, community groups, block watches—they are very outspoken...groups that are focused on stop the violence usually emanate from a particular incident. Something happened and then a group started. But the other ones are long-sustaining and are dealing with building the neighborhood."[49] Similarly, in response to a query about whether citizen groups are in regular contact with local legislators, a Philadelphia city councilwoman representing a neighborhood with a large African American population noted:

> Yes, they are....Men United for a Better Philadelphia [for example] is a group I work closely with. Their whole thing is "let's get out, let's talk to people, let's try to get people to join this group." They want people to become more involved in their neighborhood because they believe it is a deterrent to crime. That particular group meets once a month with the police commissioner. And they know what is going on across the city because it is men from a variety of different entities that belong to that group. Another group is Wister Neighborhood Council, a group that has a contract with the city to provide neighborhood services. It's like a liaison between the neighborhood and the city services. So they are involved in anything that

goes on in the neighborhood, whether it's housing rehab or block cleanup, organizing town watches and many times they call us for help, particularly as it relates to crime.[50]

One interviewee put it most succinctly: "community councils are a big source of lobbying and constituent feedback on crime issues."[51] In reference to drug-related problems in particular, a council member observed:

They are more neighborhood issues, they're more town watch groups, civic associations, in the African American community, and a lot of church-based organizations. [We have those] in non–African American communities too, but the church is a much stronger organizational component to black [communities].[52]

While different types of issues bring out different citizen groups, virtually every issue discussed during interviews and public hearings (see table 5.1) involved at least one citizen group of one kind or another. In addition, all of the topics discussed at public hearings included at least one broad citizen organization, and all but one included single-issue citizen groups as well. All 17 local respondents mentioned broad citizen organizations as active participants, and many offered specific examples of groups they worked with regularly. One Philadelphia council member, whose district includes a high-crime, predominately black neighborhood, worked with a local ex-inmate group called Ex-Offenders for Community Empowerment to produce the gun legislation discussed in chapter 1 and at the outset of this chapter. The council member described the groups as "wanting to do something positive to make a difference, going to prisons and schools."[53] A spokesman for the group testified at the 2000 city council hearing:

Ex-Offenders for Community Empowerment uses life experiences of ex-offenders in campaigns to reduce the flow of firearms into our communities and to give youth a chance at a life free of fear. In cases such as this, the community loses, the victim and the perpetrator for crimes could be prevented. Our platform is, understanding that it takes three to commit a crime: The will, the ability, and the opportunity. By removing firearms in our communities we are in taking the opportunity away for crime to happen.[54]

Specific events can also generate forces that push otherwise quiescent citizens and groups into the legislative process. One councilman noted that drug crime and violent crime in particular generate community action: "[The groups that we hear from most frequently] are more groups emanating from neighborhoods, town watch groups, civic associations, African American community groups, church-based organizations...

these groups are regular participants."[55] After the murder of her son, a local Philadelphia woman started an organization that has become active through informal contact with legislators, as well as in legislative hearings. "It was started by this woman whose son was murdered. She has this Mother's Day breakfast every year she tried to center around that, but she is pretty much a community leader," a legislative staffer indicated.[56]

Citizen Groups: The Chronic Squeaky Wheel of Local Crime Politics

Citizen groups and individuals use a wider range of tactics to contact legislators, including many that fall below the radar of most measures of group participation. E-mails, phone calls, drop-ins to local offices, and even accidental encounters are all fairly regular means through which groups and individuals make contact with their representatives. Some local legislators also attend meetings of local citizen organizations, and a few have specific staff members who do outreach and regularly attend citizen group meetings.

> People email me, I run into people, they tell me things, the telephone rings here all the time. I get letters too . . . and I go to meetings.[57]

> It's a mix. We've got a lot of people who want that one-on- one physical relationship-type contact, so they call, set up a meeting. We've got regular block watch meetings that we have [too].[58]

> We have three staff members that are outreach members. They go to block watch, community group meetings. . . . I go to every third [block watch/community council] meeting to keep in touch.[59]

Some citizen organizations are quite sophisticated and have substantial human and fiscal capital that they deploy when they target legislators.

> There are civic associations that have been around for a while. They have pretty decent budgets, they are active. If there's an issue, a lot of times they'll be out in front of it. Someone's going to be calling our office and saying, "this is a problem. We need a councilman to come to a meeting." They'll invite him to a meeting. Or in some cases we're up front of it and we're saying, "let's convene a meeting. Let's talk about this." Some of these civic associations [even] have committees that deal with certain issues. There's a noise committee, there's a zoning committee, there's a crime committee, there's a trash committee . . . and so that's the person who will call us and

deal with us. [For example] I think tonight in Queen Village, the noise committee is meeting. There'll be ten people there, they'll have some wine and they're gonna talk about noise. And then they'll call me and they'll say "these are the problems we're having.[60]

Legislators' attendance at constituents' meetings appears to be primarily focused on citizen organizations, and broad ones in particular, as opposed to business or professional organizational meetings. When queried as to his participation at community development corporation (CDC) or other business and professional organization meetings, a Pittsburgh councilman noted:

I really don't attend the CDCs, and here is the reason. They are professional in terms of their skills...and I got to be up front with you...they don't need me. Once they set the community plan in action and they tell me what they want to do, I follow them. I just facilitate their needs. They really don't need me at their meetings and plus their meetings really are more technical....Whereas the citizens groups they have daily needs. They are looking at the potholes, the trees, the new park that we are talking about. So I think that is also part of it.[61]

Broad citizen groups use a variety of other tactics as well, including some classic "outsider strategies" such as utilizing the media. One Philadelphia council member staffer noted:

It is very much a reactionary kind of thing, it's "this is happening, don't tell me it's not, do something about it or we're gonna go to the media and we're gonna make the media come out and start showing pictures of this happening." That's essentially what I hear all the time, and what the councilman hears is that "If you're not gonna do something about this, then we'll just call the press and we'll get the press involved."[62]

Who Is Represented by Citizen Groups in Local Politics?

Table 5.5 categorizes the 131 citizen groups represented at hearings and in the interviews according to their level of organizational formality, showing how many of them are officially recognized as tax-exempt organizations, how many of those that are not are mentioned in local newspapers or identifiable through a general Internet search, and how many are not identifiable in any of these three ways. Not all the citizen groups mentioned

TABLE 5.5. Citizen Groups as Identified through IRS Tax-Exempt Status, Newspaper References, and Internet Searches

	Hearings	Interviews	Both	Total
IRS tax-exempt status[a]	32 (53.3%)	33 (51.6%)	2 (28.6%)	67 (50.4%)
Newspaper reference[b]	18 (30.0%)	14 (21.9%)	5 (71.4%)	37 (27.8%)
Web-identified[c]	4 (6.7%)	5 (7.8%)	—	9 (6.8%)
Unidentified	6 (10.0%)	12 (18.8%)	—	18 (13.5%)
Total	60	64	7	131

[a] Includes all the groups that were listed as tax-exempt in the Cumulative List of Organizations of the IRS.
[b] Includes only the groups that were not in the Cumulative List of Organizations but were mentioned in newspapers.
[c] Includes only the groups that were not in the Cumulative List of Organizations or mentioned in newspapers but were identifiable through a general Internet search.

by legislators are formally organized ones. In fact, of the 131 groups, only about half (67/131) are registered as tax-exempt in the Internal Revenue Service's Cumulative List of Charitable Organizations. This leaves a substantial number (64) that are less formal, ad hoc, or loose coalitions that may or may not have a long-term presence in local politics. Some of these groups were formed in the wake of violent crime, for example Mothers United Through Tragedy in Philadelphia, while others are simply less formal community organizations, such as Esplen Community Council in Pittsburgh. Of the 64 organizations not listed with the Internal Revenue Service, 37 (57.8 percent) were active enough to get at least one newspaper mention over the time period examined in this project, and some of the groups, such as Men United for a Better Philadelphia and Citizens for Police Accountability, received over 50 mentions in local newspapers for various programming, funding, or other salient activities. Another nine (13.8 percent) were identified through Google searches that turned up various online publications in which their names had appeared.[63] Six groups that appeared at city council hearings clearly had existed long enough to have their testimony recorded at a council hearing, though I could find no record of them elsewhere. A remaining 12 groups were identified by legislators but could not be identified elsewhere. Nine groups were named specifically: the Avenue Organization Corporation (community development corporation), the Center for Family Values, the Garfield Neighborhood Association, the Neighborhood Development Leadership Conference, the Shadyside Community Council, the Morrisville Block Watch, the Sonny Hill Organization, Mothers of Murder Victims, and the Police Advisory Councils. The remaining three groups appeared in more general references to types of group: gay/lesbian advocacy groups, parents' organizations, prisoners' rights groups.[64]

Tax-exempt organizations make up about half of the groups in both hearings and interviews and roughly a quarter to a third of the groups identified only in the newspaper. It is probably noteworthy that substantially fewer groups discussed in interviews had newspaper references. This illustrates the largely informal nature of at least some of these groups and their informal contact with legislators. Nonetheless, both hearings and interviews seem to be equally important channels of access for citizen organizations at the local level. Because the barriers preventing access to lawmakers are so much lower at the local level than the state or national levels, a substantial portion of groups that contact legislators through less formal means (not through legislative hearings) are likely to fall out of the legislative process once issues migrate to other levels of government.

Some group names make it clear that they represent a segment of black (and sometimes Latino) interests, for example the NAACP, Concerned Black Citizens of Pittsburgh, the African American Heritage Coalition, the National Association of African Americans for Positive Imagery, and the Congreso de Latinos Unidos. Others are explicitly organized and run by African American citizens, for example Ex-Offenders for Community Empowerment, Men United for a Better Philadelphia, the Father's Day Rally Committee, and Mothers in Charge. Still others explicitly represent low-income citizens, for example ACORN, the Lutheran Settlement House, and Project H.O.M.E. (Housing, Opportunities for Employment, Medical Care, Education).[65] But what of the groups representing neighborhoods? Whom do they represent?

In fact, many of the broad neighborhood groups represent predominately African American or Latino neighborhoods, and quite a few represent low-income white neighborhoods as well.[66] Strawberry Mansion Community Concerns, the Philadelphia Anti Drug/Anti Violence Network, the New Life Heritage Community Economic Development Corporation, Concerned Parents, Inc., Families Are Victims Too, the Point Breeze Community Development Coalition, Mothers United Through Tragedy, the Friends of Elmwood Park, and the Belmont Improvement Association all represent or are located in neighborhoods that are more than 50 percent African American, and all appeared at legislative hearings. Similarly, Congreso de Latinos Unidos, an organization that testifies before the Philadelphia city council, is located in a neighborhood that is over half Latino. Family poverty rates in these neighborhoods are also high, ranging from 22 percent to over 50 percent. Other organizations, including the Eastern Philadelphia Organizing Project and the Lutheran Settlement House, represent predominately white neighborhoods with high family poverty rates (24 percent).

Groups mentioned in interviews even more dramatically represented racial minorities and low-income citizens. The Logan Improvement

Association, the East Falls Community Council, the Wister Neighborhood Association, the Homeward Brushton Council, the East Mt. Airy Neighbors Association, Mt. Airy USA, the Safe Streets Committee, the Northern Liberties Neighborhood Association, and North Point Breeze Planning and Development all represent neighborhoods that are at least half African American. Some of the m, like Mt. Airy and East Falls, consist of solid middle-class communities. But others, such as Homeward Brushton in Pittsburgh and Northern Liberties in Philadelphia, have family poverty rates of 25 and 30 percent, more than three times the national average. Groups representing low-income white neighborhoods, such as the Fishtown Civic Association and the Kensington Action Council in Philadelphia and the Bloomfield Citizens Council in Pittsburgh, also regularly make their interests known to legislators.

Limited Presence of Police Pressure Groups

Local police departments make up a fairly small percentage of all participants mentioned by respondents, and they represent only 10 percent of all witnesses at the hearings (though they appear at more than half of them). Without being prompted, only 6 of 17 respondents mentioned the police, and even then it was almost exclusively in the context of employment benefits. More common was the following exchange in Philadelphia:

> INTERVIEWER: do you hear much from the police officers or police organizations when these issues [drugs, violence, crime] come up?
>
> RESPONDENT: No. You don't *hear* from them. You *call* them. We just don't hear from them. When we need information, we call them. There have been captains that will pick up the phone and call me in a second and say, "Hey did you hear so and so?" or they will give you a heads up. But there are other captains that you just don't hear from unless you call them."[67]

An almost identical response came from a former council member in Pittsburgh: "Oh, no, I didn't hear from them at all. Well, it depended on the commander. Sometimes they would opine and give their two cents. And some of the police worked with community groups, usually the ones assigned there. Part of their duties were to deal with the community."[68] Most local legislators in this study regarded the police as highly reactive, lobbying local legislators primarily on issues related to employment conditions.

> The police department, from what I've seen from this office is, it's more your interaction is with them when you initiate the

interaction. Most interaction with us is initiated by the community or an elected official.[69]

The FOP [Fraternal Order of Police] was very active opposing civilian review. But they are entirely *reactive*.[70]

There were instances when local police departments either initiated or advocated for particular crime policies. The chief of the Philadelphia Police Department offered strong and compelling testimony in support of the gun legislation that the council was trying to pass:

> I would like to commend the sponsors of this legislation and the members of this Committee for recognizing the grave situation we face and looking for ways to change the environment. This legislation shows that our City Council will do all it can within the confines of the law to give law enforcement the tools it needs to effectively fight the fight and reclaim our streets. We owe it to the families and friends of every victim of gun violence to do all we can to make sure we end this epidemic now.[71]

In Pittsburgh, the police became highly active in the political process at a point in the early 2000s after a police officer was shot during a hostage situation. The incident raised a lot of questions about the behavior of police administrators and actually fueled more public debate about the Police Civilian Review Board that had been established by referendum in Pittsburgh following a series of particularly violent and controversial incidents involving police officers and minority citizens.[72]

The more common pattern, however, was a relatively quiescent police advocacy, in relation to other groups. When a police lieutenant worked with the city council to revise local noise ordinances to deal with noise levels in a high-traffic area of the city, a city council staffer indicated that this was unusual. His contact with the police really "depends on the district and on the captains or lieutenants that are involved."[73]

The Role of Professional Associations

Professional groups were fairly evenly distributed across substantive areas. Combined, medical, educational, legal, social service, and business groups represented between 15 and 18 percent of the witnesses in each topic area. Though religious groups represented only 8 percent of witnesses, over half of the respondents mentioned church groups as frequent participants in local crime politics, and their presence is huge compared to the state level (1.9 percent) and Congress (1.1 percent) during roughly the same time period. As the chapter 6 will demonstrate, some religious organizations intersect with broad citizen groups in their focus on neighborhood quality-of-life issues. For the most part, professional associations represent social service agencies that join policy debates when issues that affect their interests migrate onto local agendas.

> They're issue-centered a lot of times, so it depends on the issue. A few years ago the councilman was working on legislation to include sexual orientation as part of the nondiscrimination code, so now suddenly we had the religious groups involved. Other districts will have low-income groups that get involved in specific issues, predatory lending is an example that's been a big issue. I mean, they're intimately involved in that and we'll see them on a recurring basis but I don't see them on other issues.[74]

Patterns of Access and Policy Environments

The picture that emerges from the various data sources in this chapter is of a policy environment for crime control that is heavily skewed toward citizen organizations—broad ones particularly —but that also provides pathways of access for just about every other type of group. In fact, professional associations, criminal justice agencies, individuals, and government agencies are all represented at remarkably similar levels, appearing in at least half the hearings and accounting for somewhere between 15 and 20 percent of the witnesses. Even within the professional group category, representation is fairly evenly distributed among medical, educational, legal, social service, and business groups.

Criminal justice agencies are fairly routine participants in legislative hearings, probably because they are invited by legislators. They were much less likely to be mentioned by legislators in the interviews, however, which suggests that police and prosecutors are not actively lobbying local legislators. Contrast this with the respondents at the state level, nearly all of whom mentioned prosecutors and law enforcement as primary groups for in-person contact. Though the congressional data does not include interviews, the sheer numbers of criminal justice witnesses and appearances at congressional crime hearings indicate that lawmakers are accustomed to hearing from these groups on a routine basis as well. Locally, however, criminal justice agencies are generally too busy responding to crime and addressing internal organizational issues and crises to devote full-time staff to local lobbying. Of course, local lawmakers surely know how important it is to provide local police, prosecutors, and judges with appropriate resources and tools, but these groups are clearly less involved in the day-to-day problem-definition and agenda-setting stage of the policy process at the local level.

Table 5.6 illustrates the most commonly appearing citizen groups and professional associations.[75] In contrast to the state and national levels, where broad citizen groups made up at most a third of the groups appearing at more than two hearings (4 in 11 groups in Congress but only 1 in 10 groups in Pennsylvania), locally they represented almost half of groups appearing at more than one hearing, and three of the top five "frequent fliers" were broad citizen groups. Professional associations also look somewhat different from the state level, where legal groups dominate, and the national level, where social service and research-and-policy groups do. In Philadelphia and Pittsburgh, legal and social service groups appear, but so do educational groups and a medical group—the only time across the three venues that medical groups make it into the more routine list.

The citizen groups that are present represent a wide range of organizational structures, ranging from formal nonprofit (501[c]3) organizations to less formally organized groups that appear on city neighborhood lists, to those that do not appear on any formal lists but are active enough to receive newspaper coverage, to those that are largely off the formal radar altogether and are identifiable only insofar as they appear at legislative hearings or are discussed by legislators. Clearly, not all of these groups represent poor and minority citizens. Indeed, as the interviews suggest, some of these are affluent and quite sophisticated groups whose aim is to preserve neighborhood quality. But the data also reveal the prevalence of a huge array of groups advocating on behalf of minority interests and low-income neighborhoods, as mentioned previously.

This assessment of citizen groups represents a much wider range of group activity than is typically assessed by interest groups scholars. Political mobilization by urban minorities and low-income citizens around crime concerns happens, and it happens regularly, through formal channels and informal ones. Of course, we cannot know how well these groups represent the people living in their areas or the constituents they claim to represent. It is certainly possible that some of these organizations have only a handful of members or that a few active people run several of these organizations. And certainly prior research has illustrated how much less political activity there is in chronically and severely impoverished urban areas relative to more affluent neighborhoods.[76] But there are so many different groups representing different parts of the cities that it is clear that a much greater portion of urban residents facing serious crime are represented in the local political processes than in the state and national ones. Much of the research on the urban poor or African American mobilization in the city focuses on voting, giving money to candidates, and volunteering in political organizations. These are all worthy political endeavors,

TABLE 5.6. Citizen Groups and Professional Associations That Appeared at
More than One City Council Hearing, Philadelphia and Pittsburgh,
1997–2004

	Total hearings	Total appearances	Type of group
Citizen groups			
Men United for a Better Philadelphia	4	6	Broad
ACLU	4	5	Single-issue
Woman Against Abuse	4	6	Single-issue
Congreso de Latinos Unidos	3	3	Broad
Mothers in Charge	3	3	Broad
Strawberry Mansion Community Concerns/Neighbors	2	2	Broad
Ex-Offenders Inc.	2	2	Broad
ACT-UP	2	2	Single-issue
Brady Campaign/Million Mom March	2	2	Single-issue
PA Against Handgum Violence	2	2	Single-issue
PA Prison Society	2	2	Single-issue
Women Organized Against Rape	2	2	Single-issue
Holmesburg/Enfield Civic Association	2	11	Broad
Professional groups			
Women's Law Project	6	7	Legal
Philadelphia School District	4	4	Educational
Prison Health Services	3	9	Medical
Temple University	2	2	Educational
Philadelphia Defender Association	2	4	Legal
Philadelphia Children's Alliance	2	3	Social service
Support Center for Child Advocates	2	2	Social service

but attending a rally, calling a city council member, or showing up at a
council hearing to talk about a recent shooting in the neighborhood also
constitute political activity. To the extent that citizen groups representing
the poor and minorities have difficulty engaging in this less formal political activity in state and national legislative venues, their interests will
be subverted to those highly resourced groups who can engage in more
traditional forms of political pressure.

Of course, the facts presented in this chapter reveal little about what
these groups are actually injecting into the policy process in terms of
problem definitions and solutions. The findings outlined here are not suggestive of a halcyon local political environment where there is widespread
agreement on quality-of-life concerns or an environment for crime policy

debates in Philadelphia and Pittsburgh that lacks the NIMBYism and other parochialisms that have been so well documented in local contexts. On the contrary, citizen groups are often quarreling with legislators, the police, government agencies, and, often, each other. But this process is substantially more democratized than those at other levels of government, providing opportunities for dislodging the social control frames that dominate crime policy making. These frames are simply less attractive to local lawmakers, who must juggle the twin demands for greater public safety and improved neighborhood conditions and opportunities in a concrete way. Thus, the incentives for lawmakers to emphasize single-issue crimes, to respond to agendas set by police, prosecutors, and other criminal justice personnel, to depoliticize the relationship between crime, violence, inequality, and stratification, and to draw on iconic images of victimhood are simply less dominant at the local level. Locally, the deaths of tens or hundreds of young black and Latino men in a given year and the daily fears of minority women are simply harder to ignore or transfer into existing paradigms of social control. The sheer electoral pressure from minorities, advocates for the poor, working-class whites, and educational and religious groups makes it difficult to decouple crime and violence from people's living conditions, and the easier access that these groups have to local lawmakers exposes legislators to a wider range of groups, perspectives, and problem definitions. The precise nature of citizen groups' problem definitions and agendas is the subject of the next chapter.

Six

CITIZENSHIP THROUGH PARTICIPATION

Political structures do what they are forced to do, not what good will
would have them do. And if the community that is most impacted [*sic*]
does not have the political force to make it painful for elected officials not
to do it, then they're not going to do it.

—Pittsburgh City Council member, 2003

Narratives of black urban life in the mass media and scholarly research
have tended to focus on poverty and its impact on the culture and social
organization of the black poor. In pursuing this line of inquiry, investigators have addressed an extremely narrow range of social behaviors and
relations: crime, teenage sexuality, family disorganization, and "ghetto
street life" have dominated both the research agendas of academics and
the imagery of the mass media. Historically, political organization, work
and leisure, and other everyday dimensions of urban life that de rigueur
have guided and informed the research of social scientists working elsewhere fade from view within the epistemological frontiers of the black
inner city.

—Steven Gregory, *Black Corona: Race and the Politics of Place in an
Urban Community*

Chapter 5 left unanswered two important questions about the
role of citizen groups in local crime politics, particularly the
broad groups that often represent urban neighborhood interests. First, given
that many of these groups are simply reporting crime problems to their local
legislators, can they really be compared to groups that propose and advocate
for specific policy solutions? Can they be said to be participating in the policy

process in a meaningful way? In other words, do they make up "group inter- ests" in the way early group theorists or more recent interest group scholars use the term?[1] Second, even if these groups are conceptually on a par with more formalized organizations, are they really saying anything important or substantially different from what other groups are saying? Put simply, does their absence from the state and national level really matter all that much?

This chapter offers a more in-depth analysis of the local data in an effort to answer these complicated and underexplored questions. Drawing on interviews with 17 local city council members and their staff, analysis of 45 legislative hearings on crime and justice in Philadelphia and Pitts- burgh, and observations of the groups participating in local crime politics, I argue that the groups mobilized locally around urban crime problems frequently present a decidedly pragmatic approach to crime problems and offer substantially different policy frames from those promulgated by criminal justice agencies, professional associations, and highly active single-issue groups. Indeed, the deep connection urban dwellers have to crime, its causes, and consequences gives them a perspective on crime problems that is unique and highly practical. Unlike criminal justice agencies, whose testimony before legislatures is often focused on budgets, staffing, policy, and specific programmatic needs, or single-issue groups, whose narrow focus often precludes a broader frame, broad citizen groups address a wide range of economic, political, and social issues that are tightly coupled with crime and violence at the local level. They are not especially concerned with numbers of arrests or convictions, nor are they even particularly focused on offenders. Rather, they bring up a regular, sustained set of concerns about victimization, fear, and margin- ality. In an odd twist, the policy environment for responding to crime at the local level is actually more focused on victims—specifically on harm reduction—than the environments at the state and national levels, where criminal justice agencies and narrow victims' groups dominate.

The primary focus of this chapter is broad citizen groups, but there are other groups that are infrequent in the state and national policy picture and have more salience in the local setting. Religious and educational groups, for example, play a more prominent role in local crime politics, as do some less formal, ad hoc single-issue groups formed in the wake of violence. What these groups have in common is both their consistent presence in local crime politics—in contrast to their intermittent presence in state and national venues—and their alternative policy frames, which situate crime and violence in the daily struggles for survival and social conditions from which they emerge. I quote at length from some of the interviews and legislative hearings to illustrate how clearly and consis- tently the same themes emerge from these sources. For more details about the respondents, see appendix 3.

The Meaning of "Groups" and the
Significance of Informal Associations

Many city council members and their staff described the more informal broad citizen groups as complaining about neighborhood problems, including crime, but rarely offering specific policy solutions. They indicated that citizen groups typically express concern about specific problems—drug dealing, violence, and graffiti, for example—but do not usually propose concrete policy alternatives. One respondent in Philadelphia noted: "It's a general message [from community groups]. It's like, 'we want a safe neighborhood where people don't sell drugs and kill each other.' They're kind of generalized messages about crime and safety and that kind of stuff."[2] Several council members in Pittsburgh suggested that it is the council's job to provide answers:

> It is always "clean it up, shut it down, arrest them," not so much "let's have this policy." And I don't think it's their [community groups'] responsibility, to be honest with you, to think of policy.[3]

> They're looking to this office for solutions. Very rarely does anybody call and say there's a problem and then also give us a solution.[4]

The more formally organized groups are more likely to have specific policy proposals. The Public Safety Councils in Pittsburgh, for example, will sometimes articulate specific policy ideas: "They'll take a position sometimes on legislation. Or they'll say, "legislatively, you need to tighten up the curfew law," which we did recently. Or "the graffiti situation is out of hand in Mount Washington. Please try to come up with some answer to this problem. Do something."[5] Recall from chapter 4 the legislative staffer in Pennsylvania who expressed frustration with the groups concerned with racial profiling that would contact his office. In the policy environment in which he works, there is little he can do with a general complaint that has no policy recommendations, particularly if the issue itself is not of great concern to the majority party in the state legislature. And even if it were, it would require substantial effort on his part to help the group formulate policy solutions. In contrast, while the legislators at the local level were not eager to confront these generalized complaints, they seemed resigned to them as part of the normal course of doing business in the local legislature. And *whether* to respond was less of an issue than *how*. Though local lawmakers tended to see broad citizen group messages as diffuse and often intangible, they were not generally dismissive of them. To the contrary, a number of legislators went out of their way to provide forums where they could receive these more diffuse policy messages. Some council members in Philadelphia, for example, set up offices in a range of neighborhoods within the district.

> We have two people based in our Winfield office, one in Roxborough. They are there to make our office more convenient to people so they don't have to come down to City Hall if they want to talk to somebody—and also they kind of become the eyes and ears of that neighborhood and they develop a rapport with the district.[6]

Others prioritize attendance at meetings of broad citizen groups, knowing that it is those groups that most need the legislators' time and expertise. A staff member for a Philadelphia councilman expressed this view and saw it as part of his job to help less formal organizations navigate the legislative process.

> There is a group called Young Involved Philadelphia.... They are all in their early twenties and they see an issue and they send in their comments. I have talked to them about the [skateboarding issue]...but then they start doing things like writing all the council people, and because of the dynamics we have in the city with the mayor and council members, sometimes it is *not* best if you can get all the council members. Sometimes you might want to just get certain ones [on your side].... And that is just naiveté.[7]

In chapter 5 I also mentioned a Pittsburgh city council member who regularly attends broad citizen group meetings (but rarely the business group meetings) because, as he indicated later in the interview, "the community development corporations don't need me at their meetings...the citizens' groups do."[8]

Sometimes legislators brace themselves for phone calls from groups that they know meet on a regular basis. The noise committee mentioned in chapter 5 was sure to call their council member to discuss the evening's meeting. Other legislators set up meetings with community leaders or attend citizen organization meetings. Sometimes the less formal groups do offer policy solutions, though they are often unconventional and occasionally downright illegal. At a hearing on illegal billboards concentrated in the poorer sections of the city, for example, one representative suggested hiring local community residents in need of work to simply tear the billboards down the next day![9] And at a hearing on reducing violence in the city, a witness representing a group called Don't Fall Down in the Hood urged citizens to keep agitating until they got what they wanted: "Pick up the phone and call the elected officials. Pick up the phone and call them every single day until they do what you want them to do."[10]

The picture that emerges is one in which some less formally organized groups meet to express general frustrations and concerns about crime and other neighborhood problems while other groups organize more formal policy proposals. But few groups seem content to simply inject a complaint and walk away. They are persistent and determined, and legislators are rarely in a position to ignore them, at least not for very long. In addition, lawmakers do not seem exasperated with or dismissive of these groups. They not only go out of their way to create forums to hear citizens but also understand that the responsibility for addressing citizens' concerns is theirs. One Pittsburgh councilman described in detail his weekly outings to hear from community councils and block watches in his district:

> What I try to do is that I go to every third meeting and my staff member goes to every third meeting. So we cover about two out of every three meetings. I go to every third one unless I'm invited or there is a specific issue at hand....I go, obviously, to keep in touch. And what I find is that when you sit in City Hall you get out of touch....I will do anything I can [to hear from people].[11]

One former local lawmaker turned Pennsylvania assemblyman drew this contrast between the local and state policy environments:

> At the local level, you can't hide as much [as at the state level]. Can't hide physically and can't hide politically. Can't say, "Well, my colleagues won't be for it, or the administration won't be for it." It's easier to shift the blame at the state level [than locally].[12]

Broad Citizen Groups and Their Messages

Several important and distinct messages come from broad citizen groups that are largely absent from the perspectives other types of groups offer. First, these groups have concerns about citizen safety, qualify of life, and opportunity at their core that differ substantially from groups whose members are driven primarily by professional considerations or whose focus is on one crime or one aspect of the justice system. While the problem definitions that broad citizen groups offer are far from uniform and they do often advocate straightforward criminal justice–based solutions such as more police, they nonetheless seem to find it difficult to talk about crime problems without also raising other concerns, including housing, employment, recreation opportunities, neighborhood characteristics, and land-use issues, among others.

Second, citizen groups demonstrate a pragmatism in their approach to problems of crime and violence that virtually every other type of organization present at crime hearings across the three datasets lacks, except, perhaps, for medical and religious groups, which demonstrated a singularly pragmatic approach to gun violence. Like that of others who have examined the role of citizens in crime politics, my research indicates that broad citizen groups are not punitive in a uniformly or knee-jerk way but are surprisingly practical.[13] Even neighborhoods devastated by violence or drug addiction are receptive to a wide range of policy solutions, provided they have some potential to actually work. A common theme throughout many local legislative hearings is simply harm reduction—how can we reduce the harm done to individual victims, family members, and whole communities? Finally, and perhaps most important, broad citizen groups' contribution to the policy process is their mobilization around a politics of redistribution—a redistribution of safety that reduces the likelihood that neighborhoods currently afflicted with crime and violence will remain that way. In contrast, state and national crime politics is organized more around regulation (punishing offenders) and distribution (parceling out resources to different agencies). Broad citizen groups shift problem definitions and policy debates toward underlying structural inequities and day-to-day struggles that racial and economic stratification impose on citizens, as well as reducing the harm of crime victimization.

The Connection between Crime and Quality of Life

In the many public hearings about gun violence in Philadelphia in the early 2000s, broad citizen organizations, informal, ad hoc single-issue groups, and black religious leaders not only offered personal narratives of the impact of guns on their lives but also drew broader connections between individual gun crimes and contextual factors at work in urban neighborhoods. Given the substantially higher rates of poverty and social disorganization in black neighborhoods, some legislators framed this as a racial perspective. As one council member noted, "African American groups are more focused on root causes, employment, recreation."[14] Another Pittsburgh council member who himself is white but represents one of the neighborhoods of Pittsburgh with a sizeable African American population noted:

> I have met with thirty-two ministers...all African American... basically they were just saying that we need to intervene with our kids, we need solid good programs, tutoring, computers, some

entertainment, recreation, we need funding obviously to make these things work and we are the only ones who can reach these kids and they are right.[15]

But most of the respondents denied a clear link between race and the framing of crime problems, and the data are more supportive of a relationship between proximity to crime and poor neighborhood conditions than any specific racial or ethnic perspective.[16] A legislative aide to a Philadelphia council member suggested that most local issues, including crime, simply come back to quality-of-life considerations for all citizens:

> What's inherent in any interest group is that you just want to be happy. And if you have four or five people that want to be happy and they can agree and say, "Okay, this is what we're interested in, our happiness depends on us having the supermarket and us being able to walk to a drug store that's not going to overcharge us." That's what it all breaks down to . . . everything is about quality of life.[17]

Another legislator in Pittsburgh said that all of his constituents, from his affluent Southside neighborhood to his predominantly black neighborhoods, were receptive to addressing drug addiction through nonpunitive means.[18] Similar connections between crime and housing, employment, and other neighborhood issues arose elsewhere in Pittsburgh. A 2003 city council hearing included this testimony from a woman witness: "It is not only the drugs that are killing our children. It is when our African American mothers and fathers cannot have jobs, decent paying jobs, as the white man, it is killing our children. They're turning to drugs because of depression and dissatisfaction in the home."[19]

The link between crime and larger neighborhood and even city-wide forces go beyond physical and economic infrastructure. At one of the Philadelphia hearings on gun violence, a witness from Ex-offenders Inc. said:

> My support for this ordinance [gun ordinance discussed in chapters 1 and 5] comes from my personal experience of the harm that can be caused by the proliferation of illegal guns. I am a lifer, convicted nearly 25 years ago for murder in which an illegally obtained handgun was used in a senseless act of violence. The circumstance of [that] case is a perfect testimony of what this ordinance is meant to eliminate. What started as a fistfight between two young men, myself and the victim, escalated into a senseless killing when my accomplice, a juvenile at the time, brought to bear the illegally obtained weapon in his possession. Although the gun lobbyists are quick to assert that guns don't kill and that people kill, because of my knowledge of the people in this case, I know for a fact that

presence of the illegal weapon and the ease at which the weapon was obtained was a major factor in this crime.[20]

This is essentially an opportunity structure argument—the mere presence of a gun increases the likelihood that violence will ensue, a recognition that crime originates not *only* from the bad choices people make but from the conditions in which people are making those choices. This theme of the connection of crime to broader social conditions is one that emerges in local council hearings and is frequently raised by broad community organizations.

Similarly, a variety of ad hoc groups appeared at a 2005 Philadelphia hearing on illegal billboards, connecting the prevalence of such billboards in poor neighborhoods to the overall quality of life, limited city services, lack of respect from public officials, and even alcohol and drug abuse. A witness from the National Association for African American Positive Imagery said: "This [bill] has ramifications beyond just this little piece. It affects a lot of pieces in the neighborhood, not to mention the quality-of-life issues, and the signals it gives are that this neighborhood is a trash place, not a place to be respected."[21] One group at this hearing—Society Created to Reduce Urban Blight (SCRUB)—actually had data on the number of illegal billboards in each area of the city by zip code and presented full-color maps at the council hearing indicating that illegal billboard placement followed a socioeconomic pattern.[22] As a result, the Philadelphia Zoning Board made the billboard company remove the billboards or obtain permits.[23]

Echoing the sentiment of legislators who spoke of the resource problems that arise for low-income communities trying to get things done, a member of Concerned Citizens for the Preservation of Philadelphia testified:

> We know how to get it done. We just don't have the authority, the money, the resources. We have the will, we have the knowledge, we have the energy. We have the passion.... We got everything there. We just don't have the authority. I want to live beautiful too....I want my kids and grandkids to be able to walk to a corner store like I used to do and go get some candy and go get a juice without having to push past drunks and drug dealers and blunts and malt liquor. It's just—it's unbelievable.[24]

This particular hearing turned into a general hearing about quality-of-life issues, and enforcing existing codes in Philadelphia in poor neighborhoods as much as they are enforced in wealthier ones. Witnesses talked of finding a creative ways to get authorization for the community to remove the billboards and of hiring local people to do the job. "I think they'd do it for free," said one witness from Concerned Citizens for the Preservation of Philadelphia.[25]

Well into this hearing, a discussion ensued between Councilman Frank Rizzo and the Licenses and Inspections (L & I) director about whether to cite just the owners of illegal billboards ("eight sheets") or to also cite the owner of the building to which they are attached (who is usually paid a "rent" fee).[26] As the L & I inspector described a meeting where the decision was made to go after illegal "eight sheet" owners rather than the building owner, the following exchange with Councilman Rizzo took place:

> L & I DIRECTOR: The feeling in the room [during the meeting] was that we would be more effective in dealing with [the eight sheet owners]—
>
> COUNCILMAN (INTERRUPTING): Well the feeling in *this* room is that if you're trying to get it done, you involve everybody absolutely necessary to deliver the message. And for a lawyer to say, just go after the owner of the sign and not the person who is benefiting from the sign, to me, doesn't make any sense.

This hearing is an excellent illustration of agenda setting at the local level. Recall from chapters 4 and 5 that the typical state and congressional crime hearing began with criminal justice witnesses, moved onto government and professional associations, and eventually trickled down to citizen groups. In fact, in chapter 4 I mentioned a contentious moment in a Pennsylvania legislative crime hearing when a citizen group representative expressed frustration at being preempted by a district attorney witness. While local hearings often follow a similar pattern, with police and prosecutors or prison officials starting the hearing with their expert testimony, their presence is limited relative to other groups. In this hearing, the testimony of groups advocating enforcement of city codes regarding illegal billboards and opposing the placement of billboards in their neighborhoods was so overwhelming that by the time the representative from Clear Channel—the owner of many legitimate billboards, who was concerned about regulations infringing on his rights—was called to testify, even the Republican council members were not particularly receptive to his testimony. In this case, the zoning board decided in 2005 to revise billboard rules, and the result was that 900 billboards became illegal. After a legal battle involving the city, billboard corporations, and community groups, the city entered into a consent agreement with the billboard companies that allowed for the removal of many billboards but also reduced future fees for legal billboard use.[27]

Thus, while broad citizen groups often come into the policy process without specific policy proposals, local lawmakers nonetheless frequently try to offer concrete legislative responses, as both the gun bill and illegal billboard rule changes illustrate.[28] Such intense citizen pressures can hardly be ignored by local lawmakers. As one former Pittsburgh city council member (who later won election to the Pennsylvania General Assembly) noted, "There is more to worry about from grassroots [at the local level] because they can really hurt you at the polls."[29] Another council member described a series of meetings with community groups in Bloomfield, a low-income neighborhood of Pittsburgh with a substantial black population, in which groups and individual residents had expressed a great deal of anger about the loss of their community police officer:

> It was a very difficult meeting and they were right. They talked about lots of examples of crime in Bloomfield and they harkened back to the 1950s and [19]60s when there was a beat cop. They wanted the beat cop back because it gives the community some comfort. And you know what? We gave it to them.[30]

Another Philadelphia council member saw her role almost as conflict manager at times:

> A lot of what we try to do is facilitate. [You have to say] no, some of these things are not against the law [referring to teenagers noisily playing basketball in the alleyways], so, you bring out the community relations officer, you try to have a conversation. You try to set some ground rules. You try to create mutual respect. This is what happens in row house neighborhoods. They're very crowded and people get on each other's nerves, especially as the temperature rises. The kids are out of school, and there's less opportunities for summer jobs in this city. So all that has a ripple effect.[31]

Punishment and Harm Reduction

One major perspective that is conspicuous in its absence from citizen group advocacy at the local level is the punitiveness exhibited in state and national crime politics. In the past few decades, most states have passed mandatory minimum sentence laws for drug offenses, 23 states have Three Strikes You're Out laws, and some have done away with parole and have limited commutations (Simon 2006). Interestingly, however, broad citizen groups, even—or perhaps especially—those representing black neighborhoods in Philadelphia and Pittsburgh, are not typically pressing legislators to punish offenders more harshly. Perhaps the most striking aspect of the local crime policy environment is its focus on the people who have to live with both the realities of day-to-day threats of victimization as well as the contentious and often unproductive encounters with the justice system. As already noted, in an ironic twist, while single-issue groups focused on crime victims, such as MADD, have gained prominence in state and national venues (as chapters 3 and 4 demonstrated), their interests often intersect with those of criminal justice agencies and, as a result, the focus in those venues often centers on punishment for offenders, which is not the same agenda as reducing victimization. It is the local environment, where groups represent citizens who face serious victimization on a more routine basis, that focuses most explicitly on victims, in particular on the environment factors that make victimization more likely.

For example, a March 2004 hearing on gun violence in Philadelphia gave substantial attention to harm reduction and had virtually no discussion of punishing offenders. One witness after another talked about the harm gun violence does to children in the neighborhoods and to the community writ large. A representative from the Million Mom March indicated that urban kids have much more experience with guns than is typically acknowledged: "They all have an intimate knowledge with guns in their homes and on their streets. . . . We try to give these children, these kids, these young adults, the realization that they have a choice in their actions, but many times they don't see the choices."[32] A representative from Mothers in Charge spoke about the impact of gun violence on the family members who are left behind:

> I must speak on the devastation that follows the death of a child on the other children, their siblings that they left behind. The siblings sometimes can't sleep. Their grades fall. They separate themselves from their peers. It's a devastating situation. And then there's the parents. They fear they're overly protective of their living children. It's a devastating situation. They can't cope with everyday things.[33]

Much of the testimony provides a visceral sense of what it means to be at one's wits' end living with crime, violence, drugs, and gangs. A representative from the Father's Day Rally Committee at a 2000 Philadelphia hearing said, referring to gun violence,

> Until you witness it—we can all hear about, but until you witness and a lot of communities in the City of Philadelphia do witness what I'm saying, but until you personally witness someone die in front of you. . . . I think that incident has renewed my strength to continue to bring some kind of sense to this madness that's going on in our communities.[34]

Despite the rising homicide rates, even the gun hearings focused pragmatically on getting guns off the streets rather than just punishing gun users. A representative from Men United for a Better Philadelphia testified:

> Every gun that we prevent from reaching the streets begins the healing process for neighborhoods demoralized by gun violence over the years. We join with you in working to make our streets safer. We also ask that you join with us in creating the momentum necessary to convince Harrisburg that political expediency around firearms, although cheap in Harrisburg, the cost remains too high on the streets of Philadelphia.[35]

During the interviews, legislators and their staff members were asked where they would place these groups' proposals for dealing with those who were committing violent crimes in their neighborhoods on a broad continuum from "Help them out" to "lock them up." No one responded with an unqualified "Lock them up," and many offered the same kind of nuanced perspective that characterized the groups' testimonies at hearings.

> You very seldom get those that say "lock them up and throw away the key." We were talking this morning...what are we doing to do with these kids, what are we going to do with these kids that grow up and become drug dealers and shooting in neighborhoods and whatnot? And most people tend to try to figure out what alternatives we can provide. What alternatives can we put together as a deterrent and a prevention mechanism. I think people are more into the prevention than the criminal justice part of this. For some [kids], I don't care what you do they are still going to do it. And for those, you know, people feel that the strong arm of the law should come down. Others, you want to try to do something deterrent.[36]

> I think the community associations are very much behind cracking down on these quality of life crimes...but [they appreciate] having these courts [drug and mental health courts] where you're doling out the punishment and kind of realizing that the punishment for a kid who rips out a plant or something, shouldn't go to jail. The person is now going to go clean that area, or is going to be involved in some kind of community service.[37]

> Help them out. Don't lock them up and throw away the key. They [citizen groups] aren't about building bigger jails. They want really bad guys to go away. But you can't just do something extreme just for the sake of it. You have to look at the fallout. The community groups that I dealt with...don't want to hurt the kids that were selling drugs and gangbanging. They want them to stop it. But

they don't think that dragging them through the court system or building bigger jails was the answer.... The community really wants the bad guys locked up. They didn't want their lives to be in jeopardy—but they also wanted us to get to the root of the drug dealing. Keep getting the stems and the really teeny-weeny branches, kindling—that's what you're getting to the root of it. They really wanted to press the root issues.[38]

I don't think people have any kind of *sympathy* for the [street drug dealers], but—it's just that they are not the ones who are bringing it in, they're not the ones who are running the enterprise, and there's no visible effort to crack that system systematically.[39]

I don't think [punitiveness] is organic to the public.... I think that the vast majority of people, when given the facts, would be more supportive of a CJS [criminal justice system] that actually worked [laughs] to prevent crime.[40]

In response to a question about whether these groups worry that the police can't distinguish the good kids doing bad things from the genuinely bad criminals:

I'd say it just a little different. The different slant that I observe is not that those who are targeted are good kids doing bad things, they are bad kids doing bad things, but they're at the low level of the totem pole...many programs choose to chase the low-level runners back and forth across the street. Because that's the low-hanging fruit, you can easily find them. It's not as easy to find the upper guys and the guys who wear the suits and briefcases.[41]

One legislator in Philadelphia went into a long exposition about class and race differences in attitudes toward crime:

It's different in different neighborhoods. I think in the white community it's more severe as far as "lock 'em up" kind of attitude. I think in the African American community, the minority community, the Latino community, there're many parents whose kids are having these problems and they're not really advocating them being locked up. Although I've found, and I don't want to speak in general terms, I've found African American, more senior citizens as right-wing as strict or stricter than some of the Caucasian. So I mean, it varies, it varies with experience, it varies with age. You know, you have a black World War II vet and his wife who are under siege and he wants them all locked up. But you know a single mother who's got four kids and one's selling drugs cause they can't get a job somewhere, she's gonna be a little more lenient and understanding. You know, a white senior citizen who's got neighborhood graffiti, they're angry and they want to lock everybody up. Then you know, you have ethnic Italian American, Irish American parents whose kids are fourteen, fifteen, the police are picking them up, you know, what are they supposed to do about that. They're more "What do you want my kids to do?" They want to argue with you.... It's class difference, it's age difference. Look, there's always a race difference because of the historical relationship of the police with minority communities. At one point in time back in the fifties and sixties and seventies, the police department was a white occupying force, in the black neighborhood with no diversity. There were very few African American police officers, they were under siege in their minds, and in reality in many ways.[42]

This lengthy discussion reveals a nuance and complexity that is largely absent from state and national crime politics. While some of the comments about the relationship between race, class, and attitudes are borne out by empirical evidence (racial minorities and those in lower socioeconomic classes tend to have more hostility toward the police, for example), the statement's wholesale accuracy is less important than the observation that where people are situated in relation to crime, neighborhood, family status, class, race, and a whole host of other factors will probably influence attitudes toward crime and the police. Local lawmakers confront this wide range of opinions and priorities on a regular basis. Such diversity of perspective is frequently lost at the state and national levels, where policy frames reflect more simplistic narratives in response to the narrower range of interests represented in policy debates. This law-and-order script is easier to maintain when the object of the state's social control mechanism is not your family member, your neighbor's daughter, or the son of someone in your church. On the ground level, the punishment response to crime is often tempered by a desire to see alterations to the contexts in which people are making choices in the first place.

Local Groups' Pragmatism

In place of heavy punitiveness is a kind of pragmatism that is consistent across issues and neighborhoods. Some groups, for example, seemed willing to tackle problems in a piecemeal fashion, taking on aspects of the problem that were amenable to practical action rather than demanding that legislators solve everything at once. For example, during a Philadelphia council hearing on prohibiting billboard advertisements for alcohol in locations that are frequented by children, many witnesses raised questions well beyond the capacity of the city council to address, such as banning advertisements in local transportation systems. A representative from Philadelphia Citizens for Children and Youth urged the council to maintain a pragmatic focus on what they could accomplish: "We have to be careful that the perfect doesn't become the enemy of the good. You have before you something that you have jurisdiction over and that you can act [on]."[43] Perhaps most stark, even a council hearing on escapes from a local Philadelphia prison revealed a pragmatism one would hardly expect from a working-class neighborhood with a medium-security prison in its backyard. The Curran-Fromhold Correctional Facility (formerly Holmesburg Prison) is in the Holmesburg section of Philadelphia, which is about three-fourths white and has a moderate rate of violent crime relative to the rest of the city. A representative from a local citizens' group, the Enfield Civic Association, expressed the following concerns about the lines of communication between the neighborhood and the prison system:

> We are here today to deal specifically with the breaches of security at the various institutions within the Philadelphia Prison System. Ladies and gentlemen, we live in Holmesburg twenty-four hours a day. Our neighbors are fed up at the protracted struggle we continue to endure regarding safety issues. We have not asked for much. The right to feel safe, the right to truthful answers, the right to be treated decently. If walkaways from the Philadelphia Prison System are the norm, don't expend your energies in covering it up. Tell us, that's all we ask, then we will know what we are dealing with [applause]. If inmates are permitted certain latitudes in our neighborhood, we have a right to know. The Enfield community has always acknowledged the formidable responsibilities of operating such a large correctional system.[44]

Such pragmatism appears alive and well in Pittsburgh as well. A white city council member in a mixed district expressed his surprise at how well his ideas about treating drug abuse as a public health epidemic (as opposed to an effort focused more on punishment) were received among his constituents:

> It's easy to stand in front of a group of people and say "We're gonna have cops, we're gonna bust them [drug dealers] and put them in jail." And it sells well. But I just can't do that.... I've seen neighbors and I've talked to moms and dads and I made a conscious decision that I'm gonna stand up and say what I believe in. And I always start this way, "We gotta be hard, we gotta be tough, we've gotta get the dealer off the street, we gotta make sure that dealer gets punished," but starting a few years back, I started saying "But, it's a public health epidemic. And the only way we're gonna solve this is by helping that person that's addicted." I never thought it would

play well. But guess what? It does. I'm in shock. When I stand in front of an audience that's been terrorized by what's happening and I say that, I get agreement. And you know what that's shown me? That's shown me addictions have hit families themselves. They see it. It's hit their families, it's hit their extended families, it's hit their friends.[45]

"We Want More Police"

Many legislators also commented on how frequently citizen groups demand more police. A Pittsburgh council member said starkly: "Oh, they all ask for more police. They ask for more police, they ask for more undercover, they ask for, at times, something as drastic as just bulldoze the house down."[46] And a representative in the Pittsburgh mayor's office when asked what citizen groups are looking for, simply said, "More police, more police, more police."[47]

It would be easy to use these responses as evidence of a highly punitive public—but only if we ignored the rest of the comments offered by both lawmakers and citizen groups. In fact, part of the problem when issues are on all levels of government simultaneously is that it creates opportunities for citizen interests at one level to be translated into fragmented and partial versions in another. The narrower goals of single-issue groups such as the NRA or gun opponents, for example, or the policy priorities of criminal justice agencies, can all draw on neighborhood calls for more police as evidence of support for their interests. However, the refrain "more police" is a desperate plea for a heightened sense of safety, and simply adding police with no sense of broader community development goals or without tethering that increased police presence to some kind of community accountability would not be consistent with the message these groups bring to the legislative process. An exchange with an African American Pittsburgh councilman provides a useful perspective. He began by carefully explaining how little sympathy his constituents have for criminals:

RESPONDENT: Well I've been around long enough to remember, not too long ago, a significant level of activism around prisoners' rights, both at the prosecutorial level as well as the institutional level, inside the joint. That attitude has changed. People no longer associate prisoners' rights with civil rights. They [criminals] have so terrorized the community that people want them gone. And people have a great deal of sympathy for innocent bystanders and very little sympathy for criminal actors, whether they are the shooter or the shot.... It's because their victims are black. And the base of that civil rights protection movement was the black civil rights movement, but when they began to victimize their base, they eroded the sympathy that was coming from that base.

INTERVIEWER: What about crime issues that don't involve violence?

RESPONDENT: Take 'em all out. Take 'em all. The shooters, the druggies, the purse-snatchers. Take 'em all. There's very little sympathy.

INTERVIEWER: And so they're supportive of aggressive police tactics, the kind of big sweeps that come in and sweep them up, even if they cast the net pretty wide?

RESPONDENT: They just want to know, were they *reasonably* tough? They understand that these cops gotta be tough. They want them to be tough enough to be effective, *but don't kill people.*

Later in the interview, when asked about the kind of messages he hears from citizen groups about public safety, he said:

They want community policing. And frequently that means officers walking the beat. And officers who are partners in community improvement, not just overseers. They want a sufficient number of police to get a call responded to in a reasonable amount of time. They want local police to have a good reputation. Very polite. They explain to you why they stopped you, what the charges are. You're gonna get a ticket just the same, but they're gonna be nice. And people want to be treated that way. They want police to have clear rules about when you use force, especially lethal force. And to obey those rules and not misuse your police authority. That authority comes from us and you have no right to misuse it.[48]

Another Pittsburgh council member, in response to a question about increased presence of federal law enforcement and aggressively prosecuting local criminals with federal laws, said: "Oh, no, I know for a fact that they [groups in the African American community] would be concerned that it would be mostly black kids going down the chute....I think they would be very fearful that this was pinpointed towards hurting them rather than helping them."[49]

All this suggests that broad citizen groups bring a more nuanced perspective than the simplistic "good cop, bad cop" frame that polarizes much public discourse.[50] This feeling of being "over-policed and under-protected," as the Kerner Commission originally put it, is consistent with a wide range of scholarly literature.[51] Indeed, young people in high-crime urban areas express quite nuanced views of the police, holding negative attitudes while simultaneously wishing they were around more.[52] In fact, neighborhood satisfaction and quality-of-life concerns are deeply intertwined with attitudes toward the police and a willingness to engage in social and political activity.[53]

But this problem definition is so rooted in larger dissatisfactions with quality of life that it becomes difficult to maintain when crime issues are framed in more stark terms in national and state politics. The plea for more police is taken as a blank check for aggressive policing styles that are largely distrusted in low-income, particularly black, communities. In response, lawmakers at the state level often respond with incentives to reorient police to more community-friendly styles. These approaches— aggressive police stings and walk-the-beat neighborliness—oscillate back and forth depending on the prevailing political pressures. But both approaches miss the larger message that local citizen groups offer, which is easily decipherable if we take into consideration the context in which the citizens represented by these groups must live and work. What begins as complex agitation about a wide range of public issues—safety, neighborhood quality, public services, educational and employment opportunity, and so on—is transformed in state crime politics to more dichotomous "good cop, bad cop" debates. This, in turn, maps neatly onto the notion that there are decent, law-abiding citizens and then there are criminals. This "good citizen, bad citizen" framework obscures the criminogenic neighborhood conditions that contribute to violence and other forms of criminal offending.

Political Mobilization, Civic Engagement, and Policy Frames

This discussion highlights several important aspects of the local crime policy environment that are essentially lost in state and national venues. First, the tough rhetoric about getting rid of the "shooters, druggies, and purse snatchers" is bracketed by the twin concerns of seeking improved community relations with law enforcement and willingness to promote preventive actions that might mitigate the need for more police. This is most noticeable in the responses to my queries about constituents' attitudes toward punishment. While sympathy for criminals is extremely low, this sentiment coexists with a sense that many of the kids "going down the chute" are the "low-hanging fruit" and that the neighborhood's problems might be better solved by focusing more resources and attention at other levels in the criminal conspiracy. This is consistent with comments by other respondents and testimony at hearings that expressed deep and unforgiving frustration with crime and violence but was grounded in the realities of inner-city street life and the challenges of getting from government the kind of proper policing and neighborhood quality that residents desire.

I do not wish to minimize the emphasis on policing in local crime politics. Both citizen groups and lawmakers regularly invoked police as important players in addressing crime and violence. As one legislator noted, sometimes citizens express interest in having police do things that go well beyond their jurisdiction or even their lawful capacity, for example, bulldozing houses that are used for drug dealing.[54] But the call for more law enforcement must be seen in the context of neighborhoods awash with drugs, gangs, guns, and violence. In some respects, it is astonishing that citizen groups have the capacity to talk about anything *but* law enforcement in that context.

Second, this discussion illustrates, in part, why the presence of the single-issue citizen groups, particularly the highly active ones such as the NRA, Handgun Control, Inc., and the ACLU, in state and national politics does little to alter the standard framework of criminal justice politics. These groups enter on one side or another of a civil liberties debate in which the problem has already been defined and the agenda already set. In this frame, individuals and rights are a central part of the discussion. The debate remains focused on inequities within the criminal justice system, centering the discussion on offenders and on courtroom procedure. The capacity to talk about the broader choices or structural conditions that created opportunity for criminal behavior is essentially lost, in part because the major groups representing constituencies' interests are still largely locked into the good/bad narratives that dominate state and national crime politics. The problem definition in those legislative venues is very different from the one that points to the underlying economic, social, and political disempowerment that structures criminal behavior, drug activity, and violence on a day-to-day basis.

Third, while the negative effect of poverty on political participation is widely recognized, many scholars have found that the poor are not as demobilized as is often assumed and that even in deeply impoverished areas, mobilization is not only possible but may also contribute to political engagement.[55] Others have argued that black political participation increases when blacks occupy positions of leadership.[56] To the extent that blacks are more likely to have representation in local municipalities than in state and national offices, black political mobilization might be expected to remain higher at the local level as well.

To be sure, some of the citizen groups active in local politics operate in a highly constrained environment, struggling to keep active under extreme conditions, including stress from losing loved ones to violence, fear of violence, and limited resources. While these active citizen groups may not be as mobilized or organized as single-issue citizen groups or professional associations, they are, arguably, substantially more democratized. By virtue of their limited organization, they provide an unfiltered version of citizen interest that is less tainted by the bias of mobilization.[57] In addition, they present concrete policy ideas only infrequently, and when they do they often run afoul of bureaucratic interests or capabilities, as when they ask for drug houses to be bulldozed, for asset forfeiture funds to come back to the community, or for local unemployed persons to tear down billboards.

Of course, to the extent that many of these groups represent neighborhoods, they are likely to be concerned with their own geographic space, making them, by definition, somewhat narrow and possibly very parochial. There is an inherent tension between neighborhood mobilization and broad coalitions, to the extent that the latter want to focus attention on issues that may not be of interest—indeed may sometimes be in opposition—to issues the former want to address, and there is little question that some groups foster race and class exclusivity.[58]

I offer no resolutions to the problem of local parochialism that has demonstrated its exclusivity and narrowness repeatedly throughout American history and in contemporary studies of urban politics, except to note that *the empirical chapters in this book demonstrate that such parochialism is not confined to neighborhood politics.* To the contrary, state and national levels of government can also be narrow with professional associations and criminal justice agencies exhibiting their own forms of professional or single-issue parochialism in ways that often run directly counter to the day-to-day interests of urban neighborhoods facing serious crime. While urban neighborhood groups have a strong and sustained presence in local politics, local lawmakers operate at the bottom of a multi-layered political structure that provides them with virtually all of the feedback and almost none of the control.

Seven

DEMOCRATIC ACCOUNTABILITY
AND SOCIAL CONTROL

I am an invisible man. No, I am not a spook like those who haunted
Edgar Allan Poe; nor am I one of your Hollywood-movie ectoplasms.
I am a man of substance, of flesh and bone, fiber and liquids—and I
might even be said to possess a mind. I am invisible, understand, simply
because people refuse to see me.

—Ralph Ellison, *The Invisible Man*

Legal scholars have been highly critical of what they term the
"federalization" of crime control, by which they mean the
increasing jurisdiction of Congress over more crimes and the growing
influence of the Justice Department in state and local crime fighting. This
process, they argue, is constitutionally suspect and has produced highly
punitive legislation that may serve strategic electoral interests but is nonetheless unwarranted and unproductive.[1] As noted in chapter 1, I use the
term "federalization" differently in this book—to refer to the presence of
a policy issue on all three legislative agendas simultaneously. A more apt
term for what legal scholars are describing would be the "nationalization"
of crime policy.

As I hope this book has illustrated, the problem is not just with the
nationalization of crime policy but with its *federalization*—its presence on
multiple legislative agendas that renders invisible the very groups whose
lives, safety, and *quality of life* depend on their ability to achieve political
representation in the legislative venues that matter most. These groups
need the power, resources, policy advocacy, and political muscle that state
and national governments can offer, but they are the least likely to have

a place at the policy table in congressional and state politics, and this fact is rooted in the structure of the U.S. political system. In a political system that divides power among national, regional, and subregional governments, citizen groups with diffuse interests and limited resources are likely to have difficulty translating their preferences into policy in part because they cannot hold accountable all of the elected officials who might play an important role in the policy process.[2]

This final chapter gives a brief summary of the book's main findings and situates its empirical work in the context of broader discussions of policy agendas, federalism, urban politics, crime control, and governance. In conclusion I offer a revised typology for assessing group participation across legislative venues.

Summary

The gradual and sudden development of crime as a national policy issue opened up opportunities for some groups and foreclosed them for others. This process drew in bureaucratic agencies with specific goals and policy frames. In addition, as the national government grew in size and scope, so did criminal justice agencies. The fluid congressional jurisdiction on crime meant that the issue ebbed and flowed, responding in part to crime rates but also to active groups representing symbolic values shared by a substantial portion of the electorate. As others have argued, the public regards some groups as more worthy of government largesse than others, and those with limited resources and negative constructions (e.g., criminals, some racial groups, the poor) are particularly disadvantaged in the policy process.[3]

As a result, when crime rates rose, urban riots flared, the backlash against civil rights raged, and the scope of the national government's attention to a wide range of social problems grew, crime found a permanent place on the policy agenda. As criminal justice agencies expanded in size and scope and legislation increased their budgets and jurisdiction, their presence in the policymaking process solidified. As a result, police and prosecutors, in particular, have become well represented across a wide range of crime issues that go well beyond executive oversight and agency budget requests. Their expertise is given routinely on every substantive crime issue, even in the absence of pending legislation, and reinforces a law-and-order frame that focuses policy attention on arrests, prosecutions, and convictions. At least two of the dominant professional groups—legal and research—also reinforce this law-and-order frame by maintaining a focus on the effectiveness of criminal justice agencies. Though single-issue citizen groups have gained strength over the past 40 years, citizen participation is largely confined to groups concerned with gun rights, civil liberties, and, more recently, the victimization of women, and these groups' policy priorities often do not conflict with and sometimes even intersect with the interests of police and prosecutors. For example, while police departments often support stricter gun control measures, both police and prosecutors are also likely to support stiffer penalties for gun crimes, joining forces with the NRA's major policy agenda of deflecting attention away from more regulation. To the extent that the gun issue is framed around penalties for gun crimes, the NRA has a significant advantage, because it can focus on a policy alternative that is acceptable to a wide range of interest groups, including the ever-present criminal justice agencies. The paucity of broad citizen groups in the process makes it difficult to dislodge this punishment frame. While broad citizen groups had a brief spike in access during the period of heightened attention to civil rights and urban riots, they have largely fallen off the national legislative agenda. Black victims, in particular, have had difficulty becoming visible in national crime politics for any extended period of time.

In the states, crime became a more regular agenda item beginning in the 1960s and 1970s but really exploded in the 1980s and 1990s, with determinate sentencing schemes, mandatory minimum sentences, Three Strikes You're Out, and truth-in-sentencing legislation.[4] In this context, the growing power of elected district attorneys, as well as burgeoning women's organizations and other single-issue citizen groups, coalesced into a policy environment that is highly sensitive to the needs and interests of prosecutors and a few well-organized citizen groups. In some respects, the state-level data I examined revealed an even narrower policy domain than that of Congress. Prosecutors, for example, are particularly active in Pennsylvania legislative politics. In addition to Pennsylvania, 28 other states have active district attorneys' associations, and 37 have registered lobby groups that represent court reporters, judges, magistrates, and other criminal justice actors.[5] In fact, of all of the lobby groups listed in the law category of Gray and Lowry's lobby list from 1997, more than 1 in 5 (177/780) represent criminal justice interests. As I argued in chapter 4, the problem is not that prosecutors or other criminal justice agencies are inappropriate actors in public policy debates. Naturally, as enforcers of the law with firsthand experience in trying to keep communities safe, they form an important part of the policy landscape. The vast majority of the time, as Robert Cover aptly notes, the balance of power between suspected criminals and the government is probably just as we would want it to be.[6] But as legal scholars have argued, prosecutors frequently have a narrow set of interests focused on making it easier for them to get convictions.[7] The intractable problems of drugs, violence, juvenile delinquency, theft, and other such ills require more than conviction of known criminals.

Single-issue citizen groups and the ACLU dominate the Pennsylvania state-level policy process even more than the national-level one. Only one broad citizen group appeared more than twice at the Pennsylvania hearings in my dataset between 1990 and 2004—the Alliance for the Mentally Ill—in staggering contrast to the total of nine single-issue citizen groups, including MADD, the NRA, Pennsylvanians Against Handgun Violence, and the Pennsylvania Prison Society.[8] This is particularly important given how much recent research has been dedicated to crime policy at the national level. To the degree that Pennsylvania is at all representative (and certainly California and Texas are as likely, if not more so, to over-represent criminal justice agencies), it is the state level that appears to need more attention from criminology, policy, and sociolegal scholars, if the nature and extent of democratic accountability for state-sanctioned use of force and social control are to be fully understood.[9]

It is also worth noting that the dominant type of professional group in Pennsylvania is legal associations, mostly representing criminal defendants. Whereas we might see this as a counterbalance to the ubiquity of criminal justice agencies, the actions of local chapters of these associations reveal that in fact, debates about what to do with offenders are largely irrelevant to local groups representing neighborhoods with serious crime. To be sure, most citizens probably know that their local city council cannot do much about state sentencing policies, but there are few issues these local groups don't raise, so their lack of discussion of sentencing policy and the rights of criminal defendants is more likely to be one of preferences and interests rather than strategic focus. In fact, as I mentioned regarding their pragmatism, these groups seem less concerned with what happens to offenders than with keeping people from getting hurt in the first place and finding solutions that have results, regardless of the implications for offenders. If the answer is locking people up forever, there are plenty of citizen groups that would support such strategies. But if that is not going to work, then they will advocate some alternative. Thus, criminal defender associations do little to dislodge the law-and-order, police-centered framing of crime and victimization. Worse, they may serve to reinforce it, as they monopolize lawmakers' attention so that they have little left to give to the entirely different frames that are presented by broad citizen groups, less mobilized single-issue groups, and less routine professional associations.

Finally, the chapters on local crime politics provided a stark contrast to the other two levels. Broad citizen groups form the backbone of this process, appearing at legislative hearings, contacting legislators, holding meetings, calling the media, and otherwise making themselves known to local lawmakers in far greater numbers than any other type of group, including single-issue citizen groups. Other organizations that are seldom seen at the state and national levels—for example religious groups, particularly black churches, and education groups—appear more frequently at the local level as well, intersecting with the broad range of quality-of-life concerns that are raised by broad citizen organizations.

In fact, what is most striking about the different policy environments across legislative venues is that the local level is much less fragmented and compartmentalized. Hearings about illegal billboards devolve into hearings about urban blight more generally. Hearings about local prisons slip into hearings about economic decline. The problem with limited access of broad citizen groups to the larger policy venues is not so much that citizens in high-crime areas bring different policy solutions (although that is sometimes true, too) but, rather, that *they are pressing legislators on entirely different policy terrain*: on a broader range of quality-of-life concerns, including housing, blight, police-community relations, economic development, education, and services. The devastating effects of criminal violence and the impact of the criminal justice system fall disproportionately on blacks, Latinos, and the poor, and the impact of a wide range of social pathologies—drug and alcohol addiction, teen pregnancy, family violence, incarceration—all have deeper and longer lasting consequences in these communities than they do in middle-class ones.[10] Citizens in these neighborhoods are mobilized, albeit often in informal and loosely organized groups, and they pressure governments to ameliorate the neighborhood conditions that give rise to crime and a host of social pathologies and negative consequences. In short, the local crime policy process is all about *politics*—the redistribution of resources and the allocation and exercise of power.

As Katznelson has persuasively argued, the emergence of black political power in urban areas in the 1960s posed a challenge to the twin political powerhouses of urban politics at the time—the politics of work (labor unions) and the politics of community (political parties and machine politics in neighborhoods).[11] Indeed, since that time, cities have declined further in economic and social capital, leaving urban blacks and Latinos with even more limited opportunities for meaningful work. Thus, the work/community cleavage that diluted the political power of working-class whites, allowing an opening for black political power to grow, has largely disappeared, and the urban poor lack strong work environments in which to generate a workplace politics. In this vacuum, as a result of rising crime rates and devastating violence, the *politics of crime* has become a focal point for a wide range of political activity that encompasses claims about the absence of work and opportunity as well as the limits of social and political power.

In the state policy process, crime policy making is largely decoupled from these political concerns, focusing more narrowly on utilizing state resources to identify worthy victims and punish offenders. In Congress, crime issues wax and wane, partially in response to issue entrepreneurs—advocates for juveniles, women, and occasionally urbanites—while police and prosecutors advance their agency imperatives and resources. In fact, as single-issue groups representing primarily white victims have become routinized players in the policy process at the state and national levels, black victims *and all they represent* have remained largely invisible. Black victims' groups, of course, would represent the historic injustice of white-on-black crime committed with impunity; the transformation of southern lynchings into northern whites' race riots; the long-standing economic and social segregation of blacks in the harshest living conditions in the United States; the inner cities' staggering impoverishment and isolation and all of the violence they engender; the historic (and contemporary) victimization of blacks and Latinos by police and other state agents—to name just a few.

Though the subtitle of this book suggests that it is about the poor and minorities, it is largely about their *absence* from the policy venues that have the greatest capacity to affect change. This invisibility of blacks, in particular, as victims of violence in historic and contemporary contexts has significant implications for how we conceptualize crime and its consequences—not to mention its origins. In a broader sense, the absence of groups representing the broad quality-of-life concerns of the urban poor and minorities illustrates a more profound problem in U.S. democracy, as it raises questions about the legitimacy of governmental institutions at the state and national levels that fail to take into account the day-to-day needs of such a large segment of the population.[12] Not only do citizens facing crime and violence on a sustained basis have few opportunities for direct representation in two of three legislative policy venues but also other groups that do try to represent their interests—such as the ACLU or the Prison Society— often truncate a broad range of concerns into narrow, readily accessible frames that are continually reproduced by the policy process at the state and national levels. As if this state of affairs were not bad enough, these citizens are then exposed to the most forceful of all state institutions—the criminal justice apparatus—at a much higher rate than other citizens, further weakening the already fragile social contexts in which they must forge a community.

One of surprising findings of the research reported in this study is the relative absence of groups at any level of government that advocate alternatives to incarceration in an effort to alter the law-and-order, punishment frame of other policy venues. With the exception of the Pennsylvania Prison Society, I found few groups with such a mission and virtually no such groups at the local level. One Pittsburgh councilman noted in response to a query about whether groups were lobbying for alternatives to incarceration: "No, no, they're not. We don't tend to get that too much. I mean, the one issue that came up was...the jail problem with not having a place to take them. But that's the only interaction we've had on that."[13] What is interesting, however, is that the reason that these groups don't seem to have much of a presence in the local policy process is not that local policy is so heavily laden with punishment and law-and-order policy frames but that it simply isn't particularly focused on offenders at all. As chapter 6 demonstrated, the bulk of information local lawmakers get from broad citizen groups—and other groups that state and national legislators rarely hear from, such as religious groups and more diverse single-issue groups—is about conveying the pain and suffering of victims. They offer very little perspective on what to do with offenders.

When such groups did talk about offenders, the message lawmakers received was just as likely to push for uprooting the causes of crime as to push uniformly for punishment—as a Pittsburgh councilwoman's comments demonstrate:

> The community wants the bad guys locked up, they don't want their lives to be in jeopardy but they also want us to get the root of the drug dealing.... They really want to press the root issues. A lot of people feel it is a conspiracy to destroy African American communities and low-income communities. We don't make the drugs, we don't manufacture the drugs. It seems like there is somebody who is doing this to us. I don't buy into conspiracy theories but I do see their point. Guns and drugs aren't manufactured in those neighborhoods. The big boys and roots are in areas you'd never suspect.[14]

The tight coupling of victims' and potential victims' needs with the punishing of offenders has been widely cited as a key element of state and national crime policy making, where "the implicit assumption is that anything that is bad for offenders must be beneficial to victims."[15] But at the local level, where the damage of crime is felt in personal, familial, and community terms, such a coupling is much more tenuous. Recall that even the white working-class community with a prison in its backyard seemed less interested in skewering prison escapees than establishing an effective method for notifying community members of the escape. Similarly, a Pittsburgh councilman found a receptive audience for his public health message among his diverse constituents living in neighborhoods with high drug crime. And recall the Philadelphia legislator who described his black constituents' disdain for criminal offenders yet heard them as less interested in removing all the "low-hanging fruit" through aggressive law enforcement than in pursuing more serious offenders, and in reducing opportunities for people to become involved in criminal activity in the first place. And this appeared to be true not just for blacks but for residents in a wide range of neighborhoods where people live with the very real possibility of serious crime victimization. This does not mean that broad citizen groups are never punitive in their approach. Sometimes they want houses bulldozed, and they certainly want violent criminals removed from their streets permanently. But their typical calls for action rarely indicate that they see punishment of the corporeal being that is the offender as having any connection to the reduction of harm to victims.

This might seem counterintuitive, until one considers that public opinion on crime might be far less punitive than our policies would suggest.[16] The connection between crime, quality of life, and the limitations of punishment are more acute at the local level, where citizen groups have the most expansive representation but legislators are most constrained. In addition, broad citizen groups—representing not just African Americans but also Latinos, the poor, and otherwise marginalized groups (like the homeless)—also present a policy frame that is much closer to redistributive than the regulatory and distributive frames of state and national politics. These groups recognize that their neighborhoods are worse off than others (as illustrated by the presentation of data on illegal billboards by zip code, or the testimony about people having the desire to change their neighborhoods but not the capacity to do so), and they want the government to do something about it. This is plain, old-fashioned redistributive politics. While it is coupled with a strong desire for regulatory agency (i.e., police), citizen groups are not simply lining up for a distribution of some City Hall resources. They advocate for more police, but in the context of cleaner neighborhoods, more opportunities, and better schools, which requires a reallocation of power and resources. As the issue migrates to other legislative venues, the police message resonates, but much of the rest is left behind.

Federalism and Group Politics

In their classic book, *Agendas and Instability*, Baumgartner and Jones (1993) describe a porous political system in which issues come and go from multiple political agendas and internal and external pressures create new contexts, new groups, and new policy environments. By calling attention to these dynamics, Baumgartner and Jones have provided a crucial foundation for more accurate assessments of the U.S. policy process. As they note, policy debates in this process are often multidimensional, with some groups articulating particular claims and other groups responding on different dimensions. The fluidity of our federal system thus broadens opportunities for some as it narrows them for others. As E. E. Schattsch-neider aptly said, "organization is itself a mobilization of bias."[17]

The porous nature of federalism, however, renders power more accessible for some groups than others. While Paul Peterson's important work *City Limits* observed that federalism creates a unique policy environment for cities, limiting their legislative capacity, the research presented here suggests that state and national venues are also structurally limited and that, at times, cities represent citizen interests better than other levels of government.[18] By tracking one issue across the local, state, and national legislative venues, this book has shown that while fluidity has some democracy-enhancing features, it also has some limiting ones: the more mobilized groups have to be, the fewer opportunities will be available to groups that have diffuse interests, few resources, or negative stereotypes to overcome.

This is the fundamental issue of democratic politics explored in this book. *Federalism may provide multiple pathways of access, but it also divides and conquers, isolating poorly resourced groups from one another and making it difficult for them to hold legislators accountable to their interests.* At the same time, this structure allows more organized groups, sometimes quite narrow in focus, to access debates in the venues that are most hospitable to their interests and to migrate across venues when they see opportunities for gaining a policy advantage. As the preceding chapters have demonstrated, citizens facing serious crime—and all of its causes and collateral consequences—have greater democratic control over what the local government does to address crime than they do over any other level. In fact, their say is so minuscule at those other levels as to be practically nonexistent. Thus, federalism exacerbates the classic collective action problem by increasing the number of potential veto points for single-minded, narrow interests and by isolating potential allies from one another.

This division of power also allows more mobilized groups to shift their policy frames to suit the policy venue, an opportunity that is far less available to groups with more diffuse interests and few specific policy solutions readily at hand. Consider the chameleon tactics of the NRA, which not only navigates across state and national venues with ease but also shifts its framing of the gun issue according to where the debate is taking place. In Pennsylvania, the NRA joined suit to bar Philadelphia and Pittsburgh from banning assault weapons in their jurisdictions, arguing for the importance of uniformity across the state, and effectively denying these cities the capacity to regulate and prosecute gun criminals in their own way (see chapter 1). In Congress, the NRA argued just the opposite—that Congress should severely curtail its gun regulations because variation across the states is more appropriate with our federal political system.[19] As Kristin Goss notes, in her excellent study of the limited nature of gun control advocacy in the United States, the NRA exploited the "political inconveniences of a fragmented federal system" better than gun opponents.[20] The same may be said for advocates for women and children in the second half of the twentieth century, who have had some success across legislative venues.[21] The poor (with their limited resources and social capital) and racial minorities (with their association with criminality in the minds of many whites) are severely disadvantaged in such a system, and among the many consequences is their highly constrained ability to force government to deliver on one of its most cherished and fundamental social contracts: helping citizens live free from random violence.

In this sense, the policy environments at the state and national levels provide a kind of cover for lawmakers that allows them to marginalize those groups that they do not hear from regularly or will eventually run out of steam. The policy process at these levels can sometimes move at a glacial pace, and groups without the lobbying force to stay with it can easily fall off the radar. One Pennsylvania general assemblyman who is a former Pittsburgh city council member noted:

> I felt more of a lobbying effort at local level than I do at the state level. When grassroots push happens, they want it done overnight. At the state level, things happen much more slowly...there is very little will to get what some groups want done actually done. It's too big, too complex, people feel like they never get a straight answer. Locally [Pittsburgh], there are only nine members and the mayor. The runaround is shorter, there are fewer people to point the finger to. Eventually someone has to fess up to reason why they're blocking what [these groups] want. Whereas with over two hundred—or at federal level, over four hundred legislators, it's easy to pass the buck. There is a faster return on the grassroots at the local level. It's harder to pass the buck locally. Legislators are in closer proximity to each other.[22]

Of course, progressive groups—often working on behalf of the poor or racial and ethnic minorities—have exploited these aspects of federalism as well. Over the course of 40 years, leaders of the civil rights movement proved masterfully adept at exploiting the multiple venues of our federal political system and concentrating resources in the places where they would make the most difference. Other left-wing groups, for example environmental activists and education reformers, have forged similar opportunities.[23] But this is one of the key findings of this book: *federalism structures group representation in ways that vary across time and issue*, and this structure can reinforce existing race and class stratifications and political hierarchies as much as it can provide opportunities for resisting them.

Arguably, civil rights groups won some victories not *because* of federalism but *in spite* of it. Substantial transformations in domestic and global politics were important underpinnings for the successes of the civil rights movement, which advocated the same basic policy goals since before the Civil War.[24] Claims that the federal system helps the poor and the marginalized because it provides multiple points of access must be balanced against analyses of how well those groups fare in nonfederal systems. While the U.S. federal system has, at times, generated opportunities for public interest pressures to balance narrower, material group interests, in the long run, its fragmented nature reverts power to those who have the greatest organizational capacity to identify and interact with the level of government that can best respond to their interests.[25]

To be clear, this book is not a defense of localism. It is not an argument about the intrinsic value of smaller political entities over larger ones, nor does it offer an idealized picture of local politics where citizens come to consensus on important issues and willingly set aside self-interest for the greater good. To the contrary, as chapters 5 and 6 illustrated, local crime politics is a mess of self-interested, frustrated groups eager to hold lawmakers' feet to the fire in any way they can. Groups come and go sometimes without leaving any trace of their presence, save a few lines at a legislative hearing or a vague name imprinted in the minds of a local lawmaker. Many groups inject complaints and rage into policy debates with little sense of how to resolve them. Groups (and individuals) run up against recalcitrant public officials or simply make demands that administrators are unable to meet. Sometimes they insist on policy solutions that have demonstrably little impact but simply make them feel better. They demand more and more police while simultaneously criticizing police for inadequacy and corruption. They seem to know little about the policy solutions they want and even less about how to get them.

They do, however, know what they do not want, and it is, at its core, what none of us want: a life in which bursts of violence streak across the daily landscape without warning, criminality offers itself to young people more frequently than professional opportunities, the siren call of drug addiction is persistent and pervasive, neighborhoods are flooded with empty lots, abandoned cars and buildings, unsightly billboards, and graffiti, and few opportunities for economic progress exist. Local lawmakers simply cannot avoid being called on to remediate these intolerable conditions, and they have little choice but to respond. Citizen groups in local jurisdictions all over the country register remarkably similar messages of concern over public safety and quality of life, but their voices are so distant from one another that they rarely produce a collective noise, much less an audible signal. While the problems of localism are well documented and legion, chapters 4 and 5 demonstrate that *state and national policy venues*

can exhibit their own kind of localism, narrowly responding to a small segment of interests. At least local-level crime politics includes a wide assort-
ment of citizen interests and policy priorities, which cannot be said of the
state- or congressional-level ones.

In fact, this analysis of groups across legislative venues may provide
a useful illustration of what Iris Marion Young refers to as "perspective,"
as distinguished from interests or opinions.[26] Interests, in this formulation, usually provide for certain specific policy outcomes and goals, while
perspectives provide a starting point for debate. Perhaps scholars have
assumed too much correspondence between perspectives and interests—
assuming, for example, that citizen groups that pursue an *interest* effectively represent the *perspectives* of citizens. Many groups represented in
local crime politics, however, seem to be presenting primarily a perspective—one that informs legislators of the challenges of living in poor neighborhoods or of facing serious crime but offers few specific proposals for
ameliorating the problem. This perspective could come with a wide range
of policy interests or preferences, but citizens themselves may not be fully
certain of their interests or preferences on how to resolve the problem.
It may be that citizens can offer *perspectives* most effectively in settings
where there is close proximity between legislators and their constituents
or when accountability is more direct. In that context, the process is less
formal, and citizens can raise concerns without having to make choices
between different, complex, and competing policy solutions or channel
them into specific policy frames. In addition, this setting allows for perspectives to be understood as a function of particular citizens' social locations rather than as universalized experience. The problem with interests,
Young suggests, is that they are often perceived as universal and neutral,
not as simply vehicles of one social perspective among many. This phenomenon is nicely illustrated here by the notion that single-issue groups
effectively represent citizen interests on crime, when in fact, they appear
to represent the perspectives of whites, women, and the middle class more
than those of blacks, particularly black men, and poor people, particularly when those groups intersect. And even then, it is not at all clear that
single-issue citizen groups are all that representative of the wide range of
even white or middle-class citizen perspectives on crime. One of the consequences of federalism, then, is this: when state and national policy venues
narrow perspectives to interests, citizens are left with little choice but to
simply support or oppose existing options. The resultant policy outcomes
are perceived as representative of citizen perspectives when, in fact, they
may represent highly mobilized and often narrow interests.

Skocpol (2003) has argued that in the early part of the twentieth century, many of the locally active groups were not, in fact, organic to local
communities but were the product of organized, concerted efforts by

elites to generate active, densely populated, translocal organizations that could serve constituencies' needs and address political concerns across the spectrum of federal institutions. To the extent that these groups have disappeared and been replaced by highly professionalized advocacy organizations that target narrow policy goals and specific policy venues, the urban poor are missing the one opportunity they may have for forging alliances and political power across legislative venues. That so many of the citizen groups that populate state and national policy environments are single-issue (with the notable exception of the ACLU) represents a real loss to the policy process, as groups with more diffuse and expressive interests have given way to narrow, instrumental groups.

While the perils of federalism are potentially a problem in a lot of policy areas, those involving the poor—a category blacks and Latinos fall into disproportionately—are most likely to feel its effects. It is one thing to rally your friends and neighbors to the Tuesday city council meeting or get a dozen people to show up and call themselves Citizens for Less Crime, More Safety, and a Better Quality of Life. It is quite another to gain tax-exempt status, a lobbyist in the state capital, specific policy proposals, knowledge about the criminal code, and complex legislative sessions, not to mention the savvy to frame policy solutions in ways legislators might respond to. In fact, coming up with any practical policy solution to crime at all is beyond most of us. So while black teenagers are seven times more likely to experience violent crime than whites, black and Latino citizens are exposed to illegal drugs, criminal conspiracies, and routine street crime on a regular basis, and the worst living conditions for urban whites are about average for blacks, a cavernous structural gap separates the groups formed on their behalf from the legislators who can help them.[27]

Some legislators no doubt see themselves as responding to the needs of inner-city crime victims when they impose mandatory minimums or increase police budgets. And surely some of those policies have an impact, though not always in the intended way. But the research presented in this book shows that those policy responses have goals and outcomes that are far removed from the visible reduction in harm and increased quality of life for which groups representing routine crime victims advocate. These responses are also not generally organic to the communities that experience crime the most, and while those communities may be supportive if they can see these responses working, they do little to strengthen community mobilization efforts, reinforce the local groups that are already organized in opposition to crime, promote civic engagement that generates social capital, or address the structural conditions that generate crime and violence in the first place. As a result, the federalization of crime generates bloated criminal justice agency budgets and crime frames fixated on punishing offenders and depoliticizes citizen engagement. Arresting criminals and increasing sentence lengths may be crucial elements of crime reduction strategies, but few groups that testify in the local legislative hearings or contact city council members see them as ends in and of themselves.

Given this analysis, we might fairly ask what valued political commodity federalism provides. In his classic work *A View from the States*, Daniel Elazar argued that

> by requiring that basic policies be made and implemented through a process of negotiation that involves all polities concerned, the federal system enables all to share in the overall system's decision-making and executing processes. In its simplest form, federalism means political integration through the compounding of political systems that continue to exist within the new whole. In a larger sense, however, federalism is more than an arrangement of governmental structures; it is a mode of political activity that requires the extension of certain kinds of cooperative relationships throughout any political system it animates.[28]

The analysis presented here suggests that the multiple venues for representation and decision making that federalism creates are not necessarily additive. That is, *the addition of new legislative venues does not necessarily increase opportunities for representation.* In fact, in a very real sense, it may decrease those opportunities if issues migrate to the levels of government where there is little opportunity for a full spectrum of participants, particularly if the levels of government with the most resources are also the ones with the most limited ability to accommodate groups with diffuse, expressive interests. The political representation that Ex-Offenders Inc., for example, has in the city of Philadelphia is not only isolated from that of other similarly situated groups around the country, it is further depressed by the capacity of powerful nationally based groups, like the NRA, to hold lawmakers accountable across a range of venues. In this respect, it is not unreasonable to suggest that the local Philadelphia city government is more representative of the citizens of Philadelphia than the U.S. Senate is of the citizens of the United States.

In comparative context, some scholars have argued that in other countries, including Britain, the presence of a strong bureaucratic class of experts has contributed to a less politicized policy environment that has mitigated the trends toward harsher punishments.[29] But the data presented here suggest that bureaucratic agencies in the United States are at least as active in policy making as they are elsewhere (perhaps more so) but their agency priorities are largely insulated from public pressure for actually resolving crime problems. As a result, they are able to press for more arrest and prosecution power—the tools they have most readily at their disposal—and are less likely to be held accountable by the groups who are most deeply affected when such approaches fall short of community expectations. In other words, the problem is not that in the United States bureaucratic agencies of the criminal justice system are not sufficiently insulated from public pressure. Rather, the problem may very well be that they are *too* insulated from the people who are most exposed to crime and violence on a regular basis and whose policy priorities are less likely to equate punishing offenders with reducing harm to victims. While some have fretted over how to insulate punishment practices from democratic impulses, this book suggests that the problem is less one of avoiding too much democracy and more one of the *nature* of that democratic process.[30] The problem in the United States is that public opinion is filtered through political institutions that magnify narrow interests whose advocates can provide tangible or feel-good benefits to their constituents and supporters but diminish the representation of groups representing the broad public interest in establishing and maintaining safe and viable communities. Social movement scholars have long recognized the difficulty in sustaining legislative attention to movements and groups focused on broad public goods because they provide only limited material benefits to members, making mobilization more difficult, and because any concessions from government are widely dispersed, making the free-rider problem especially likely.[31]

Thus, as the place of crime on state and national legislative agendas has become institutionalized, the relationships between institutions and particular sets of interests have smoothed the path for participation such that what is good for lawmakers is good for prosecutors is good for single-issue citizen groups. Even the ACLU hardly dislodges this policy dynamic, because its focus is primarily on improving conditions and practices of existing criminal justice institutions. I do not mean to minimize this worthy goal but simply to note that it bears little relationship to the broader policy agendas presented by broad citizen groups and religious and educational organizations at the local level. In fact, taking this argument further, the elite rhetoric that criticizes current crime control policies by focusing on civil liberties, the problems of the "drug war," high incarceration rates, and aggressive police tactics is not particularly responsive to the deep anxieties about drugs, gangs, violence, and social disorganization that many of the local groups bring to the policy process. Inequities and unjust practices within the justice system no doubt occur and deserve scrutiny, but focusing on these problems instead of the larger, more fundamental socioeconomic differences that structure citizen interaction with the justice system in the first place will not generate useful solutions to the ongoing suffering that crime brings into people's day-to-day lives in the inner cities. Perhaps the ACLU's efforts have intersected best with those of urban broad citizen groups when it has advocated policing strategies that are more responsive to community needs and local drug and mental health courts. The Pennsylvania chapter of the ACLU has advocated for both.[32] But in the absence of other citizen groups supporting such policies at the state level, the ACLU probably appears overly sympathetic to offenders in a context in which single-issue victim advocacy and criminal justice agencies dominate.

Crime, Law, Political Mobilization, and the Urban Poor

As noted in chapter 1, some sociolegal scholars have argued that over the course of the twentieth century, the iconic crime victim—innocent, middle-class, generally white—has become the central citizen subject around which a wide range of public policies are designed.[33] The centrality of the crime victim as the focal point of public policy severely reduces the range of social problems that can be addressed and the spectrum of possible policy solutions. On the one hand, the limited nature of the congressional crime agenda (less than 2 percent of all hearings are about crime and justice) and its relatively stable, if not declining, presence since the early 1990s suggests that the topic of crime is not so ubiquitous after all.[34] And while crime as an agenda topic has grown in Pennsylvania politics, few interest groups scholars have identified criminal justice agencies or victims' groups as central to the policy process more generally. In addition, the decline of individual witnesses in both venues, many of whom used to represent victims and their families, along with the limited role of citizen groups, including victims' groups, suggests that victim citizens do not occupy the privileged position some would suggest they do.

On the other hand, the national and state studies provide some compelling evidence that law-and-order frames dominate the crime policy process, precisely because of the increasing strength of prosecutors and single-issue citizen groups, whose victim-centered orientations end up focusing primarily on punishing offenders, save for the repeated assertions of civil liberties concerns by the ACLU. The findings here are thus consistent with recent research demonstrating the growing influence of prosecutors and the executive branch in crime policy making over the past 30 years.[35] In this sense, chapter 2 shows the ways some voices and narratives about crime and victimization have come to be privileged over others, and chapters 3 and 4 provided empirical support for this analysis. The channeling of policy energy into legal frames was most dramatically illustrated by the exchange at the Pennsylvania General Assembly hearing presented in chapter 4 in which citizen groups who had waited a long time for their turn to testify were asked to allow a district attorney—who "would basically support" their position, it was said—to speak ahead of them. The justification for moving the district attorney ahead of citizens' groups because his time was valuable and he would essentially articulate their message anyway suggests that citizen groups are largely irrelevant members of the policy process whose messages can be squeezed in if there is time but who are easily replaced by other, more legitimate witnesses. To be sure, the underenforcement of the criminal law among blacks has been a historic problem, and no one mindful of this history would advocate for prosecutors to be less aggressive in pursuing convictions of violent offenders in urban neighborhoods.[36] Indeed, the research I have presented reveals that groups representing urban minorities and the urban poor are not at all opposed to aggressive law enforcement and removing known criminals from the streets. But the prosecutorial verve for conviction is deeply linked to professional norms, expectations, and ambitions, and to the extent that prosecutors and other criminal justice agencies dominate the policy process, policy frames will be skewed and severely limited in their ability to offer genuine harm reduction and community revitalization.

This framing offers a profoundly limited understanding of the policy priorities of broad citizen groups, as the subsequent testimony in the hearing suggests. Citizen groups are frequently the last to testify and, unlike criminal justice agencies who usually provide lawmakers with a tangible place to locate resources, often present a laundry list of concerns and complaints that intersect with few existing policies. Clearly not all groups are created equal in terms of the political muscle they bring to the policy process. What is the testimony of a district attorney worth? That of two police officers? Five citizen groups? Not only do criminal justice agencies dominate the policy process at the state and national levels in terms of sheer numbers, their expertise is valued in ways that broad citizen groups are not. The problem is not with expert testimony per se. Rather, the limitation federalism imposes is the inability of local groups to reframe the crime issue beyond the reactive, punishment-oriented frame that characterizes most policy making.

While the state level, in particular, seems to illustrate a shift in policy focus to victims as the citizen subjects (though policy outcomes end up focusing on offenders), I find less evidence for this shift at the local level. Here, local groups are not only mobilized around a wide range of social issues; both lawmakers and the groups they hear from connect crime to a broad spectrum of social ills. This is actually quite consistent with public opinion research that finds that citizens are far less punitive than the nation's crime policies would suggest. As one of the state respondents suggested, when confronted with generic bad guy, most citizens just want him locked away. But on a practical level, citizen groups exhibit a more pragmatic streak, pressing for policy *solutions*, not simply waste management—as Jonathon Simon (1993) so poignantly termed our current state- and national-level justice practices. Local crime politics is a focal point for a wide range of concerns about social conditions and political marginalization, and this is not a recent phenomenon. In fact, crime concerns have animated urban politics for much of the twentieth century, and there is little evidence that the anxieties and demands of ethnic immigrants about public safety and neighborhood conditions in the early twentieth century look much different from those demands by urban blacks and Latinos in the early twenty-first.[37] Urban crime victims and their advocates—typically low-resourced populations made even more so by their living conditions, including the prevalence of crime— have long faced difficulties translating their needs and preferences into political action, in part because of a political structure that divides and conquers, pitting diffuse urban interests against more mobilized ones and also against one another, as individual cities compete for scarce resources rather than collectively advancing their common interests.

Typology of Group Representation

Chapter 2 offered a typology of group representation in federalism. Some patterns emerge from the empirical chapters that require some revisiting of that typology. First, not all types of mobilization are observable in the crime policy process. The most notable types of mobilization are *hyper- and top-heavy mobilization* (criminal justice agencies, social service organizations, and single-issue groups are largely top-heavy, with a few groups within those categories, such as police, women's anti-violence groups and the ACLU migrating down to the local level); *national mobilization* (research-and-policy groups); *state mobilization* (legal groups, a few narrow single-issue groups like the Pennsylvania Prison Society); and *local mobilization* (broad citizen groups, educational groups, religious groups). Thus, groups seem to either mobilize primarily on a single level or are fairly active in all three.

Given the findings about different types of groups and their mobilization capacities across levels of government, we can construct a matrix at the intersection of group resources and the narrowness or diffuseness of a group's interests that shows the type of mobilization we might expect from each type. Table 7.1 presents this modified typology.

This matrix provides a way of locating different groups in the policy process in a federal system. In order for citizen groups to have an active presence on all three legislative agendas, they must be highly resourced

TABLE 7.1. Types of Group Mobilization across Legislative Venues, by Resources and Interests

	Resources	
	Low	High
Interests		
Narrow	*Local/state mobilization*, e.g., some single-issue citizen groups, some professional associations (SCRUB, PA Prison Society, Citizens for Police Accountability, teachers' organizations)	*Hypermobilization*, e.g., government agencies, some single-issue citizen groups, professional associations (Pennsylvania District Attorneys' Association, Fraternal Order of Police, single-issue, ACLU, MADD, NRA)
Diffuse	*Local mobilization*, e.g., most broad citizen groups, some professional organizations, religious organizations (Belmont Improvement Association, Mothers Against Tragedy, black churches, public schools)	*State/national mobilization*, e.g., a few broad citizen organizations, policy/research, social service, legal, religious organizations (NAACP, American Bar Association, Cato Institute, Heritage Foundation, Boys and Girls Club)

and, for the most part, narrowly focused. There are exceptions, of course. But the barriers to regular and sustained participation across multiple legislative venues are significant enough that few citizen groups with broad interests will make it across that threshold on a regular basis. Professional associations, too, vary in their resources and interests, and those with greater means and more finely tuned messages (such as legal and research groups) will find the migration easier. Those with interests that intersect across a wide range of social issues—such as educational groups—will find hypermobilization difficult.

Conclusion

This study describes only the tip of a very large iceberg: the way federalism structures group representation, political accountability, and the democratic process. It also has provided a roadmap for understanding the crime policy process across all three legislative venues. While I have emphasized the challenges that *broad* citizen groups face in accessing legislative venues outside the local level, the data reveal that citizen groups of *any* kind have only limited representation in crime politics outside urban politics. Though there are a few highly mobilized groups—the ACLU, the NRA, Handgun Control, Inc., MADD, PCAR—that clearly represent large chunks of the public, the fact that a mere handful of citizen groups are visible across the state and national crime policy landscapes is somewhat surprising and is evidence of how effectively bureaucratic agencies have locked in their centrality to the policy process on this important issue. As I have argued, these agencies surely have a role to play in deciding how to respond to crime and violence. But their professional priorities should not be confused with the kind of broad-range problem solving on crime that legislatures can engage in if they are pressured to do so. And in other policy areas, the limited capacity of citizen groups to sustain a presence across legislative venues may dilute the capacity of our political institutions to develop and nurture public interest policy goals.

While federalism may have solved a crucial problem at the founding of the republic, today it seems to overrepresent narrow citizen interests and make it hard for groups representing broad, diffuse citizen concerns to stake out a place at the policy table in the venues that matter most. Since this state of affairs is unlikely to change, it seems worthwhile to encourage broad citizen groups with deep local ties to forge alliances with other local groups, creating the kind of translocal associations that can exert a collective will in state and national policy process more readily than individual groups alone. One of the founders of Ex-Offenders Incorporated expressed his desire to broaden his constituency base to neutralize groups like the NRA by persuading suburban and rural voters that the policy priorities of his group are a public good:

> [The problem with gun control groups is] they're mostly reactive. They don't have original ideas. Our problem is—we got the ideas and strategies but just don't have the money to implement the strategy. But we do want to take this show on the road. We want to go toe to toe with NRA and go into the heartland of their territory.[38]

A Philadelphia city council member most clearly articulated the need for a political strategy that could overcome the obstacles imposed by state and nationally organized groups:

> What's true is that we have a hard-boiled campaign ahead of us and this is an issue in which sides have pretty much been picked, and we're not going to win by convincing NRA members that they ought to think of Philadelphia kids first or Pittsburgh or Erie kids first. I think we've got to do it by political muscle. That's what I see in the city's taking the leadership, finding a legal issue by which we can challenge the decision made back in 1996 that this had to be decided by state law rather than a local law. I think the city has to take a leadership. We hope Mayor Street will play a strong role in it and authorize the Law Department to move ahead. And then

I think you have the issue that will enable you to mobilize the people in Philadelphia. *I think we've got to win this by brute political force.*[39]

Given the policy processes described in chapters 2, 3, and 4, clearly Ex-Offenders would benefit greatly by connecting with other, similar groups in localities throughout Pennsylvania and the rest of the nation. There are models for such groups; ACORN and the Industrial Areas Foundation, for example, have a strong national core that is supported by active local member organizations.

Of course, there is more at work here than just federalism. The United States has a single-member-district, winner-take-all electoral system that makes multiple parties that might better represent the interests of the poor unlikely to be sustained for any length of time. We elect our president through a system that overrepresents small states where rural citizens are more common than urban dwellers (even though, on the whole, more people live in cities). And the nation has a limited social welfare tradition, making movements for broad public goals like health care, education, transportation, employment security, and public safety difficult to sustain. Federalism clearly isn't the only culprit keeping broad citizen groups from having a more sustained presence in public policy. But it is a contributing factor, and failure to take account of the obstacles and opportunities presented by the level of government in which an issue is salient risks misrepresenting the actual possibilities for democratic participation, political representation, and accountability. It is my hope that future research will take up these questions in more detail and offer further nuance and understanding of the relationship between federalism, group representation, political accountability, and democratic institutions, as well as more detailed analysis of specific crime policies and the group interests represented therein.

Appendix 1

CONGRESSIONAL HEARINGS DATA

S tudying legislative hearings is an important and systematic way of observing group participation in the policy process. In his extensive analysis of citizen interests in Congress, Jeffrey Berry notes that

> there is reason to believe that hearings capture much of the over-all roster of lobbying participants. Testifying at hearings helps to legitimize a group's participation in the policymaking steps that follow.... Scholzman and Tierney's survey of Washington lobbyists showed that 99 percent of their respondents indicated that their organization testified before the Congress.[1]

The data used in this chapter draw on a dataset that was originally collected by Frank R. Baumgartner and Bryan D. Jones, with the support of National Science Foundation grant number SBR 9320922, and distributed through the Center for American Politics and Public Policy at the University of Washington and the Department of Political Science at Pennsylvania State University. Neither the National Science Foundation nor the original collectors of the data bear any responsibility for the analysis reported here.

I initially extracted all hearings in the category Law, Crime, and Family. For a full description of each subcategory of the hearings, see www.policyagendas. org. The total number of hearings in this category from 1947 to 2002 is 3,586. However, I excluded several types of hearings from the dataset (subtopic codes are listed hereafter): all hearings about children and family (subtopics 1207 and 1208) were excluded unless they had a specific relationship to crime and criminal justice. Thus, hearings about custody disputes and family dysfunction were excluded, whereas hearings about child sexual abuse, parental kidnappings, or child witness testimony at trials were included. I also excluded hearings on child abuse unless they were explicitly about the criminal justice system or criminal code. These hearings are numerous and include topics well beyond the criminal justice system. My intention was to ensure that the dataset did not overstate the attention to child victims, so I focused on hearings that were specifically addressing crime, violence, or criminal justice institutions. Hearings related to the civil justice system, tort reform, tax and bankruptcy proceedings, and firefighters (unless the hearing related to arson or other criminal activity) were also excluded. This left 2,903 hearings between 1947 and 2002. I divided the hearings into two categories: substantive crime hearings (organized crime, drugs, juvenile crime and delinquency, riots and crime prevention, criminal code) and procedural crime hearings (executive branch, courts, police, prisons, general, other), making up the first dataset. For the second dataset, I took a random sample of hearings, sorting the file by type (procedural and substantive) and by date. Because substantive hearings outnumbered procedural ones, I took every fifth substantive hearing and every fourth procedural hearing. This process resulted in 574 hearings. Table A1.1 lists the percentage of each topic in the total hearings and in the sample illustrating their comparability.

Each hearing was then identified through CIS identification numbers provided in the Policy Agendas Project, and witnesses at each hearing were coded and recorded according to the coding scheme outlined in chapter 1 (n = 5,764). My final dataset for the congressional level consists of all legislative hearings on drugs, crime prevention and riots, juveniles, crimes against women and children, police/weapons, and the criminal code between 1991 and 1998 (n = 301 hearings, 2,385 witnesses).

New York Times Data

The data on *New York Times* stories also comes from the Agendas Project. The sample is a random selection of entries in the *New York Times* index from

TABLE A1.1. Percentage of Each Topic in Total Hearings and Sample and Their Comparability

	Total hearings		Sample hearings	
Hearing Topic	Number	Percentage of total	Number	Percentage of total
Drugs	619	21.3%	128	22.3%
Courts	573	19.7%	110	19.2%
Executive	450	15.5%	73	12.7%
White Collar	271	9.3%	46	8.0%
Juveniles	246	8.5%	48	8.4%
Police/weapons	178	6.1%	41	7.1%
Code	158	5.4%	36	6.3%
Riots/CP	152	5.2%	27	4.7%
Prisons	114	3.9%	27	4.7%
Women/children	95	3.3%	25	4.4%
Other	47	1.6%	13	2.3%
Total	2903		574	

1947 to 2000. The sample is derived from coding the first entry on every odd-numbered page of the index. Between 1947 and 2000, 2,389 entries were coded, of which 2,083 were stories about crime and justice (as opposed to family). Stories about divorce, child custody, the civil justice system, and other family-related matters were eliminated from the dataset, as were stories about the investigation of President Clinton and his relationship with Monica Lewinsky.

Appendix 2

PENNSYLVANIA LEGISLATIVE
HEARINGS AND INTERVIEW
DATA

Hearings

I sought Pennsylvania House and Senate Judiciary Committee hearings on crime and justice from several sources and identified 479 hearings in both chambers between 1965 and 2004. A list of all Senate judiciary hearings from 1985 to 2004 was provided by the office of the Chair of the Judiciary Committee. Senate hearings prior to 1985 were archived, and a comprehensive list from 1965–84 was provided by the Senate library. For House judiciary committee hearings, I received lists of hearings of the period 1979 through 2004 from administrative assistants in the House Judiciary Committee office and the chief clerk's office. For hearings prior to 1979, I received a list from the State Archives identifying all House Judiciary Committee hearings. I also searched the Pennsylvania State Archives website for any additional hearings. I am particularly grateful to Judy Sedesse, Peggy Nissly, and Jackie Jumper in the Pennsylvania General Assembly and Pennsylvania Archives for their enormous assistance in helping me locate these hearings. I would never have been able to compile this dataset without their kind, generous, and able assistance. There are obvious limitations to these data. By acknowledgment of the archivists in the Senate Archives and the State Archives, it is unlikely that the lists of hearings prior to the 1980s are complete. However, both archivists indicated that major hearings are most likely to have been recorded.

Physically retrieving the hearing transcripts was difficult, time-consuming, and expensive. As a result, the hearings from which witness lists were analyzed do not make up a random sample but rather a careful selection of hearings that includes a wide range of topics (n = 309). Since the earlier years had fewer hearings, I obtained a range of hearings covering a diverse set of topics that included both bill and nonbill hearings. In particular, I included as many hearings on substantive crime topics as I could from both periods, in order to avoid undersampling hearings that were most likely to include the citizen groups of particular interest in this project.

TABLE A2.1. Number of Hearings by Time Period, Chamber, Bill, Topic, and Percentage of Witness Dataset

Time period	Total hearings	Included in dataset
1965–1980	96	61 (63.5%)
1981–2004	351	248 (70.7%)
House	289	233 (80.6%)
Senate	158	76 (48.1%)
Bill	233	176 (75.5%)
Nonbill	209	133 (63.6%)
Substantive issues	141	116 (80.5%)
Procedural issues	294	193 (65.6%)

Table A2.1 shows the number of hearings identified by time period, chamber, bill, and topic and what percentage were included in the witness dataset.

Types of crime were categorized as follows:

"Crimes against women/children": domestic violence, sexual assault, family violence, stalking, pornography, sexual predators, child witness testimony, and so on

"Urban violence": drugs, juveniles, gangs, guns, and policing. "Criminal procedure and prison issues": wiretapping, search and seizure, insanity defense, prison overcrowding and reform

"Court and prison administrative issues": judicial procedure, selection of judges, compensation, appellate court reform, prerelease programs, furlough programs, crime commission reports, community corrections, probation and parole

Interviews

For the interviews, I selected members of the House and Senate Judiciary committee. The oversampling of Democrats was to ensure that the areas from which citizen groups, particularly broad citizen groups, might emerge were sufficiently represented. The interviews were recorded and transcribed, and analysis of the hearings consisted of review of the written transcripts as well as searches of the texts for various group names and organizations. I also counted all groups mentioned in the interviews and have included data on the total number of groups as well as the frequency with which different types appear. Given the sensitive nature of crime victimization and the disinclination of legislators to criticize popular groups mobilized on crime issues, I promised my respondents confidentiality in the interview process. As a result, I identify the respondents by interview numbers. Table A2.2 shows the respondent interviews by party, chamber, and date of interview.

Mean differences in Herfindahl scores for each time period, chapter 4, are as shown in table A2.3.

TABLE A2.2. Respondent Interviews by Party, Chamber, and Date

Party	Chamber	Number	Date	
D	House	401	30 Sep	2003
R	Senate	402	30 Sep	2003
R	Senate	403	30 Sep	2003
R	House	404	30 Sep	2003
D	Senate	405	28 Oct	2003
D	Senate	406	28 Oct	2003
R	House	407	28 Oct	2003
D	Senate	408	28 Oct	2003
D	House	409	13 Nov	2003
R	House	410	26 Feb	2004
D	Senate	411	17 Feb	2004
D	House	412	30 Mar	2004

TABLE A2.3. Mean Differences in Herfindahl Scores for Concentration of Group Representation, by Time Period

	All groups*	Major groups
1965–1985	33.04752	49.2035
1986–2004	14.14917	34.80501

*Differences significant at $p < .05$ (two-tailed).

Appendix 3

PHILADELPHIA AND
PITTSBURGH LEGISLATIVE
HEARINGS AND INTERVIEW
DATA

Hearings

Transcripts of legislative hearings at the local level are not easy to obtain. In Philadelphia, I am grateful for the assistance of Michael Decker, who kindly sent me the bulk of transcripts I have from Philadelphia. Similarly, in Pittsburgh, Latisha Taylor helped me understand the complex system of labeling and filing of Pittsburgh city council hearings. In Pittsburgh, it was particularly difficult to isolate hearings about crime and justice. This is because most council hearings that are open to public testimony are general hearings in which a wide range of issues might be addressed. Thus, I waded through dozens of transcripts from the late 1990s to locate only a handful of hearings that were relevant for my project. As a result, my Pittsburgh hearing data is limited to only five hearings, a small fraction compared to the 40 I was able to identify in Philadelphia between 1997 and 2004.

However, the legislative hearings data in both cities is buttressed by extensive interviews. The tables in this appendix provide information on the number of interviews in each city, as well as information on respondents, including political party and race of respondent, and date of interview.

TABLE A3.1. Number of Interviews by City

	Pittsburgh	Philadelphia
District	9	7
At-large	0	2
White	7	2
African American	2	7

Interviews

Interviews were conducted in the same manner as on the state level, as described in appendix 2. Because Philadelphia and Pittsburgh are heavily Democratic cities, there are more Democratic council members in the sample. Respondents were interviewed over the course of approximately four months in 2003. The dates and locations of interviews and respondents' party affiliations are listed in table A3.2.

In addition to interviews and hearings, I acquired and read dozens of *legislative hearings* on crime and justice topics at all three levels of government in order to draw some inferences about the interaction of groups and legislative venues and the quality of testimony different groups provide. I focused primarily on hearings that were about substantive crime issues (e.g., drugs, violence, sex crimes) rather than procedural concerns (court reform, oversight of parole boards) since those hearings were more likely to include the kinds of groups who might bring policy ideas to that table that represent a challenge to the status quo and were also most likely to include the broad community groups in which I was particularly interested.

Lobby registration rolls are available for most state legislatures. While these data present obvious limitations, given my interests, they nonetheless provide additional observation points and can serve to illuminate the distinctions between formally organized groups and less formal ones. I also obtained informal lists of groups who maintain an interest in crime and public safety policies at state and local levels.

TABLE A3.2. Dates and Locations of Interviews and Respondents' Party Affiliations

Party	Interview Number	Date		Location
D	101	10 Jun	2003	Pittsburgh
R	102	10 Jun	2003	Pittsburgh
D	103	10 Jun	2003	Pittsburgh
D	104	10 Jun	2003	Pittsburgh
R	105	18 Jun	2003	Pittsburgh
D	106	16 Jul	2003	Pittsburgh
R	107	11 Jun	2003	Pittsburgh
D	108	20 Aug	2003	Pittsburgh
D	109	11 Jun	2003	Pittsburgh
D	201	29 Jul	2003	Philadelphia
R	202	29 Jul	2003	Philadelphia
D	203	29 Jul	2003	Philadelphia
D	204	30 Jul	2003	Philadelphia
D	205	30 Jul	2003	Philadelphia
D	206	30 Jul	2003	Philadelphia
D	207	20 Aug	2003	Philadelphia
D	208	29 Sep	2003	Philadelphia
D	209	28 Sep	2003	Philadelphia

Because data on groups at the local level are more difficult to identify systematically, I searched for citizens' groups that I uncovered in the hearings and interviews nonprofit organizations databases, newspaper coverage, and Web-based reference. In particularly, I utilized the Internal Revenue Service's Cumulative List of Organizations and local newspaper coverage and searched for references to groups on the Internet. This provided the opportunity to identify groups that were more or less formally organized (i.e., groups that were formal nonprofit organizations and those that were not) as well as their level of activity.

NOTES

Chapter 1

1. Executive Summary, Crime in Pennsylvania, 2006 Annual Uniform Crime Report. Commonwealth of Pennsylvania and the Pennsylvania State Police. Available on-line at: http://ucr.psp.state.pa.us/UCR/ComMain.asp

2. Public Law 571 was passed on October 4, 1994, and amended sec. 6120.

3. 545 Pa. 279 (1996).

4. Minutes of hearing, Philadelphia City Council, November 15, 2000. Hearings provided by the Philadelphia City Council Chief Clerk's Office.

5. Beer 1977; Derthick 1999, 2001.

6. Baumgartner and Jones 1993; Chong 1991; Cigler and Loomis 1983; Feeley and Rubin 1998; McCann 1986; Piven and Cloward 1979; Scholzman and Tierney 1986; Walker 1991.

7. A growing number of scholars are investigating the same policy issue over multiple legislative venues. See Goss 2006; Pralle 2007; Manna 2006.

8. See Miller 2007. Legal scholars use the term *federalization* to apply to the growth of federal jurisdiction over the criminal law, particularly during the last 40 years. I use the term more broadly here because I think it offers a strategy for understanding crime policy in a more comprehensive manner and because it provides a valuable framework for research across a range of policy issues.

9. Lowi 1977; McConnell 1967; Riker 1964; Schattschneider 1960. See also Peterson 1981.

10. Schattschneider 1960, 2; see also Miller 2007.

11. Skogan 1981; Scheingold 1991; Miller 2001a; Lyons 1999.

12. See Skocpol 1999 for a related discussion.

13. See Olson 1965 on collection action.

14. Baumgartner and Jones 1993; see also Miller 2007.

15. Peterson 1981, 15.

16. Scheingold 1991, 23.

17. Olson 1965; Schattschneider 1960; Truman 1951.

18. Berry 1997.

19. Berry et. al. 2006; Fiorina 1999; Lowery and Gray 2004; Scholzman 1984; Reckhow 2006.

20. See Miller 2007 for a more detailed discussion of this perspective; see also Lowi 1977; McConnell 1967; Riker 1964; Schattschneider 1960.

21. Amenta 1998; Mettler 1998; Skocpol 2003; Szymanski 2003.

22. Baumgartner and Leech 1998; Berry 1997, 1999; Lowery and Gray 2004; Scholzman and Tierney 1986.

23. See Amenta 1998; Baumgartner and Jones 2002; Goss 2006; Holyoke 2003; Manna 2006; Pralle 2005 for discussions of variation across legislative venues and venue shopping. For analysis of group pressure in local venues, see Berry et al. 2006. See Nownes and Cooper 2003 for analysis of urban group activity. See also Sidney 2004, which explores the impact of national housing policies on local housing advocacy groups and policy outcomes, and Manna 2006, about state and national education policy.

24. Lowi 1964.

25. See Dubber 2002.

26. Amenta 1998; Skocpol 2003.

27. Campbell 2003, 2.

28. See Soss 2000.

29. Skocpol 2003.

30. Cover 1986.

31. There is a fair amount of social science scholarship on local criminal justice politics from the 1980s, much of it from political scientists, including Jacob 1980, 1984; Feeley and Sarat 1980; Cronin, Cronin, and Milakovich 1981; Heinz, Skogan, and Maxfield 1981; Heinz, Jacob, and Lineberry 1983; Scheingold 1984, 1991; Rosenbaum 1986; Meier 1992. See also Fairchild 1981 for a discussion of interest groups in state crime politics. More recent scholarship is less common but does move beyond local settings. For more recent work, see Lin 2000; Gottschalk 2002; Morone 2003; Lyons 1999; Miller 2001b, 2004; Mendes 2004; Stolz 2002; Yates 1997. See also Stolz 2002 for a discussion of interest groups in the national crime policy process.

32. Bauer and Owens 2004; Stephan 2004.

33. Bauer and Owens 2004.

34. Bureau of Justice Statistics, 2005. See also Mauer and Chesney-Lind 2002.

35. *Homicide Trends in the U.S., 2004.* U.S. Department of Justice, Bureau of Justice Statistics, www.ojp.usdoj.gov/bjs/abstract/htus02.htm; Pastore and Maguire (2002), table 3.20, "Estimated Percent Distribution of Violent Victimization incidents," and table 3.5., "Estimated Number and Rate (per 1,000 persons over 12 years of age) of Personal Victimization by Type of Crime and Sex of Victim."

36. There are important exceptions: see Barkow 2005; Zimring, Hawkins, and Kamin 2001.

37. *Homicide Trends in the U.S., 2004*. U.S. Department of Justice, Bureau of Justice Statistics. www.ojp.usdoj.gov/bjs/abstract/htus02.htm.

38. Pastore and Maguire (2000), table 3.11, "Estimated Number and Rate (Per 1000 Persons in Each Group) of Violent Victimization by Type of Crime, Hispanic Origin and Race."

39. Pastore and Maguire (2002), table 3.5, "Estimated Number and Rate of Personal Victimization."

40. Pastore and Maguire (2002), table 3.16, "Estimated Rate of Personal Victimization (Per 1000 Persons Age 12 and Older) by Type of Crime, Size of Population and Locality of Residence," and table 3.15, "Estimated Rage of Personal Victimization (Per 1000 Persons Age 12 and Older) by Type of Crime and Annual Household Income of Victim."

41. Walker, Spohn, and DeLone 2004.

42. Thacher, 2004.

43. Mauer and Chesney-Lind 2002; Mauer 2006; Gottschalk 2006; Murakawa 2005; Western 2004, 2006; Western et al. 2001.

44. Walker, Spohn, and DeLeone 2004; Weitzer and Tuch 2005.

45. Mauer and Chesney-Lind 2002.

46. Strazzella 1998; Baker 1999; Beale 1995; Brickey 1995; Clymer 1997; Curtis 1996; Heller 1997; see also Cronin 1981; Miller and Eisenstein 2005; Ligurio 1995; Windlesham 1998.

47. Caplow and Simon 1999; Feeley and Simon 1994; Garland 1996; 2001; Simon 1993, 2006.

48. See Miller 2001a for a related discussion of the pitfalls of macro-theorizing about crime policy.

49. On the other end of the spectrum, ground-level crime control research has exposed the inner workings of police organizations, the institutional arrangements of criminal courts, and the peculiarities of urban crime politics. These studies have provided valuable contributions to the understanding of the day-to-day operations of criminal justice institutions and the ways local political processes interact with those institutions. But their specific focus on criminal justice agencies offers limited opportunity for more general theorizing about the crime policy process in political institutions. On police, see Bell 2002; Goldstein 1990; Kelling et al. 1974, 1996; Kelling and Coles 1996; Manning 1977; Skogan and Hartnett 1997; Skolnick 1966; Skolnick and Fyfe 1993; Walker 1999, 2001; Wilson 1968, 1975. On criminal courts, see Blumberg 1967; Casper 1972; Eisenstein and Jacob 1977; Feeley 1979; Heumann 1977; Jacoby 1979. On urban crime politics, see Heinz, Jacob, and Lineberry 1983; Jacob 1980, 1984; Lyons 1999; Miller 2001b; Scheingold 1991; Skogan and Maxfield 1981; Wilson 1968.

50. Barker 2006; Gottschalk 2006; Murakawa 2005.

51. See Baumgartner and Jones 1993 and Rochefort and Cobb 1994 for excellent discussions of the central role of problem definitions and agenda-setting in policy outcomes.

52. Campbell 2003.

53. Gottschalk 2002; see also Caplow and Simon 1999.

54. There are a few exceptions: Fairchild 1983; Gottschalk 2002, 2005; Melone and Slagter 1983; Miller 2004; Stolz 2002.

55. See also Miller 2004.

56. See Simon 2006; Garland 2001. See Stuntz 2001 for an excellent discussion of the convergence of legislators' and prosecutors' interests. See also Miller 2004 for an empirical assessment of criminal justice agencies in congressional crime politics.

57. Baumgartner and Leech 1998; Gray and Lowry 1996.

58. Lowery and Gray 2004.

59. I use the broad definition of *interest group* commonly used by interest groups scholars: "An interest group is any association of individuals or organizations, whether formally organized or not, that attempts to influence public policy" (Hrebrenar 1993, 9).

60. Berry et al. 2006.

61. Manna 2006; Pralle 2006.

62. See Goss 2006. In 2004, 31 states had laws barring cities from enacting new laws that regulate guns in any way. See 2004 State Report Cards, www.bradycampaign.org.

63. While research suggests that conflict between law enforcement and prosecutors across levels of government is common, these tensions typically arise over how cases are processed. When resources are at stake, these actors may present fairly consistent priorities.

64. Miller and Eisenstein 2005. Chapter 2 takes up the federalization of criminal justice in detail.

65. See Gottschalk 2006, Morone 2003, Murakawa 2005, and Simon 2006 for important exceptions.

66. Beckett 1997; Scheingold, Olson, and Pershing 1994; Yates 1997; Zimring et al. 2001.

67. Pierson 2004; Steinmo, Thelen, and Longstreth 1992.

68. Beckett 1997; Murakawa 2005.

69. Jacobson 1998; Morone 2003; Smith 1997.

70. Gilens 1999; Peffley and Sniderman 1997.

71. Entman and Rojecki 2000; Gilliam and Iyengar 2000; Greenberg and West 2001; Jacobs and Carmichael 2002; Williams and Holcomb 2001; Yates 1997.

72. Wacquant 2005.

73. King 1995; King and Smith 2005; Lieberman 1998.

74. Frymer 2005, 374.

75. Massey and Denton 1993.

76. See Miller 2007.

77. See Walker, Spohn, and DeLeone 2004 for a comprehensive review of recent research. See also Demuth and Steffensmeier 2004; Steffensmeier, Ulmer, and Kramer 1998.

78. Frymer 2005, 385.

79. There are virtually no systematic data on local interest groups in any policy area, much less crime control. Given the proximity of local elected officials to their constituents, group participation in local politics can take many forms that are difficult to measure. Letters, faxes, appearances at council hearings, and formal lobbying campaigns occur, but so do routine phone calls, e-mails, impromptu office visits, and ad hoc protests. The state and national level data are also a problem but for different reasons. While there is a great deal of interest group research at the national level and growing attention to states, the most common source of information is lobby disclosure reports, which are frequently used to assess interest group participation. These data, however, overlook less formally organized groups—precisely the type of groups I seek to include.

80. Here I draw on King, Keohane, and Verba (1994, 48) who suggest that "our data need not be symmetric . . . just so long as each is an observable consequence of our theory. In this process, we go beyond the particular to the general, since the characterization of particular units on the basis of common characteristics is a generalizing process." These data are not always uniform across the levels of government, but a framework that assesses the same types of groups across these different data sources can draw comparisons among them.

81. A rival approach—what I might term the *jurisdictional hypothesis*—is worth noting here. This suggests that to the extent that interest group participation varies across levels of government, this merely reflects strategic choices on the part of groups to choose an appropriate venue for their concerns, rather than a systematic mobilization of bias in federalism. For example, local city councils can address policing because the local police department is often under the political control of mayors and this generates broad citizen group attention. In contrast, state legislatures can address the criminal code, and this attracts the interest of prosecutorial associations. In that case, the mobilization of groups in or out of policy environments has to do with levels of government only insofar as each level of government is confined to particular jurisdictional terrain. I offer several points in response. First, the distinction between national, state, and local jurisdiction on crime is largely a matter of 200 years of constitutional jurisprudence, statutory interpretation, and group pressure, rather than clearly and objectively delineated space, and continues to evolve today. The Supreme Court has given Congress a wide berth to pursue many of the same crime issues as state governments. The local level certainly has less legislative authority when it comes to the criminal code, but this again has been more a matter of negotiation between cities and state governments than clearly delineated law, and cities regularly engage in policy making on crime (concealed weapons laws, loitering and curfew regulations, for example). Furthermore, cities that exercise home rule have considerably more leeway in policy making. In addition, all three levels of government operate law enforcement agencies and correctional facilities and employ prosecutors. In fact, as the subsequent empirical chapters show, the legislative agendas of

all three levels of government encompass a full range of policy discussions that policy scholars analyze and that have the potential to draw a wide range of interests, including the state of the problem (general discussions about the scope or severity of a problem), specific bills, and legislative oversight of agencies. Thus, while each level of government may emphasize different terrain, all three regularly pursue each aspect of the policy process. If at least some groups from each type target legislators for a full range of needs at a variety of levels of government, then the jurisdictional hypothesis has less support.

82. Thomas and Hrebenar 2004, 102.

83. Berry. 1999.

84. Fiorina 1999.

85. Salisbury 1984; Gray and Lowry 1996.

86. See Miller 2004.

87. There is the potential for overlap between social service agencies and some citizen groups. In general, if an organization was primarily a service organization or if the organization represented social service providers themselves, it has been coded as social service, not citizen.

88. The bulk of the groups that fall into this category in this project are groups that represent the interests of urban poor, urban minority, or working-class populations. This is no doubt a function of the disproportionate impact of crime and criminal justice institutions on these populations. Of course, other policy domains would observe different broad citizen groups, and the extent to which their representation follows similar patterns is a subject for future research.

89. Gottschalk 2006 does this as well, though her focus is largely on social movements.

Chapter 2

1. Beale 1995; Beckett 1997; Brickey 1995; Garland 2001; Marion 1994; Mauer and Chesney-Lind 2002; Strazzella 1998. For important exceptions see Gottschalk 2006; Murakawa 2005.

2. Baumgartner and Jones 1993; Gottschalk 2006.

3. See Steinmo, Thelen and Longstreth 1992; Pierson 2004.

4. Murakawa 2005, 46.

5. Gottschalk offers a similar approach in her study of the rise of mass incarceration and finds that the contemporary fact of high incarceration has its roots in the historic underdevelopment of the U.S. welfare state, the rise of the public prosecutor, the various social movements of the 1960s and 1970s, and the periodic moral crusades that swept through national institutions (Gottschalk 2006). My approach builds on her findings but focuses more narrowly on the congressional crime agenda.

6. Gottschalk 2002, 5–6.

7. Friedman 1993; Henderson 1985; Schwartz 1948; Zimring and Hawkins 1997. This discussion is not intended as a comprehensive overview

of national involvement in crime and justice but, rather, a more focused discussion trained on the interests and institutions whose attention to violence, crime, and punishment runs deep through U.S. history. For additional scholarship on this topic, see Friedman 1993; Gottschalk 2006; Henderson 1985; Murakawa 2005.

8. Schwartz 1948; Zimring 1996.

9. 1 Stat. 112 (1790).

10. 2 Stat. 593 (1810).

11. "If any offense shall be committed in any of the places aforesaid, the punishment of which offense is not specially provided for by any law of the United States, such offense shall, upon a conviction in any court of the United States having cognisance thereof, be liable to, and receive the same punishment as the laws of the state in which such fort, dock-yard, navy-yard, arsenal, armory, or magazine, or other place, ceded as aforesaid, is situated, provide for the like offence when committed within the body of any county of such state"; 4 Stat. 115. See 4 Stat. 121 for statute outlawing rape on the high seas.

12. Kurland 1996, citing the Federal Judicial Center, notes: "The history of federal jurisdiction reveals no bright lines that have traditionally divided the business of the federal courts from that of the states. The so-called traditional role of the federal courts, on closer examination, is much less distinct from that of the state courts than might be supposed. Much conduct that can be prosecuted under federal criminal statutes has long been equally subject to prosecution under state law, although perhaps under different labels" (p. 63).

13. Annals of Congress, 17th Cong., 2d Sess. (1822–1823) 929.19. *Williams v. U.S.* 327 U.S. 711.

14. "The only question which this case presents is, whether the Circuit Courts of the United States can exercise a common law jurisdiction in criminal cases. We state it thus broadly because a decision on a case of libel will apply to every case in which jurisdiction is not vested in those Courts by statute. Although this question is brought up now for the first time to be decided by this Court, we consider it as having been long since settled in public opinion. In no other case for many years has this jurisdiction been asserted; and the general acquiescence of legal men shows the prevalence of opinion in favor of the negative of the proposition." 11 U.S. 32 (1812). *U.S. v. Hudson and Goodwin.*

15. See Murakawa 2005 for an excellent overview of federal criminal legislation.

16. Henderson 1985, 40–41.

17. Henderson 1985, 13.

18. See *Civil Rights Cases,* 109 U.S. 3 (1883).

19. Author's collection of data on congressional hearings from the Civil War to 1920. *U.S. Congressional Committee Hearings Index,* pt. 1, 1825–1917, secs. 1–5. Washington, D.C.: Congressional Information Service.

20. See Murakawa 2006.

21. Hearings on rape were confined to crimes on land under federal or military jurisdiction, such as Indian reservations or the Philippine Islands. Prostitution hearings centered primarily on the District of Columbia, though a few hearings also dealt with immigration locales, such as Ellis Island.

22. See Serial Set at note 19, vol. no. 1727, sess. vol. no. 6, 44th Congress, 2nd sess., S.Misc.Doc. 48 pt. 1, p.11; Serial Set vol. no. 1491, sess. vol. no. 2, 42nd Congress, 2nd sess., S.Rpt. 41 pt. 8, p. 1016.

23. Hearing before a subcommittee of the Committee of Privileges and Elections, U.S. Senate, 68th Congress, 2nd sess., S. Res. 97, Authorizing the investigation of alleged unlawful practices in the election of a senator from Texas, December 8, 9, 10, 1924, pt. 4.

24. Foner 1988. See Brandwein for an excellent, nuanced discussion of the role of courts and black civil rights in the nineteenth century.

25. *Slaughter-House Cases,* 86 U.S. 36 (1883), *U.S. v. Cruickshank,* 92 U.S. 542 (1875), *U.S. v. Harris,* 106 U.S. 629 (1882), *Civil Rights Cases* 109 U.S. 3 (1883).

26. *Civil Rights Cases,* 109 U.S. 3 (1883).

27. *U.S. v. Cruikshank.* 92 U.S. 542 (1875).

28. *Champion v. Ames,* 188 U.S. 321.

29. Morone 2003.

30. Morone 2003, 239.

31. The White Slave Traffic Act, 18 U.S.C. sec. 2421, 1910. It was upheld by the Supreme Court as a legitimate exercise of Congress's interstate commerce power in *Hoke v. United States,* 227 U.S. 308, 322 (1913).

32. Wells 1892; Ferrell 1986.

33. Civil Rights Act of 1866, 14 Stat. 27–30; Ku Klux Klan Act 31 U.S.C. 1983; Civil Rights Act of 1875, 18 Stat. 335.

34. See Kennedy 1997; Ferrell 1986; Wells 1892.

35. 203 U.S. 1 (1906). See also the *Slaughter-House Cases,* 86 U.S. 36 (1873).

36. Quoted in Ferrell 1986, 119.

37. Nonetheless, there was, naturally, opposition to the Mann Act as well, though it never gained enough traction to reject the bill (see Morone 2003).

38. Ferrell 1986, 150.

39. See *United States v. E.C. Knight Company,* 156 U.S. 1 (1895), *Hammer v. Dagenhart,* 247 U.S. 38 (1918).

40. *U.S. v. Cruickshank* (1876).

41. "To Protect Citizens against Lynching." Hearing before the Committee on the Judiciary, House of Representatives, 64th Congress, H. R. 11279 (Dyer Bill), ser. 66, June 6, 1918, 12–13.

42. Quoted in Interstate Immorality 1947,718–753. H.R. Rep. No. 47, 61st Congress, 2nd sess. (1909), 9–10.

43. Paris agreement of May 1904, signed by Pres. Theodore Roosevelt on June 15, 1908 35 Stat. 1979 (1908). Interstate Immorality 1947, 718–753.

44. Mark Graber argues persuasively that the Constitution was designed to permit the elimination of slavery only when the proslavery contingent agreed to it (Graber 2006).

45. Morone 2003; Ferrell 1986.

46. See Ferrell 1986 and Murakawa 2005.

47. Constitutionality of Anti-lynching Law, Hearing before the Committee on the Judiciary, 67th Congress, ser. 10, pt. 1, June 18, 1921.

48. Congress did hear from black victims on occasion. During Reconstruction, Congress held hearings on Klan violence and efforts to suppress the black vote, and blacks sometimes testified at these hearings, as did current and former Klan members. See Henderson 1985.

49. To Protect Citizens against Lynching, Hearing before the Committee on the Judiciary, House of Representatives, 64th Congress, H. R. 11279, June 6, 1918.

50. Constitutionality of Anti-lynching Law, Hearing before the Committee on the Judiciary, 67th Congress, ser. 10, pt. 1, June 18, 1921; Constitutionality of Anti-lynching Law, Hearing before the Committee on the Judiciary, 67th Congress, ser. 10, pt. 2, July 20, 1921.

51. Ferrell 1986.

52. Murakawa 2005.

53. 16 Stat. 162.

54. Hearings before the Subcommittee of the House Committee on Appropriations...for Deficiency Appropriations for 1908 and Prior Years on Urgent Deficiency Bill, January 17, 1908, 202–203. See also Attorney General Charles Bonaparte to President Roosevelt, January 14, 1909, Dept. of Justice File, 44-3-11-Sub 3, 12/5/08–4/6/09, www.fbi.gov/libref/historic/history/historic_doc/chron.htm.

55. *U.S. v. Beach* 1945, 324 U.S. 193, upholding a conviction under the Act that involved prostitution wholly within the District of Columbia.

56. *Caminetti v. U.S.*, 242 U.S. 470 (1917).

57. Federal Kidnapping Act, 18 USC sec. 1201(a)(1), 1932. See Scott 2003 for a discussion of the role of the Lindbergh kidnapping case in the expansion of federal involvement in crime control.

58. 38 Stat. 785.

59. Morone 2003.

60. Wilson 1978.

61. Wilson 1978.

62. Key 1938.

63. National Firearms Act 1934, 48 Stat. 1236, 26 U.S.C. 5801, Federal Bank Robbery Act, 1950, 18 U.S.C. 2113; Hobbs Act, 1946, 18 U.S.C. 1951. See also Friedman 1993, 267.

64. *Brooks v. U.S.*, 267 U.S. 432 (1925), and *Gooch v. U.S.*, 297 U.S. 124 (1936). For a nice summary of the court's history of reviewing congressional authority to regulate criminal activity under the commerce clause, see *Heart of Atlanta Motel, Inc. v. United States*, 379 U.S. 241 (1964).

65. Key 1938. More recently, the Department of Homeland Security was created by the Homeland Security Act of 2002 after the attacks of September 11, 2001. The Act transferred the Bureau of Alcohol, Tobacco, Firearms (and now Explosives) as well as the Immigration and Naturalization Service (renamed U.S. Citizenship and Immigration Service) and the Secret Service,

among others, to the new department. Homeland Security Act of 2002, Pub. L. No. 107-296, 116 Stat. 2135.

66. See Feeley and Rubin 1998 for an excellent discussion of federalism and U.S. politics.

67. Friedman 1993, 268.

68. In April 1999, two students at Columbine High School in Columbine, Colorado, shot and killed 12 students and a teacher and injured another 24 before committing suicide in the school.

69. Campbell 2003.

70. Miller 2007.

71. Morone 2003, 283.

72. Miller and Eisenstein 2005.

73. Jacob 1984, 81.

74. A massive spike in spending on federal law enforcement in the late 1960s, which tripled between 1968 and 1973, precipitated a dramatic decline in spending on this item over the next ten years, but budget allocations never fell to their levels prior to the initial spending spike. See Policy Agenda Project, www.policyagendas.org.

75. Frymer 2005; Lieberman 1998.

76. Graber 2006; Smith 1997; King and Smith 2005.

77. O'Reilly 1982; Morone 2003.

78. Nourse and Schacter 2002.

79. Fairchild 1981; Miller 2004; O'Reilly 1982; Stolz 2002.

80. Morone 2003; see also Gottschalk 2006.

81. The evolution of the federal criminal law as an extension of Congress's commerce powers is itself an interesting tale, one that has been extensively pursued by legal scholars. See Baker 1999; Beale 1995; Brickey 1995; Maroney 2000; Scott 2003. In *Perez v. United States*, 402 U.S. 146 (1971), the Supreme Court determined that Congress can regulate, under its interstate commerce powers, entire classes of activities that, taken as a whole, affect interstate commerce.

Chapter 3

1. See appendix 1 for details on the data collection, sampling, and coding.

2. Feeley and Simon 1994; Garland 2001; Simon 1993.

3. Baumgartner and Jones 1993, 2002.

4. See Baumgartner and Jones (1993) for an excellent overview of these changes. See also Berry 1997; Peterson 1990; Salisbury 1984; Walker 1991.

5. Figures are by congressional year to avoid the large fluctuations in hearings that result from election years.

6. The data are drawn from the Policy Agendas Project; see appendix 1.

7. I use homicide rate because it follows a similar trend to violent crime, extends farther back in time than measures of violent or property crime, and

is generally regarded as a good proxy for crime rates over the long term. The homicide rate and the percentage of congressional hearings devoted to crime become negatively correlated and nonsignificant around the mid-1980s.

8. See appendix 1 for details of the Policy Agendas Project dataset on *New York Times* stories.

9. Some scholars have noted the problematic nature of official crime data, and these are no doubt important critiques, particularly as they relate to shifting police reporting (Beckett 1997). Other scholars have argued that media and elite attention to crime has driven the congressional agenda as much or more than crime rates (see Beckett 1997; Murakawa 2005). These arguments are compelling, and clearly the relationship between underlying crime rates, media coverage, and framing and legislative attention needs more attention.

10. Flamm 2005; Phillips 2006.

11. Baumgartner and Jones 1993; Flamm 2005.

12. The total number of hearings in the Law, Crime and Family category of the Baumgartner and Jones dataset from 1947–2002 is 3,586. However, I excluded several types of hearings from the dataset. See appendix 1 for details.

13. 755 Stat. 5762, Public Law 87-274. See also Bernard 1992; Flamm 2005.

14. Some argue that the juvenile delinquency issue simply morphed into urban riots and policing as black teenage crime escalated in the 1960s (Flamm 2005).

15. 82 Stat. 197.

16. Beckett 1997; Murakawa 2005; Simon 2006.

17. See Flamm (2005) for a discussion of how and why the more intensive law-and-order politics declined around this time period.

18. See Musto 1987 for an overview of political attention to drug policy.

19. H381-10 (1987); H781-15 (1987); H381-67 (1987); 381-54 (1987); H381-14 (1988); S181-29 (1988); H381-74 (1988); H641-41 (1988); S181-33 (1988); S201-16 (1989); H561-11 (1989); S401-48 (1990).

20. Comprehensive Drug Abuse Prevention and Control Act (1970), Pub. L. No. 91-513, 84 Stat. 1236.

21. Jenness and Grattet 2001. One hearing in 1969–70 concerned the mailing of pornographic material to minors. See also S521-15 (1978), hearing on protecting children from sexual exploitation; H341-68 (1982), hearing on teenage prostitution and child pornography; H521-10 (1986), hearing on rape law reform; S541–27 (1986), hearing on domestic violence.

22. Violent Crime Control and Law Enforcement Act, 1994. P.L. 103-322.

23. Flamm (2005) argues that the changing social and political landscape, including economic worries of the white middle-class, liberals' embrace of law-and-order rhetoric, and steadying or declining crime rates reduced attention to the more overtly racialized dynamics of national law-and-order politics.

24. Baumgartner and Jones 1993.

25. This is true for most policy issues, not just crime.

26. While more than 4 out of 5 House hearings before 1968 were referral hearings, that percentage declined to a third. Bill hearings in the Senate also declined, from about half of the hearings to just over a third.

27. Sfo.t.62; S181-2.

28. Baumgartner and Jones 2000. A perfect monopoly—all hearings in a given congressional year taking place in one committee—would represent a score of 100. Dramatic declines in the index over a period of time, from 85 to 40 for example, represent growing interest in the issue. An index score for any given congressional year can range from 0 to 1, but following Baumgartner and Jones 2000, I multiply the scores by 100 for ease of presentation. Note that because the Herfindahl index is based on squared proportions, changes in the index are exponential. The lowest possible committee clarity score is difficult to calculate since, theoretically, every committee in Congress could hold hearings on crime and justice, and the number of committees varies over time. If we assume approximately 50 standing committees, if hearings were spread evenly among those 50 committees, the Herfindahl score would be 2. If select committees are included, this number would be further reduced.

29. Senate crime hearings are more likely to be held in the Judiciary Committee in both periods, but the percentage of hearings held in the Judiciary Committees fell dramatically in both chambers of Congress.

30. Baumgartner and Jones 1993; see also King 1997.

31. As hearings proliferate across committees, the committee clarity score decreases. Thus, as the homicide rate increases, more committees hold crime and justice hearings, reducing the clarity score.

32. The Boggs Act (1951), the Narcotics Control Act (1956), Gambling Devices Act (1961), and the Juvenile Delinquency Act (1961). See Murakawa 2005 for an excellent overview of major congressional legislation on crime since the early founding of the republic.

33. House Committee on International Relations, "Effectiveness of Turkish Opium Control, Part I," July 28, 1975, Y4.In8/16:Op3/2/pt.1; Senate Committee on Appropriations, "Oversight Hearing on Border Drug Interdiction, Special Hearing," February 24–25, 1993, Y4.AP6/2:S.HRG.103-83. Customs agents were coded as law enforcement, but Immigration and Naturalization agents, whose work is more multifaceted, were coded as government.

34. Hearing before the House Committee on Education and Labor, "Investigation of Riot at Shakespeare Co., Kalamazoo, Michigan," December 1948, CIS 80 H1125-7.

35. Senate Special Committee to Investigate Organized Crime in Interstate Commerce, "Investigation of Organized Crime in Interstate Commerce, Florida," May 1950, CIS 81 S955-0-A.

36. Appellate court jurisdiction, H115-6 (1955), H 216-19 (1958); juvenile delinquency hearings, S216-34 (1959), S216-6 (1954).

37. H115-6 (1971), H108-4 (1974), H115-6 (1972), H115-2 (1974).

38. S216-9 (1967).

39. S217-11 (1980), S216-17 (1978).

40. H115-3 (1972), H115-2 (1973).

41. H120-6 (1978).

42. S216-17 (1978), H108-28 (1971).

43. H341-32 (1974).

44. H521-8 (1974), H521-38 (1975), H341-21 (1971).

45. S216-0 (1985), H115-7 (1995), H115-0 (1997), H115-0 (1999), H115-3 (1983).

46. H115-3 (1983), H115-2 (1986).

47. Baumgartner and Jones 1993.

48. Berry 1997, 1999.

49. Senate hearing S521-25, 1984, pretrial detention of juveniles, and Senate hearing S521-42, 1975, school violence and vandalism.

50. Two-tailed test, $p < .05$.

51. S211-0.

52. Harrison Narcotics Act, 28 Stat. 785. See Musto 1987.

53. As with the larger dataset, criminal justice agencies dominate crime and justice hearings on substantive crime topics in the 1990s. They make up 38 percent of the witnesses (916/2,385) and appear at more than 4 out of 5 hearings (260/301). The representation of witnesses in these hearings parallels the range of witnesses from the post–World War II time period, except for fewer representatives of business and labor and a few more individuals. Individuals are much more heavily represented in these hearings than in the overall sample discussed in the previous section. This is probably because of the large number of executive branch and court hearings in that dataset that are excluded from this one.

54. Hearing before the subcommittee on National Security, International Relations and Criminal Justice of the Committee on Government Reform and Oversight, House of Representatives, 104th Congress, 2nd sess., September 23, 1996, 9; H401-52.

55. Wilson 1989.

56. It might be argued that the ACLU is, in fact, representing minority interests. They have been on the vanguard of racial profiling and anti–death penalty activism and have raised issues involving police-community relations. I will take up this concern more thoroughly in chapter 6. For my purposes here, they represent only 2 of 291 witnesses in the riots/crime prevention category.

57. Citizens for Law and Order testified on behalf of Clarence Thomas at his nomination hearing, describing him as a "voice of reason, fairness and balance in the area of criminal justice"; Testimony of John Collins, East Regional Director, Citizens for Law and Order, September 19, 1991. The Law Enforcement Alliance of America is a nonprofit organization whose aim is primarily to promote public education about law enforcement issues and to reduce violent crime while reserving the right to self-defense. The organization opposes most gun control legislation.

58. Feeley and Rubin 1998; Kennedy 1997; Lyons 1999.

59. Feeley and Rubin 1998, 368.

60. "Total justice employment per 10,000 population by activity, for all governments, 1980–1999." Department of Justice, Bureau of Justice Statistics, December 12, 2001.

61. Feeley and Simon 1994.

62. The Hate Crimes Statistics Act, P.L. 101–275.

63. Beckett 1997; Cronin et al. 1981; Flamm 2005; Murakawa 2005.

64. Murakawa 2005.

Chapter 4

1. Pennsylvania General Assembly Public Hearing on Proposed Anti-Drug Legislation, May 18, 1989. House of Representatives Office of the Chief Clerk.

2. See appendix 2 for detailed description of hearings and interviews.

3. Most of the hearings were public hearings. However, a few were termed "Information meetings," which are held on a wide range of topics and are more likely to target a broad topic area than a particular piece of legislation.

4. Witnesses are coded in the same manner discussed in chapter 1.

5. Thomas and Hrbrenar 2004.

6. Squire 1992.

7. Mooney 1995, 48–49.

8. Treadway 2005.

9. Treadyway 2005.

10. See Baumgartner and Jones 1993 for a similar discussion at the national level.

11. King 2000.

12. Treadway 2005.

13. Treadway 2005; King 2000; Mooney 1995; Squire 1992.

14. This section summarizes the findings of Patricia Crotty in her 1993 analysis of interest groups in Pennsylvania Politics.

15. Crotty 1993, 298–299.

16. Barkow 2005; Stuntz 2001; Heinz, Gettleman, and Seeskin 1969; Zimring, Hawkins, and Kamin 2001.

17. Heinz et al. 1969, 343.

18. Barkow 2005; Stuntz 2001.

19. Barkow 2005.

20. Stuntz 2001, 510.

21. Berk, Brackman, and Lesser 1977, 152: "While the interests of police and of prosecutors sometimes differ, our qualitative analysis reveals them as members of the same coalition."

22. Zimring et al. 2001.

23. Greene 2002.

24. Barkow 2005; Heinz et al. 1969.

25. Jacob 1984, 147.

26. Berk et al. 1977, 285.

27. See Gottschalk 2006, Simon 2006.

28. Jacob 1984; see also Gottschalk 2006; Simon 1993, 2006. See also Cohen 1985 for a discussion of the ways small changes to the criminal law can dramatically widen the number of citizens exposed to the criminal justice apparatus.

29. Mauer 2006; Jacob 1984.

30. *Gregg v. Georgia*, 428 U.S. 153 (1976). See Gottschalk 2006.

31. Zimring 2005.

32. Zimring 2005.

33. Torbet and Szymanski 1998.

34. Three Strikes You're Out, Title 42, 9714 (a)(2). Megan's Law, 42 Pa.C.S. sec. 9791.

35. Barker 2006.

36. Barker 2006.

37. Given the long history of states as subregional governments with distinct political, economic, and cultural features, every one of the 50 states has unique features that could be highlighted in this context (Gray 2004).

38. Crotty 1993, 281.

39. Crotty 1993.

40. Hamm and Moncrief 2004, 158.

41. Berry et al. 2006; Nownes and Cooper 2003. A final point here is that, as indicated in chapter 1, the purpose of this project is to compare interest groups across legislative venues, not to utilize a single case study to generalize about a single policy environment. Thus, the findings suggest that policy environments will vary across local, state, and national levels, not that each state or local environment will look precisely like the ones here.

42. Author's interview (403). Transcript maintained by author. See appendix 2 for details on respondents.

43. Berry 1999; Flamm 2005.

44. *Pastore and Maguire (2004*, table 6.29.

45. See appendix 2 for subtopics within each crime topic category.

46. See Jacob 1984; Cronin et al. 1981; Zimring 2005. Unlike the congressional data, at present there is no way to determine the denominator—the full range of hearings held in Pennsylvania during this time period—in order to assess whether this is a rise in hearings on crime or simply an increase in hearings in general. Extensive data on the policy process in Pennsylvania—including hearings and policy outcomes—is being compiled by Joseph P. McLaughlin, J. Wesley Leckrone, and Jason Bossie at Temple University.

47. Goss 2006; Gottschalk 2005; Jenness 1997.

48. See appendix 2 for sampling details.

49. See appendix 2 for details about the interview schedules.

50. Author's interview (402). Transcript maintained by author. See appendix 2 for details on respondents.

51. Author's interview (401). Transcript maintained by author. See appendix 2 for details on respondents.

52. Author's interview (412). Transcript maintained by author. See appendix 2 for details on respondents.

53. Formed in 1970 to bring together community and neighborhood organizations around the country and focus on issues like housing, schools, neighborhood safety, health care, and job conditions, ACORN operates in 75 cities around the country with 850 neighborhood chapters.

54. The PCADV may not technically qualify as a citizen group according to the criteria I established in chapter 1. It is a coalition of service organizations and agencies that coalesce into a formidable lobbying and advocacy presence. I count it here as a citizen group for several reasons. First, many lawmakers consider it an important representation of citizen views and refer to it as a citizen interest group. Second, though members are technically service organizations, the groups engages in a great deal of policy advocacy on behalf of women and children victims of domestic violence, and individuals can and do participate in a range of lobbying activities that the groups engage in. Third, while the group could be categorized as a social service agency, that category consists almost exclusively of organizations that have service as their primary organizational goal. The PCADV was formed precisely to serve as a representation of the interests of women victims in legislative politics. Removing the PCADV from the citizen category would simply reduce the number of citizen organizations represented in Pennsylvania legislative crime politics even further, strengthening my argument that citizen organizations as a whole have little presence in state crime politics. But it seems appropriate to consider it with other groups that represent citizens as victims and potential victims.

55. An index score for any given congressional year can range from 0 to 1, but following Baumgartner and Jones 2000, I multiply the scores by 100 for ease of presentation.

56. Note that because the Herfindahl index is based on squared proportions, changes in the index are exponential. The lowest possible concentration score for all groups—which would mean each type of group is equally represented at the hearings in that year—would be 6.25. The lowest concentration score for just the major groups would be 20.

57. See appendix 2 for mean differences in Herfindahl scores for the two time periods.

58. Obviously a much larger portion of groups on the "interested parties" list and the lobby registration lists are businesses and lobbyists than is true of the original data presented in this chapter. Since these lists are compiled for *any* issue that might come onto the Judiciary Committee or the state legislature as a whole, it is not surprising that the number of business groups that actually participate in crime hearings is much smaller than the broader list of groups that might want to participate in legal matters in the state.

59. Author's interview (407). Transcript maintained by author. See appendix 2 for details on respondents.

60. Many respondents also noted that the ACLU has a paid lobbyist in Harrisburg, though the ACLU was not listed in Gray and Lowry's dataset.

61. Author's interview (407). Transcript maintained by author. See appendix 2 for details on respondents.

62. Author's interview (405). Transcript maintained by author. See appendix 2 for details on respondents.

63. The website of the Association has an extensive description of its activities: www.pdaa.org/history.html.

64. Author's interview (404). Transcript maintained by author. See appendix 2 for details on respondents.

65. Author's interview (407). Transcript maintained by author. See appendix 2 for details on respondents.

66. See www.pcar.org/about/index.html.

67. Author's interview (407). Transcript maintained by author. See appendix 2 for details on respondents.

68. See www.aclupa.org/home/abouttheaclu.

69. YES See www.prisonsociety.org.

70. Author's interview (407). Transcript maintained by author. See appendix 2 for details on respondents.

71. "Prosecutors often endorsed legislation permitting the use of 'illegally' obtained evidence. Police usually supported wiretap legislation that would facilitate the apprehension of suspects and opposed efforts to limit the use of 'necessary' force. Defense attorneys, on the other hand, opposed legislation that took advantage of the insecurity and confusion of newly arrested suspects. In short, the location of individuals within the criminal justice system determined the nature of their jobs, which in turn directly affected their support for legislation" (Berk et al. 1977, 286).

72. Pennsylvania General Assembly Public Hearing on Proposed Anti-Drug Legislation, House of Representatives, Judiciary Committee, May 19, 1989, 118. House of Representatives Office of the Chief Clerk.

73. Pennsylvania General Assembly Public Hearing on Proposed Anti-Drug Legislation, House of Representatives, Judiciary Committee, May 19, 1989, 145. House of Representatives Office of the Chief Clerk.

74. Pennsylvania General Assembly Public Hearing on Proposed Anti-Drug Legislation, House of Representatives, Judiciary Committee, May 19, 1989, 110–112. House of Representatives Office of the Chief Clerk.

75. The transfer of asset forfeiture funds to groups engaged in community development may have originated in Chicago, where a community organization, National People's Action, in collaboration with ACORN, pressured the Chicago Police Department and eventually the Justice Department to craft new regulations allowing local police departments to transfer as much as 15 percent of asset forfeiture monies to community organizations for crime prevention programs (Anner 1995).

76. Pennsylvania General Assembly Public Hearing on Proposed Anti-Drug Legislation, House of Representatives, Judiciary Committee, May 19, 1989, 138–139. House of Representatives Office of the Chief Clerk.

77. Pennsylvania General Assembly, Public Hearings House Subcommittee on Courts, December 3, 1997, 86. House of Representatives Office of the Chief Clerk.

78. Author's interview (405). Transcript maintained by author. See appendix 2 for details on respondents.

79. Author's interview (411). Transcript maintained by author. See appendix 2 for details on respondents.

80. Pennsylvania General Assembly, Public Hearing debating House Resolution 67, Special Committees to Investigate Gang Violence, August 8, 21, 22, September 26, November 21 and 30, 1973. Pennsylvania State Archives.

81. Senate Bill 595 P.N. 645, Senate Bill 446 P.N. 493, House Bill 89 P.N. 113, House Resolution 200 P.N. 1243.

82. Press Release on Domestic Violence Fatality Review Board Legislation, PCADV, April 42, 2007.

83. Gottschalk 2006, chap. 5.

84. See Gottschalk 2006; see also Goss 2006.

85. The nine hearings in which both groups appeared were: June 9, 1987, Senate (drug), September 25, 1989, Senate (death penalty for juveniles), January 24, 1996, Senate (prison overcrowding), May 11, 1994, Senate (violent repeat offenders), January 7, 1990, House (lethal injection), September 10, 1992, House (mandatory sentencing), April 1, 1998, House (sexual assault in prison), April 24, 1996, House (private prisons), February 5, 2003, House (topic unknown).

86. Dubber 2002; Scheingold, Olson, and Pershing 1994; Zimring, Hawkins, and Kamin 2001.

Chapter 5

1. No. 070442 (May 24, 2007), proposing to prohibit the possession of firearms by persons charged with certain offenses; No. 070348 (April 26, 2007), to provide for certain reporting requirements on the application to carry a firearm; No. 07034700 (April 26, 2007), to require sales of firearms to be reported to the Philadelphia police and for the police to maintain a registry for such reports; No. 070346 (April 26, 2007), to regulate acquiring and transferring of firearms; No. 070345 (April 26, 2007), providing for prohibition on certain assault weapons; No. 070344 (April 26, 2007), prohibiting straw purchases and limiting handgun purchases to one a month; No. 070343 (April 26, 2007), requiring prompt notification of firearms theft; No. 070336 (April 26, 2007), prohibiting sale of firearms to persons subject to protection-from-abuse orders; No. 070335 (April 26, 2007), permitting the temporary removal of firearms from people posing a risk of imminent injury to self or others; No. 060804 (October 26, 2006), prohibiting adults from allowing children to have unsupervised access to firearms; No. 060700 (September 21, 2006), requiring prompt notification of lost or stolen firearms; No. 060584 (June 15, 2006), requiring certain licensing of persons who sell firearms. A useful resource for up-to-date information about Philadelphia city council hearings, bills, and other city business is www.hallwatch.org.

2. Because of the nature of record keeping at the local level, an analysis of hearings dating back to the 1960s—or even the 1980s, for that matter—was not possible for my two local sites. However, research on local crime politics as well as the brief reviews of citizen activism in Philadelphia and Pittsburgh presented in this chapter help illustrate the dynamic interaction between local legislative institutions and group interests over time.

3. Full details about the data are listed in appendix 3.

4. See Dilworth (2006) for an outstanding collection of essays on the relationship between urbanism, social capital, and political mobilization.

5. Dahl 1961; Hunter 1953; Truman 1951.

6. Browning et al. 1984; DeLeone 1992; Swanstrom 1985; Ferman 1996; Berry, Portney, and Thomson 1993; Reckhow 2006; Berry et al. 2006; Dilworth 2006.

7. Eisinger 1976; Aberbach and Walker 1970.

8. Berry et al. 2006.

9. Gray and Lowry 2004.

10. Schattschneider, 1960, 30.

11. Campbell 2003; Goss 2006; Lowi 1977.

12. Jacob 1984; Scheingold 1991.

13. Heinz, Jacob, and Lineberry 1983.

14. Heinz et al. 1983.

15. Heinz et al. 1983, 4.

16. Heinz et al. 1983; Lyons 1999; Scheingold 1991; Skogan and Hartnett 1997; Skogan and Maxfield 1981; Wilson 1968.

17. Jacob 1980; Scheingold 1984; Lyons 1999; Rosenbaum 1986; Miller 2001b; Skogan and Hartnett 1997.

18. Heinz et al. 1983.

19. See Boyle 2004 and Escobar 1999 for thorough discussions of the interaction of local police with urban political regimes and the use of police to maintain racial hierarchy.

20. Kennedy 1997, p. 152.

21. In 1992, Rodney King, an African American motorist, led police on a high-speed chase down a Los Angeles freeway. After finally being pulled over, King was badly beaten by over a dozen police officers. During the trial of the officers involved, prosecutors presented evidence that several of the officers made racially derogatory remarks after the beating. For a detailed account of the event, see Lawrence (2000). Abner Louima, a Haitian immigrant, was sodomized in 1997 by a New York City police officer in the bathroom of a precinct house after his arrest for involvement in a brawl outside a nightclub.

22. Pastore and Maguire (2004). Table 2.12, "Reported Confidence in the Criminal Justice System, by Demographic Characteristics," table 2.13, "Reported Confidence in the Police, by Demographic Characteristics," table 2.24, "Attitudes Toward Fair Treatment of Persons of Different Races by Police in Own Community," and table 2.25, "Respondents Fear That Police Will Stop Them and Arrest Them When Innocent."

23. See Walker et. al. 2004; Weitzer and Tuch 2005.

24. Buffum and Sagi, 1983, 125.

25. Rosenbaum 1986; Miller 2001b; Lyons 1999; see also Skogan and Hartnett 1997.

26. Jacob 1980.

27. This section draws heavily on social and political histories of Philadelphia and Pittsburgh: Buffum and Sagi 1983, Countryman 2006, Dilworth 2006, and Ferman 1986. This chapter addresses Philadelphia and Pittsburgh, but they are hardly the only urban areas with long histories of citizen mobilization. For a discussion of political mobilization in Milwaukee, see Eisinger 1976; for Chicago, Philadelphia, and San Francisco, see Skogan and Maxfield 1981; for Seattle, see Scheingold 1991; for Newark, Minneapolis, Phoenix, and Los Angeles, see Heinz et al. 1983; for San Francisco, see DeLeone 1992.

28. Countryman 2006; Dilworth 2006; Ferman 1996.

29. Buffum and Sagi 1983.

30. Countryman 2006.

31. Buffum and Sagi 1983; Countryman 2006.

32. Countryman 2006.

33. Countryman 2006, 819.

34. Countryman 2006.

35. The ministers' strategies included selective patronage campaigns in which they urged black constituents to boycott businesses that refused to address black hiring demands. Among the first targets was the classic Philadelphia institution the Tasty Baking Company (makers of Tastykakes). After a two-month boycott, the company agreed to all of the demands, "including the hiring of the first blacks to the lucrative position of salesman-driver" (Countryman 2006, 822).

36. Countryman 2006, 813.

37. Buffum and Sagi 1983.

38. Buffum and Sagi 1983, 127, quoting Daughen and Binzen 1977, 102.

39. Countryman 2006.

40. Ferman 1996.

41. Ferman 1996; Zahniser 2005.

42. Cunningham 1981.

43. Cunningham 1981; Ferman 1996.

44. Collins 2003; Cunningham 1981.

45. There was some evidence in my interviews that the district council members heard from broad citizen groups more than the at-large members, but I do not have a large enough sample of at-large members to draw definitive conclusions.

46. Some obvious missing issues are criminal procedures, staffing of courts and corrections, and the death penalty.

47. Author's interview (204). Transcript maintained by author. See appendix 3 for details on respondents. See also, Philadelphia City Council hearing, December 6, 2005. Office of the Chief Clerk.

48. Author's interview (209). Transcript maintained by author. See appendix 3 for details on respondents.

49. Author's interview (108). Transcript maintained by author. See appendix 3 for details on respondents.

50. Author's interview (109). Transcript maintained by author. See appendix 3 for details on respondents.

51. Author's interview (102). Transcript maintained by author. See appendix 3 for details on respondents.

52. Author's interview (201). Transcript maintained by author. See appendix 3 for details on respondents.

53. Author's interview (107). Transcript maintained by author. See appendix 3 for details on respondents.

54. Philadelphia city council hearing, November 15, 2000. Office of the Chief Clerk.

55. Author's interview (201). Transcript maintained by author. See appendix 3 for details on respondents.

56. Author's interview (208). Transcript maintained by author. See appendix 3 for details on respondents.

57. Author's interview (201). Transcript maintained by author. See appendix 3 for details on respondents.

58. Author's interview (104). Transcript maintained by author. See appendix 3 for details on respondents.

59. Author's interview (107). Transcript maintained by author. See appendix 3 for details on respondents.

60. Author's interview (202). Transcript maintained by author. See appendix 3 for details on respondents.

61. Author's interview (107). Transcript maintained by author. See appendix 3 for details on respondents.

62. Author's interview (202). Transcript maintained by author. See appendix 3 for details on respondents.

63. Five of these groups also appear on Pittsburgh's neighborhood group list obtained from the Pittsburgh mayor's office.

64. Some of these groups may be misnamed duplicates of other groups already in the dataset. I did search for a variety of possible alterations—for example, with Shady Side Community Council I also looked for Shady Side Citizen Council, Association, and Organization. Some of these references may simply be erroneous. Even assuming that half of them are, this means that less than 5 percent of all the groups identified in the interviews and hearings were nonexistent.

65. More information on ACORN, an organization of low and moderate-income families "working together for social justice," is at www.acorn.org. Lutheran Settlement House in Philadelphia was established and run by the Lutheran Social Mission Society as part of the settlement movement in 1902. It provides services for low-income children, adults, and families (www.lutheransettlement.org). Project H.O.M.E. is an organization dedicated to empowering homeless and poor citizens (www.projecthome.org).

66. Demographic data are drawn from the 2000 U.S. Census, on the basis of zip codes.

67. Author's interview (206). Transcript maintained by author. See appendix 3 for details on respondents.

68. Author's interview (108). Transcript maintained by author. See appendix 3 for details on respondents.

69. Author's interview (209). Transcript maintained by author. See appendix 3 for details on respondents.

70. Author's interview (103). Transcript maintained by author. See appendix 3 for details on respondents.

71. Philadelphia City Council hearing, Joint Committee on Public Safety and Education, April 6, 2004. Office of the Chief Clerk.

72. Author's interview (109). Transcript maintained by author. See appendix 3 for details on respondents.

73. Author's interview (202). Transcript maintained by author. See appendix 3 for details on respondents.

74. Author's interview (202). Transcript maintained by author. See appendix 3 for details on respondents.

75. I include groups here who appeared at more than one hearing, in contrast to the tables in chapters 3 and 4 in which only groups that appeared in more than two hearings are listed, for two reasons. First, my legislative hearing data at the local level are not nearly as extensive as those at the state and national levels, where I have roughly 10 hearings per year. At the local level, I have only 40 hearings over five years, and they are spread between two cities; and we would not necessarily expect to find precisely the same groups in the two cities (though they are mostly from Philadelphia). In addition, at the state and national levels, there seemed to be an important analytic distinction between groups that appeared more than twice and groups that appeared only once or twice, in that only a few groups appeared more than twice, whereas a substantial number of groups appeared twice. At the local level, the distinction appeared to be more between one-timers and those appearing more than once.

76. Cohen and Dawson 1993.

Chapter 6

1. Truman 1951; Dahl 1961; Berry 1999; Gray and Lowry 1996.

2. Author's interview (201). Transcript maintained by author. See appendix 3 for details on respondents.

3. Author's interview (107). Transcript maintained by author. See appendix 3 for details on respondents.

4. Author's interview (204). Transcript maintained by author. See appendix 3 for details on respondents.

5. Author's interview (102). Transcript maintained by author. See appendix 3 for details on respondents.

6. Author's interview (204). Transcript maintained by author. See appendix 3 for details on respondents.

7. Author's interview (205). Transcript maintained by author. See appendix 3 for details on respondents.

8. Author's interview (107). Transcript maintained by author. See appendix 3 for details on respondents.

9. Philadelphia City Council hearing, December 6, 2005, Office of the Chief Clerk.

10. Philadelphia City Council Hearing, June 15, 2006, 59, Office of the Chief Clerk.

11. Author's interview (107). Transcript maintained by author. See appendix 3 for details on respondents.

12. Author's interview (411). Transcript maintained by author. See appendix 2 for details on respondents.

13. Gottschalk 2006, Barker 2006.

14. Author's interview (102). Transcript maintained by author. See appendix 3 for details on respondents.

15. Author's interview (107). Transcript maintained by author. See appendix 3 for details on respondents.

16. The nature of the data in this project does not lend itself to causal analysis of the relationship between race and attitudes about causes of crime. There is considerable research documenting that both class and race play a role in attitudes toward the police (Weitzer 2005). And previous research links some of the rise of community policing to black political agitation (Lyons 1999, Miller 2001b). As I suggested in chapter 5, the research presented here suggests a more nuanced approach. While race and class no doubt filter one's attitudes toward crime and its causation, one's proximity to routine violence may be equally important in shaping one's attitudes.

17. Author's interview (203). Transcript maintained by author. See appendix 3 for details on respondents.

18. Author's interview (107). Transcript maintained by author. See appendix 3 for details on respondents.

19. Pittsburgh City Council hearing, Jan 22, 2003, municipal record, 131st council. City Clerk's Office, 4.

20. Pittsburgh City Council hearing, November 14, 2000, City Clerk's Office.

21. Philadelphia City Council hearing, December 6, 2005, 61, Office of the Chief Clerk. The Association's goal is to "mobilize African-American communities around the nation to support healthy media and advertising images. The mission is to mobilize communities to live a healthy lifestyle, promote positive imagery among individuals and communities and to foster environments free of health disparities." NAAAPI website: www.naaapi.org/default.asp.

22. The Society's website uses the phrase "Working with Citizens to Improve Philadelphia's Visual Environment and Quality of Life"; www.urbanblight.org/.

23. Philadelphia City Council hearing, Joint Committee on Public Safety and Public Health and Human Services, December 6, 2005, 80, Office of the Chief Clerk.

24. Philadelphia City Council hearing, December 6, 2005, 102–104, Office of the Chief Clerk.

25. Philadelphia City Council hearing December 6, 2005, 109, Office of the Chief Clerk.

26. At-large councilman Frank Rizzo is the son of the late mayor Frank Rizzo.

27. Anthony S. Tyman, "City Again Orders Billboards Removed," *Philaddelphia Inquirer,* September 30, 2005.

28. I am grateful to Bill Lyons for urging me to speak more directly to the issue of how citizen group presence in local crime politics may actually translate into real policy outcomes. While this is primarily a study of agenda-setting, not policy, outcomes, it is nonetheless important to pay attention to whether citizen groups are simply creating public spectacles that are then channeled into traditional police-centered frames. As I and others have noted elsewhere (Carr et. al. 2007; Lyons 1999; Miller 2001b), it is in fact difficult for citizen groups mobilized around crime to change traditional law-and-order policy frames that typically place police in the center of crime prevention and control. However, as this chapter demonstrates, lawmakers seem at least moderately responsive to citizen group preferences that link crime to broader structural issues and challenge dominant frames of policing.

29. Author's interview (409). Transcript maintained by author. See appendix 2 for details on respondents.

30. Author's interview (106). Transcript maintained by author. See appendix 3 for details on respondents.

31. Author's interview (204). Transcript maintained by author. See appendix 3 for details on respondents.

32. Philadelphia City Council Hearing, March 9, 2004, 83–85, Office of the Chief Clerk.

33. Philadelphia City Council Hearing, March 9, 2004, 113–114, Office of the Chief Clerk. Mothers in Charge, an antiviolence group started by an African American woman whose son was murdered in 2001, has a membership that includes over 300 women. The founder of the group, echoing the pragmatic approach described later in this chapter, has been quoted as saying: "I think police need community support. I don't think that a cop on the corner would have prevented my son from being murdered. We need to work with the police around the issues of violence—please make that point. We need to work with them and not expect them to do it all for us." Quoted in Michael Matza, "Homicides Surge Past 2006 Rate," *Philadelphia Inquirer,* February 27, 2007.

34. Philadelphia City Council hearing, November 15, 2000, Office of the Chief Clerk. The Father's Day Rally Committee is a local grassroots African American group aimed at providing community support for fathers. Matthew P. Blanchard, "Fathers and Children Bond in Fairmount Park Ritual," *Philadelphia Inquirer,* June 17, 2002.

35. Philadelphia City Council hearing, November 15, 2000, 57–58, Office of the Chief Clerk. Men United for a Better Philadelphia is a city-wide activist organization dedicated to reducing violence, withprimarily African American membership. www.menunited.org/. See also Robert Moran, "War of Words

on Drug Dealing: Men United for a Better Philadelphia Aims to Complement the Current Police Campaign," *Philadelphia Inquirer*, May 9, 2002.

36. Author's interview (206). Transcript maintained by author. See appendix 3 for details on respondents.

37. Author's interview (202). Transcript maintained by author. See appendix 3 for details on respondents.

38. Author's interview (108). Transcript maintained by author. See appendix 3 for details on respondents.

39. Author's interview (103). Transcript maintained by author. See appendix 3 for details on respondents.

40. Author's interview (411). Transcript maintained by author. See appendix 2 for details on respondents.

41. Author's interview (103). Transcript maintained by author. See appendix 3 for details on respondents.

42. Author's interview (201). Transcript maintained by author. See appendix 3 for details on respondents.

43. Philadelphia City Council hearing, December 6, 2005, 51. Office of the Chief Clerk.

44. Philadelphia City Council hearing, June 16, 1998, 43–36. Office of the Chief Clerk.

45. Author's interview (107). Transcript maintained by author. See appendix 3 for details on respondents.

46. Author's interview (107). Transcript maintained by author. See appendix 3 for details on respondents.

47. Author's interview (101). Transcript maintained by author. See appendix 3 for details on respondents.

48. Author's interview (103). Transcript maintained by author. See appendix 3 for details on respondents.

49. Author's interview (107). Transcript maintained by author. See appendix 3 for details on respondents.

50. See Heumann and Cassak 2003. added.

51. National Advisory Commission on Civil Disorders 1968. See Stuntz 2001, 2006.

52. Carr, Napolitano, and Keating 2007.

53. Silver and Miller 2004.

54. I heard this several times in my research on a federal crime program called Weed and Seed in Seattle in the late 1990s as well. See Miller 2001b.

55. Cohen and Dawson 1993.

56. Gilliam and Bobo 1990.

57. See Schattschneider 1960; Miller 2007.

58. Ferman 1996.

Chapter 7

1. Baker 1999; Beale 1995; Brickey 1995; Heller 1997; Strazzella 1998.

2. Of course, this is not the only challenge for groups representing poorly resourced citizens. As Alfred Stepan notes (1999), federalism comes in many

different forms, and in the United States it is particularly nonconducive to broad citizen interests because of its overrepresentation of small states in the upper chamber (Senate) and its single-member-district, winner-take-all electoral system. The precise relationship between different types of federal and electoral systems and the representation of broad citizen interests is a subject for future research, though there is already some empirical verification of the limitations that federalism imposes on broad social welfare state policy goals (see Immergut 1992).

3. Schneider and Ingram 1993.

4. Gottschalk 2006; Jacob 1984; Simon 2006; Zimring, Hawkins, and Kamin 2001.

5. Very few registered lobbyists are police organizations, though law enforcement organizations do form an important part of the crime policy environment in Pennsylvania, as shown in chapter 4.

6. Cover 1995.

7. Barkow 2005; Stuntz 2006.

8. The Alliance for the Mentally Ill testifies primarily at hearings on procedural issues such as the insanity defense and policing the mentally ill.

9. A number of important works have examined state punishment policies but few have explored the policy process itself. See Barker 2006, Yates 1997, and Zimring et al. 2001 for important exceptions.

10. Anderson 1999; Bourgois 2003; Patillo-McCoy 1999.

11. Katznelson 1981.

12. See Cohen and Dawson (1993) for a related discussion.

13. Interview 102.

14. Interview 108.

15. Zimring et al. 2001, 222; see also Drubber 2002; Henderson 1985.

16. Roberts et al. 2005.

17. Schattschneider 1960, 30.

18. Peterson 1981.

19. Hearing before the Subcommittee on Juvenile Justice of the Committee on the Judiciary, Senate, 103rd Congress, September 13, 1993, Y4.J89/2:S.HRG 103-393, 69.

20. Goss 2006, 30.

21. Gottschalk 2006.

22. Interview 409.

23. Pralle 2006; Manna 2006.

24. Dudziak 2002.

25. Hall 1992.

26. Young 2000.

27. Massey and Denton 1993.

28. Elazar 1972, 2

29. Savelsberg 1994; Garland 2001.

30. Zimring et al. 2001.

31. Lowi 1964; Olson 1965.

32. Testimony on urban violence presented to Senate Judiciary Committee by Larry Frankel, legislative director, ACLU of Pennsylvania, September 25, 2006.

33. Simon 2007; see also Garland 2001; Lyons and Drew 2006.

34. Simon persuasively argues that scholars should look for governing through crime frameworks in policy venues other than crime control. In this sense, it is possible that other policy areas—welfare, environment, health care, national security, immigration, social security, and other important topics of the twenty-first century—are increasingly framed in citizen-victim terms. This is outside the scope of this project but makes for an important future research project.

35. Gottschalk 2006; Simon 2006.

36. See Kennedy 1997.

37. See Boyle 2004 for a particularly rich discussion of the relationship between crime, race, and local machine politics in 1920s Detroit.

38. Wayne Jacobs, phone conversation with author, August 25, 2005.

39. Councilman Cohen, Philadelphia City Council Public Hearing on Straw and Multiple Gun Purchases, March 9, 2004, 90.

Appendix 1

1. Berry 1999, 374.

WORKS CITED

Abney, Glenn, and Thomas P. Lauth. 1985. Interest Group Influence in City Policy-Making: The Views of Administrators. *Western Political Quarterly* 38: 148–161.

Amenta, Edwin. 1998. *Bold Relief: Institutional Politics and the Role Origins of Modern American Social Policy.* Princeton, NJ: Princeton University Press.

Anderson, Elijah. 1999. *Code of the Streets: Decency, Violence and the Moral Life of the Inner City.* New York: Norton.

Anner, John. 1996. "Linking Community Safety with Police Accountability." In John Anner, 1986, *Beyond Identity Politics: Emerging Social Justice Movements in Communities of Color.* Boston: South End Press.

Aberbach, Joel, and Jack Walker. 1970. Political Trust and Racial Ideology. *American Political Science Review* 64: 1212.

Baker, John S. 1999. State Police Powers and the Federalization of Local Crime. *Temple Law Review* 72: 675–713.

Barker, Vanessa. 2006. The Politics of Punishing: Building a State Governance Theory of American Imprisonment Variation. *Punishment and Society* 8 (1): 5–32.

Barkow, Rachel E. 2005. Federalism and the Politics of Sentencing. *Columbia Law Review* 105 (4): 1276–1314.

Bastian, Lisa D., and Bruce M. Taylor. 1994. *Young Black Male Victims: National Crime Victimization Survey.* Office of Justice Programs, U.S. Department of Justice. NCJ 147004. Washington, DC: Bureau of Justice Statistics.

Bauer, Lynn, and Steven D. Owens. 2004. *Justice Expenditures and Employment in the United States, 2001.* Office of Justice Programs, Department of Justice. NCJ 202792. Washington, DC: Bureau of Justice Statistics.

Baumgartner, Frank R., and Bryan D. Jones, eds. 2002. *Policy Dynamics.* Chicago: University of Chicago Press.

Baumgartner, Frank R., and Bryan D. Jones. 2000. The Evolution of Legislative Jurisdictions. *Journal of Politics* 62: 321–349.

Baumgartner, Frank R., and Bryan D. Jones. 1993. *Agendas and Instability in American Politics.* Chicago: University of Chicago Press.

Baumgartner, Frank R., and Beth L. Leech. 2001. Interest Niches and Policy Bandwagons: Patterns of Interest Group Involvement in National Politics. *Journal of Politics* 63: 1191–1213.

Baumgartner, Frank R., and Beth L. Leech. 1998. *Basic Interests: The Importance of Groups in Politics and Political Science.* Princeton, NJ: Princeton University Press.

Beale, Sara Sun. 1995. Too Many and Yet Too Few: New Principles to Define the Proper Limits for Federal Criminal Jurisdiction. *Hastings Law Journal* 46: 997–1018.

Beckett, Katherine. 1997. *Making Crime Pay: Law and Order in Contemporary American Politics.* New York: Oxford University Press.

Beer, Samuel H. 1977. Federalism, National and Democracy in America. *American Political Science Review* 72: 9–21.

Bell, Jeannine. 2002. *Policing Hatred: Law Enforcement, Civil Rights and Hate Crime.* New York: New York University Press.

Bennett, W. Lance. 1995. *News: The Politics of Illusion.* White Plains, NY: Longman.

Bentley, Arthur. 1949. *The Process of Government: A Study of Social Pressures.* Evanston, IL: Principia Press.

Berk, Richard A., Harold Brackman, and Selma Lesser. 1977. *A Measure of Justice: An Empirical Study of Changes in the California Penal Code, 1955–1971.* New York: Academic Press.

Bernard, Thomas J. 1992. *The Cycle of Juvenile Justice.* New York: Oxford University Press.

Bernstein, David E. 2005. Thoughts on *Hodges v. U.S. Boston Law Review* 85: 811–819.

Berry, Jeffrey M. 1999. The Rise of Citizen Groups. In Theda Skocpol and Morris P. Fiorina, eds., *Civic Engagement in American Democracy.* Washington, DC: Brookings.

Berry, Jeffrey M. 1999. *The New Liberalism: The Rising Power of Citizen Groups.* Washington, DC: Brookings Institute Press.

Berry, Jeffrey M. 1997. *The Interest Group Society.* New York: HarperCollins.

Berry, Jeffrey M. 1977. *Lobbying for the People.* Princeton, NJ: Princeton University Press.

Berry, Jeffrey M., Kent E. Portney, Robin Liss, Jessica Simoncelli, and Lisa Berger. 2006. Power and Interest Groups in City Politics. Paper presented at the annual meetings of the American Political Science Association, Philadelphia, August 30–September 3.

Blumberg, Abraham S. 1967. *Criminal Justice.* Chicago: Quadrangle Books.

Bourgois, Philippe I. 2003. *In Search of Respect: Selling Crack in El Barrio.* Cambridge: Cambridge University Press.

Boyle, Kevin. 2004. *Arc of Justice: A Saga of Race, Civil Rights and Murder in the Jazz Age.* New York: Holt.

Brandwein, Pamela P. 2007. A Judicial Abandonment of Blacks? Rethinking the "State Action" Cases of the Waite Court. *Law and Society Review* 41 (2): 343–86.

Brickey, Kathleen F. 1995. Criminal Mischief: The Federalization of American Criminal Law. *Hastings Law Journal* 46: 1135–1174.

Browne, William P. 1990. Organized Interests and Their Issue Niches: A Search for Pluralism in a Policy Domain. *Journal of Politics* 52: 477–509.

Browning, Rufus P., Dale Rogers Marshall, and David H. Tabb. 1984. *Protest is Not Enough: The Struggle of Blacks and Hispanics for Equality in Urban Politics*. Berkeley: University of California Press.

Buckley, Frank. 1925. The Department of Justice: Its Origin, Development and Present-Day Organization. *Boston University Law Review* 5: 177–185.

Buffum, Peter C., and Rita Sagi. 1983. Philadelphia: Politics of Reform and Retreat. In Anne Heinz, Herbert Jacob, and Robert L. Lineberry, eds., *Crime in City Politics*. New York: Longman.

Campbell, Andrea Louise. 2003. *How Policies Make Citizens*. Princeton, NJ: Princeton University Press.

Caplow, Theodore, and Jonathon Simon. 1999. Understanding Prison Policy and Population Trends. In Michael Tonry and Joan Petersilia, eds., *Prisons*. Chicago: University of Chicago Press.

Carpenter, Daniel P. 2001. *The Forging of Bureaucratic Autonomy: Reputations, Networks and Policy Invocation in Executive Agencies, 1862–1928*. Princeton, NJ: Princeton University Press.

Carr, Patrick J., Laura Napolitano, and Jessica Keating. 2007. We Never Call the Cops and Here Is Why: A Qualitative Examination of Legal Cynicism in Three Philadelphia Neighborhoods. *Criminology* 45 (2): 701–735.

Casper, Jonathan D. 1972. *American Criminal Justice: The Defendant's Perspective*. Englewood Cliffs, NJ: Prentice-Hall.

Chandra, Kanchan. 2006, Spring. Mechanisms v. Outcomes. *Qualitative Methods: Newsletter of the American Political Science Association Organized Section on Qualitative Methods* 4 (1): 00–00.

Chong, Dennis. 1991. *Collective Action and the Civil Rights Movement*. Chicago: University of Chicago Press.

Cigler, Allan J., and Burdett A. Loomis. 1983. *Interest Group Politics*. Washington, DC: CQ Press.

Clemens, Elisabeth S. 1997. *The People's Lobby: Organizational Innovation and the Rise of Interest Group Politics in the United States, 1890–1925*. Chicago: University of Chicago Press.

Clymer, Steven D. 1997. Unequal Justice: The Federalization of Criminal Law. *Southern California Law Review* 70: 643–735.

Cohen, J. Cathy, and Michael C. Dawson. 1993. Neighborhood Poverty and African American Politics. *American Political Science Review* 87 (2): 286–302.

Cohen, Stanley. 1985. *Visions of Social Control: Crime, Punishment and Classification*. Cambridge: Polity Press.

Collins, James. 2003. Taking the Lead: Dorothy Williams, NAACP Youth Councils and Civil Rights Protests in Pittsburgh, 1961–64. *Journal of African-American History* 88: 126–137.

Countryman, Matthew. 2006. From Protest to Politics: Community Control and Black Independent Politics in Philadelphia, 1965–1984. *Journal of Urban Affairs* 32 (6): 813–861.

Cover, Robert. 1986. Violence and the Word. *Yale Law Journal* 95: 1601–1629.

Cronin, Thomas E., Tania Z. Cronin, and Michael E. Milakovich. 1981. *U.S. v. Crime in the Streets*. Bloomington: Indiana University Press.

Crotty, Patricia McGee. 1993. Pennsylvania: Individualism Writ Large. In Ronald J. Hrebenar and Clive S. Thomas, eds.,*Interest Groups in the Northeastern States*. University Park: Pennsylvania State University Press.

Cunningham, Constance A. 1981. Homer Brown: First Black Political Leader in Pittsburgh. *Journal of Negro History* 66: 304–317.

Curtis, Dennis E. 1996. The Effect of Federalization on the Defense Function. *Annals of the American Academy of Political and Social Science* 543: 85–96

Dahl, Robert. 1961. *Who Governs?* New Haven, CT: Yale University Press.

Daughen, Joseph R., and Peter Binzen. 1977. *The Cop Who Would Be King: Mayor Frank Rizzo*. Boston: Little Brown.

Deering, Christopher J., and Steven S. Smith. 1997. *Committees in Congress*. 3rd ed. Washington, DC: Congressional Quarterly Press.

DeLeone, Richard Edward. 1992. *Left Coast City: Progressive Politics in San Francisco, 1975–1991*. Lawrence: University of Kansas Press.

Demuth, Stephen, and Darrell Steffensmeier. 2004. Ethnicity Effects on Sentence Outcomes in Felony Cases: Comparisons among White, Black, and Hispanic Defendants. *Social Science Quarterly* 85: 994–1011.

Derthick, Martha. 2001. *Keeping the Compound Republic: Essays on American Federalism*. Washington, DC: Brookings Institution Press.

Derthick, Martha. 1999. *Dilemmas of Scale in America's Federal Democracy*. New York: Cambridge University Press.

Dilworth, Richardson. 2006. *Social Capital and the City: Civic Engagement and Participation in Philadelphia*. Philadephia: Temple University Press.

Downs, Anthony. 1957. *An Economic Theory of Democracy*. New York: Harper.

Dubber, Markus Dirk. 2002. *Victims in the War on Crime: The Use and Abuse of Victims' Rights*. New York: New York University Press.

Dudziak, Mary L. 2002. *Cold War Civil Rights: Race and the Image of American Democracy*. Princeton, NJ: Princeton University Press.

Eisenstein, James, and Herbert Jacob. 1977. *Felony Justice: An Organizational Analysis of Criminal Courts*. Boston: Little, Brown.

Eisinger, Peter K. 1976. *Patterns of Interracial Politics: Conflict and Cooperation in the City*. New York: Academic Press.

Elazar, Daniel J. 1987. *Exploring Federalism*. Tuscaloosa: University of Alabama Press.

Elazar, Daniel J. 1972. *American Federalism: A View from the States*. New York: Crowell.

Ellison, Ralph. 1952. *Invisible Man*. New York: Random House.

Entman, Robert M., and Andrew Rojecki. 2000. *The Black Image in the White Mind: Media and Race in America*. Chicago: University of Chicago Press.

Escobar, Edward J. 1999. *Race, Police, and the Making of a political identity; Mexican Americans and the Los Angeles Police Department, 1900–1945*. Berkeley: University of California Press.

Fairchild, Erika. 1981. Interest Groups in the Criminal Justice Process. *Journal of Criminal Justice* 9: 181–194.

Feeley, Malcolm. 1979. *The Process Is the Punishment: Handling Cases in a Lower Criminal Court*. New York: Russell Sage Foundation.

Feeley, Malcolm M., and Edward L. Rubin. 1998. *Judicial Policymaking and the Modern State: How the Courts Reformed Americas Prisons*. New York: Cambridge University Press.

Feeley, Malcolm M., and Austin D. Sarat. 1980. *The Policy Dilemma: Federal Crime Policy and the Law Enforcement Assistance Administration*. Minneapolis: University of Minnesota Press.

Feeley, Malcolm M., and Jonathon Simon. 1994. Actuarial Justice: The Emerging New Criminal Law. In David Nelken, ed., *The Futures of Criminology*. New York: Sage.

Ferman, Barbara. 1996. *Challenging the Growth Machine: Neighborhood Politics in Chicago and Pittsburgh*. Lawrence: University Press of Kansas.

Ferrell, Claudine L. 1986. *Nightmare and Dream: Antilynching in Congress 1917–1922*. New York: Garland.

Fiorina, Morris. 1999. Extreme Voices: The Dark Side of Civic Engagement. In Theda Skocpol and Morris Fiorina, eds., *Civic Engagement in American Democracy*. Washington, DC: Brookings Institute Press.

Flamm, Matthew. 2005. *Law and Order: Street Crime, Civil Unrest and the Crisis of Liberalism in the 1960s*. New York: Columbia University Press.

Foner, Eric. 1988. *Reconstruction: America's Unfinished Revolution, 1863–1877*. New York: Harper and Row.

Freedman, Robert. 1963. *A Report on Politics in Philadelphia*. Cambridge, MA: Joint Center for Urban Studies, Massachussetts Institute of Technology.

Friedman, Lawrence M. 1993. *Crime and Punishment in American History*. New York: Basic Books.

Frymer, Paul. 2005. Racism Revised: Courts, Labor Law, and the Institutional Construction of Racial Animus. *American Political Science Review* 99 (3): 373–87.

Fyfe, James J. 1988. Police Use of Deadly Force. *Justice Quarterly* 5: 165–205.

Garland, David. 2001. *The Culture of Control: Crime and Social Order in Contemporary Society*. Chicago: University of Chicago Press.

Garland, David. 1996. The Limits of the Sovereign State. *British Journal of Criminology* 36: 445–470.

Gilens, Martin. 1999. *Why Americans Hate Welfare: Race, Media, and the Politics of Antipoverty Policy*. Chicago: University of Chicago Press.

Gilliam, Frank D., and Lawrence Bobo. 1990. Race, Sociopolitical Participation, and Black Empowerment. *American Political Science Review* 84 (2): 377–393.

Gilliam, Franklin D., Jr., and Shanto Iyengar. 2000. Prime Suspects: The Influence of Local Television News on the Viewing Public. *American Journal of Political Science* 44: 560–573.

Glassner, Barry. 1999. *The Culture of Fear: Why Americans Are Afraid of the Wrong Things.* New York: Basic Books.

Goldstein, Herman. 1990. *Problem-Oriented Policing.* New York: McGraw-Hill.

Goss, Kristin. 2006. *Disarmed: The Missing Movement for Gun Control in America.* Princeton, NJ: Princeton University Press.

Gottschalk, Marie. 2006. *The Prison and the Gallows: The Politics of Mass Incarceration in America.* New York: Cambridge University Press.

Gottschalk, Marie. 2005. The Prisoners' Rights Movement and the Carceral State. Paper presented at the annual meeting of the American Political Science Association, Washington, DC, September 1–4.

Gottschalk, Marie. 2002. Black Flower: Prisons and the Future of Incarceration. *Annals of the American Academy of Political and Social Sciencies* 582: 195–227.

Graber, Mark. 2006. *Dred Scott and the Problem of Constitutional Evil.* Cambridge: Cambridge University Press.

Gray, Virginia. 2004. The Socioeconomic and Political Context of the States. In Virginia Gray and Russell L. Hanson, eds., *Politics in the American States: A Comparative Analysis.* Washington, DC: Congressional Quarterly Press.

Gray, Virginia, and David Lowery. 1996. *The Population Ecology of Interest Representation: Lobbying Communities in the American States.* Ann Arbor: University of Michigan Press.

Greenberg, David F., and Valerie West. 2001. State Prison Populations and Their Growth, 1971–1991. *Criminology* 39 (3): 615–653.

Greene, Judith A. 2002. Entrepreneurial Corrections: Incarceration as a Business Opportunity. In Marc Mauer and Meda Chesney-Lind, eds., *Invisible Punishment: The Collateral Consequences of Mass Imprisonment.* New York: New Press.

Gregory, Steven. 1998. *Black Corona: Race and the Politics of Place in an Urban Community.* Princeton, N.J.: Princeton University Press.

Gressman, Eugene. 1952. The Unhappy History of Civil Rights Legislation. *Michigan Law Review* 50: 1323–1358.

Hall, Peter. 1992. Political Structure, State Policy, and Industrial Change: Early Railroad Policy in the United States and Prussia. In Steven Steinmo, Kathleen Thelen, and Frank Longstreth, eds., *Structuring Politics: Historic Institutionalism in Comparative Analysis.* Cambridge: Cambridge University Press.

Haltom, William, and Michael W. McCann. 2004. *Distorting the Law: Politics, Media and the Litigation Crisis.* Chicago: University of Chicago Press.

Hamm, Keith E., and Gary F. Moncrief. 2004. Legislative Politics in the States. In Virginia Gray and Russell L. Hanson, eds., *Politics in the American States: A Comparative Analysis.* Washington, DC: Congressional Quarterly Press.

Heclo, Hugh. 1978. Issue Networks and the Executive Establishment. In Anthony King, ed., *The New American Political System*. Washington, DC: American Enterprise Institute.

Heinz, Anne, Herbert Jacob, and Robert L. Lineberry. 1983. *Crime in City Politics*. New York: Longman.

Heinz, John P., Robert Gettleman, and Morris A. Seeskin. 1969. Legislative Politics and the Criminal Law. *Northwestern University Law Review* 64: 277–385.

Heller, Robert. 1997. Selective Prosecution and the Federalization of Criminal Law: the Need for Meaningful Judicial Review of Prosecutorial Discretion. *University of Pennsylvania Law Review* 145: 1309–1358.

Henderson, Dwight. 1985. *Congress, Courts and Criminals: The Development of Federal Criminal Law, 1801–1829*. Westport, CT: Greenwood Press.

Hershey, Marjorie Randon, and Darrell M. West. 1983. Single-Issue Politics: Pro-Life Groups and the 1980 Senate Campaign. In David A. Rochefort and Roger W. Cobb, eds., *The Politics of Problem Definition: Shaping the Policy Agenda*. Lawrence: University of Kansas Press.

Heumann, Milton, and Lance Cassak. 2003. *Good Cop, Bad Cop: Racial Profiling and Competing Views of Justice*. New York: Peter Lang.

Heumann, Milton. 1977. *Plea Bargaining: The Experiences of Prosecutors, Judges and Defense Attorneys*. Chicago: University of Chicago Press.

Holcombe, J. E., M. R. Williams, and S. Demuth. 2004. White Female Victims and Death Penalty Disparity Research. *Justice Quarterly* 21: 877–902.

Holyoke, Thomas T. 2003. Choosing Battlegrounds: Interest Group Lobbying across Multiple Venues. *Political Research Quarterly* 56: 325–336.

Hrebrenar, Ronald J. 1993. The Role of Interest Groups in Northeast Politics. In Ronald J. Hrebranar and Clive S. Thomas, eds., *Interest Group Politics in the Northeast States*. University Park: Pennsylvania State University Press.

Hunter, Floyd. 1953. *Community Power Structure: A Study of Decision-makers*. Chapel Hill, NC: University of North Carolina Press.

Immergut, Ellen. 1992. The Rules of the Game: The Logic of Health Policy-Making in France, Switzerland, and Sweden. In Steven Steinmo, Kathleen Thelen, and Frank Longstreth, eds., *Structuring Politics: Historic Institutionalism in Comparative Anslysis*. Cambridge: Cambridge University Press.

Interstate Immorality: The Mann Act and the Supreme Court. 1947. Note. *Yale Law Journal*, 56: 718–753.

Jacob, Herbert. 1984. *The Frustration of Policy: Responses to Crime by American Cities*. Boston: Little Brown.

Jacob, Herbert. 1980. *Crime and Justice in Urban America*. Englewood Cliffs, NJ: Prentice-Hall.

Jacobs, David, and Jason T. Carmichael. 2002. The Political Sociology of the Death Penalty: A Pool Time-Series Analysis. *American Sociological Review* 67 (1): 109–131.

Jacobson, Matthew Frye. 1998. *Whiteness of a Different Color: European Immigrants and the Alchemy of Race*. Cambridge, MA: Harvard University Press.

Jacoby, Joan. 1979. *The Prosecutor*. Newbury Park, CA: Sage.

Jenness, Valerie, and Kendal Broad. 1997. *Hate Crimes: New Social Movements and the Politics of Violence*. New York: de Gruyter.

Jenness, Valerie, and Ryken Grattet. 2001. *Making Hate a Crime: From Social Movement to Law Enforcement*. New York: Russell Sage.

Katznelson, Ira. 1981. *City Trenches: Urban Politics and the Patterning of Class in the United States*. New York: Pantheon Books.

Kelling, George L., and Catherine M. Coles. 1996. *Fixing Broken Windows: Restoring Order and Reducing Crime in Our Communities*. New York: Martin Kessler Books.

Kelling, George L., Tony Pate, Duane Dieckman, and Charles E. Brown. 1974. *The Kansas City Preventive Patrol Experiment*. Washington, DC: Police Foundation.

Kennedy, Randall. 1997. *Race, Crime and the Law*. New York: Pantheon Books.

Key, Sewall. 1938. The Legal Work of the Federal Government. *Virginia Law Review* 25: 165–201.

Key, V. O. 1958. *Politics, Parties and Pressure Groups*. New York: Crowell.

King, Desmond S. 1995. *Separate and Unequal: Black Americans and the US Federal Government*. Oxford: Clarendon Press.

King, Desmond S., and Rogers M. Smith. 2005. Racial Orders in American Political Development. *American Political Science Association* 99: 75–92.

King, Gary, Robert O. Keohane, and Sidney Verba. 1994. *Designing Social Inquiry: Scientific Inference in Qualitative Research*. Princeton, NJ: Princeton University Press.

King, James D. 2000. Changes in Professionalism in U.S. State Legislatures. *Legislative Studies Quarterly* 25: 327–343.

Kurland, Adam H. 1996. First Principles of American Federalism and the Nature of Federal Criminal Jurisdiction. *Emory Law Journal* 1: 00–00.

Landy, Marc K. 1990. Local Government and Environmental Policy. In Martha Derthick, ed., *Dilemmas of Scale in America's Federal Democracy*. Cambridge: Cambridge University Press.

Lawrence, Regina G. 2000. *The Politics of Force: Media and the Construction of Police Brutality*. Berkeley: University of California Press.

Lieberman, Robert C. 1998. *Shifting the Color Line: Race and the American Welfare State*. Cambridge, MA: Harvard University Press.

Ligurio, Aurther J. 1995. Crime and Communities: Prevalence, Imapct and Programs. In Lawrence B. Joseph, ed., *Crime, Comunities and Public Policy*. Chicago: Chicago Assembly.

Lin, Ann Chih. 2000. *Reform in the Making: The Implementation of Social Policy in Prison*. Princeton, NJ: Princeton University Press.

Lineberry, R. L., and E. P. Fowler. 1967. Reformism and Public Policies in American Cities. *American Political Science Review* 6: 701–716.

Lowery, David, and Virginia Gray. 2004. Bias in the Heavenly Chorus: Interests in Society and Before Government. *Journal of Theoretical Politics* 16: 5–30.

Lowi, Theodore. 1977. *The End of Liberalim: The Second Republic of the United States*. New York: Norton.

Lowi, Theodore. 1964. American Business, Public Policy, Case-Studies and Political Theory. *World Politics* 16: 677–715.

Lyons, William. 1999. *The Politics of Community Policing: Rearranging the Power to Punish*. Ann Arbor: University of Michigan Press.

Lyons, William T., and Julie Drew. 2006. *Punishing Schools: Fear and Citizenship in American Public Education*. Ann Arbor: University of Michigan Press.

Manna, Paul. 2006. *School's In: Federalism and the National Education Agenda*. Washington, DC: Georgetown University Press.

Manning, Peter. 1977. *Police Work*. Cambridge, MA: MIT Press.

Marion, Nancy. E. 1994. *A History of Federal Crime Control Initiatives, 1960–1993*. Westport, CT: Praeger.

Massey, Douglas S., and Nancy A. Denton. 1993. *American Apartheid: Segregation and the Making of the Underclass*. Cambridge, MA: Harvard University Press.

Mauer, Mark. 2006. *Race to Incarcerate*. New York: New Press.

Mauer, Mark, and Meda Chesney-Lind. 2002. *Invisible Punishment: The Collateral Consequences of Mass Imprisonment*. New York: New Press.

McCann, Michael W. 1986. *Taking Reform Seriously: Perspectives on Public Interest Liberalism*. Ithaca, NY: Cornell University Press.

McConnell, Grant. 1967. *Private Power and American Democracy*. New York: Knopf.

Meier, Kenneth J. 1992. The Politics of Drug Abuse: Laws, Implementation, and Consequences. *Western Political Quarterly* 45: 41–69.

Melone, Albert P., and Robert Slagter. 1983. Interest Group Politics and the Reform of the Federal Criminal Code. In Stuart Nagel, Erika Fairchild, and Anthony Champagne, eds., *The Political Science of Criminal Justice*. Springfield, IL: Charles C. Thomas.

Mendelberg, Tali. 1997. Executing Hortons: Racial Crime in the 1988 Presidential Campaign. *Public Opinion Quarterly* 61: 134–157.

Mendes, Silvia M. 2004. Certainty, Severity, and Their Relative Deterrent Effects: Questioning the Implications of the Role of Risk in Criminal Deterrence Policy. *Policy Studies Journal* 32: 59–75.

Mettler, Suzanne. 2005. *Soldiers to Citizens: The G.I. Bill and the Making of the Greatest Generation*. New York: Oxford University Press.

Mettler, Suzanne. 1998. *Dividing Citizens: Gender and Federalism in New Deal Public Policy*. Ithaca, NY: Cornell University Press.

Miller, Lisa L. 2007. The Representational Biases of Federalism: Scope and Bias in the Political Process, Revisited. *Perspectives on Politics* 5 (2): 305–321.

Miller, Lisa L. 2004. Re-thinking Bureaucrats in the Policy Process: Criminal Justice Agents and the National Crime Agenda. *Policy Studies Journal* 32: 569–588.

Miller, Lisa L. 2001a. Looking for Postmodernism in All the Wrong Places: Implementing a New Penology. *British Journal of Criminology* 41: 168–184.

Miller, Lisa L. 2001b. *The Politics of Community Crime Prevention: Implementing Weed and Seed in Seattle*. Law, Justice and Power Series. Burlington, VT: Dartmouth/Ashgate Press.

Miller, Lisa L., and James Eisenstein. 2005. The Federal/State Criminal Prosecution Nexus: A Case Study in Cooperation and Discretion. *Law and Social Inquiry* 30 (2): 239–268.

Mooney, Christopher Z. 1995. Measuring U.S. State Legislative Professionalism: An Evaluation of Five Indices. *State and Local Government Review* 26: 70–78.

Morenoff, Jeffrey D., and Robert J. Sampson. 2001. Neighborhood Inequality, Collective Efficacy, and the Spatial Dynamics of Urban Violence. *Criminology* 39: 517–559.

Morlan, R. L., and L. C. Hardy. 1968. *Politics in California*. Encino, CA: Dickenson.

Morone, James A. 2003. *Hellfire Nation: The Politics of Sin in American History*. New Haven, CT: Yale University Press.

Murakawa, Naomi. 2005. Electing to Punish: Congress, Race and the American Criminal Justice State. Ph.D. diss., Yale University.

Musto, David F. 1987. *The American Disease: Origins of Narcotics Control*. New York: Oxford University Press.

Nagel, Stuart, Erika Fairchild, and Anthony Champagne. 1983. *The Political Science of Criminal Justice*. Springfield, IL: Charles C. Thomas.

National Advisory Commission on Civil Disorders. 1968, March 1. *Final Report*. Washington, DC: U.S. Government Printing Office.

Nourse, Victoria F., and Jane S. Schacter. 2002. The Politics of Legislative Drafting: A Congressional Case Study. *New York University Law Review* 77: 575.

Nownes, Anthony, and Chris Cooper. 2003. Citizen Groups in Big-City Politics. *State and Local Government Review* 2: 102–111.

O'Brien, David. 2005. *Constitutional Law and Politics: The Struggle for Power and Governmental Accountability*. New York: Norton.

Olson, Mancus. 1965. *The Logic of Collective Action: Public Goods and the Theory of Groups*. Cambridge, MA: Harvard University Press.

O'Reilly, Kenneth. 1982. A New Deal for the FBI: The Roosevelt Administration, Crime Control and National Security. *Journal of American History* 69: 638–658.

Parenti, Christian. 1999. *Lockdown America: Police and Prisons in the Age of Crisis*. London: Verso Press.

Pastore, Ann L., and Kathleen Maguire, eds. *Sourcebook of Criminal Justice Statistics*. Department of Justice, Bureau of Justice Statistics. Available on-line http://www.albany.edu/sourcebook.

Pattillo, Mary, David Weiman, and Bruce Western, eds. 2004. *Imprisoning America: The Social Effects of Mass Incarceration*. New York: Russell Sage Foundation.

Pattillo-McCoy, Mary. 1999. *Black Picket Fences: Privilege and Peril among the Black Middle Class*. Chicago: University of Chicago Press.

Peffley, M., J. Hurwitz, and P. M. Sniderman. 1997. Racial Stereotypes and Whites' Political Views of Blacks in the Context of Welfare and Crime. *American Journal of Political Science* 41 (1): 30–60.

Percival, Garrick L. 2004. The Influence of Local Contextual Characteristics on the Implementation of a Statewide Voter Initiative: The Case of California's Substance Abuse and Crime Prevention Act (Proposition 36). *Policy Studies Journal* 32: 589–160.

Peterson, Mark. 1990. *Legislating Together*. Cambridge, MA: Harvard University Press.

Peterson, Paul E. 1995. *The Price of Federalism*. Washington, DC: Brookings Institution Press.

Peterson, Paul E. 1981. *City Limits*. Chicago: University of Chicago Press.

Phillips, Julie A. 2006. The Relationship between Age Structure and Homicide Rates in the United States, 1970 to 1999. *Journal of Research on Crime and Delinquency* 43 (2): 230–260.

Pierson, Paul. 2004. *Politics in Time: History, Institutions and Social Analysis*. Princeton, NJ: Princeton University Press.

Piven, Frances Fox, and Richard A. Cloward. 1977. *Poor People's Movements: Why They Succeed, How They Fail*. New York: Vantage Books.

Pralle, Sarah. 2006. *Branching Out, Digging In: Environmental Advocacy and Agenda Setting*. Washington, DC: Georgetown University Press.

Pralle, Sarah. 2005. Shopping Around: Environmental Organizations and the Search for Policy Venues. Paper delivered at the annual meeting of the Western Political Science Association, Oakland, CA, March 17–19.

Reckhow, Sarah. 2006. Flexing Their Political Muscle: Organized Mobilization and Electoral Representation of Race and Ethnic Groups in U.S. Cities. Paper presented at the annual meetings of the American Political Science Association, Philadelphia, PA, August 31.

Riker, William H. 1964. *Federalism: Origin, Operation, Significance*. Boston: Little, Brown.

Roberts, Cheryl, John Doble, Elyse Clawson, Carol Stelton, and Andrew Briker. 2005. *Rethinking Justice in Massachusetts: Public Attitudes toward Crime and Punishment*. Boston: Doble Research Associations, Boston Foundation.

Rochefort, David A., and Roger W. Cobb. 1994. *The Politics of Problem Definition: Shaping the Policy Agenda*. Lawrence: University Press of Kansas.

Rosenbaum, Dennis, ed. 1986. *Community Crime Prevention: Does It Work?* Newbury Park, CA: Sage.

Rourke, Francis E. 1978. *Bureaucratic Power in National Politics: Readings*. Boston: Little, Brown.

Salisbury, Robert. 1984. Interest Representation: The Dominance of Institutions. *American Political Science Review* 78: 64–76.

Sampson, Robert J., and Jeffrey D. Morenoff. 2002. Assessing "Neighborhood Effects": Social Processes and New Directions in Research. *Annual Review of Sociology* 28: 443–478.

Savelsberg, Joachim. 1994. Knowledge, Domination and Criminal Punishment. *American Journal of Sociology* 99 (4): 911–943.

Schattschneider, E. E. 1960. *The Semi-Sovereign People: A Realist's View of Democracy in America*. Fort Worth, TX: Harcourt, Brace.

Scheingold, Stuart. 1991. *The Politics of Street Crime*. Philadelphia: Temple University Press.

Scheingold, Stuart. 1984. *The Politics of Law and Order*. Philadelphia: Temple University Press.

Scheingold, Stuart, Toska Olson, and Jana Pershing. 1994. Sexual Violence, Victim Advocacy, and Republican Criminology: Washington State's Community Protection Act. *Law and Society Review* 28: 729–763.

Schneider, Anne, and Helen Ingram. 1993. The Social Construction of Target Populations: Implications for Politics and Policy. *American Political Science Review* 87: 334–347.

Scholzman, Kay Lehman. 1984. Political Equality and the American Pressure System. *Journal of Politics* 46: 1006–1032.

Scholzman, Kay Lehman, and John T. Tierney. 1986. *Organized Interests and American Democracy*. New York: Harper and Row.

Schwartz, L. B. 1948. Federal Criminal Jurisdiction and Prosecutors' Discretion. *Law and Contemporary Problems* 13: 64–65.

Scott, M. Todd. 2003. Kidnapping Federalism: *United States v. Wills* and the Constitutionality of Extending Federal Criminal Law into the States. *Journal of Criminal Law and Criminology* 93: 53.

Seibel, Brian J. 1999. City Lawsuits against the Gun Industry: A Road Map for Reforming Gun Industry Misconduct. *St. Louis University Public Law Review* 18: 247–290.

Sharp, Elaine B. 1994. Paradoxes of National Antidrug Policymaking. In David A. Rochefort and Roger W. Cobb, eds., *The Politics of Problem Definition: Shaping the Policy Agenda*. Lawrence: University of Kansas Press.

Sidney, Mara S. 2004. *Unfair Housing: How National Policy Shapes Community Action*. Lawrence: University of Kansas Press.

Silver, Eric, and Lisa L. Miller. 2004. Sources of Informal Social Control in Chicago Neighborhoods. *Criminology* 42: 551–583.

Simon, Jonathon. 2006. *Governing through Crime*. New York: Oxford University Press.

Simon, Jonathon. 1993. *Poor Discipline: Parole and the Social Control of the Underclass*. Chicago: University of Chicago Press.

Simons, Michael A. 2000. Prosecutorial Discretion and Prosecution Guidelines: A Case Study in Controlling Federalization. *New York University Law Review* 75: 893–965.

Skocpol, Theda, and Morris P. Fiorina. 1999. *Civic Engagement in American Democracy*. Washington DC: Brookings Institute Press and Russell Sage Foundation.

Skocpol, Theda. 2003. *Diminished Democracy: From Membership to Management in American Civic Life*. Norman: University of Oklahoma Press.

Skogan, Wesley G., and Susan M. Hartnett. 1997. *Community Policing, Chicago Style*. New York: Oxford University Press.

Skogan, Wesley G., and Michael G. Maxfield. 1981. *Coping with Crime: Individual and Neighborhood Reactions.* Beverly Hills, CA: Sage.

Skolnick, Jerome H. 1966. *Justice without Trial: Law Enforcement in a Democratic Society.* New York: Wiley.

Skolnick, Jerome, and James J. Fyfe. 1993. *Above the Law: Police and the Excessive Use of Force.* New York: Free Press.

Smith, Rogers. 1997. *Civic Ideals: Conflicting Visions of Citizenship in U.S. History.* New Haven, CT: Yale University Press.

Smith, Rogers M. 1988. Political Jurisprudence, The New Institutionalism, and the Future of Public Law. *American Political Science Review* 82: 89–108.

Soss, Joe. 2000. *Unwanted Claims: The Politics of Participation in the U.S. Welfare System.* Ann Arbor: University of Michigan Press.

Squire, Peverill. 1992. Legislative Professionalism and Membership Diversity in State Legislatures. *Legislative Studies Quarterly* 17: 69–79.

Stannard, David E. 2005. *Honor Killing: How the Infamous Massie Affair Transformed Hawaii.* New York: Penguin Books.

Steffensmeier, Darrell, Jeff Ulmer, and John Kramer. 1998. The Interaction of Race, Gender, and Age in Criminal Sentencing: The Punishment Cost of Being Young, Black, and Male. *Criminology* 36: 763–797.

Steinmo, Steven, Kathleen Thelen, and Frank Longstreth. 1992. *Structuring Politics: Historical Institutionalism in Comparative Analysis.* New York: Cambridge University Press.

Stepan, Alfred. 1999. Federalism and Democracy: Beyond the U.S. Model. *Journal of Democracy* 10 (4): 19–34.

Stephan, James J. 2004. *State Prison Expenditures, 2001.* Office of Justice Programs, Department of Justice., Special Report. NCJ 202949. Washington, DC: Bureau of Justice Statistics.

Stolz, Barbara Ann. 2002. The Role of Interest Groups in U.S. Criminal Justice Policymaking. *Criminal Justice* 2(1): 51–69.

Strazzella, James A. 1998. The Federalization of Criminal Law. Washington, DC: Task Force on the Federalization of Criminal Law. American Bar Association, Criminal Justice Section.

Stuntz, William J. 2006. The Political Constitution of Criminal Justice. *Harvard Law Review* 119: 780.

Stuntz, William J. 2001. The Pathological Politics of Criminal Law. *Michigan Law Review* 100: 505.

Swanstrom, Todd. 1985. *The Crisis of Growth Politics: Cleveland, Kucinich and the Challenge of Urban Populism.* Philadelphia: Temple University Press.

Szymanski, Ann-Marie E. 2003. *Pathways to Prohibition: Radicals, Moderates, and Social Movement Outcomes.* Durham, NC: Duke University Press.

Thacher, David. 2004. The Rich Get Richer and the Poor Get Robbed: Inequality in U.S. Criminal Victimization, 1974–2000. *Journal of Quantitative Criminology* 20: 89–116.

Thelen, Kathleen, and Sven Steinmo. 1992. Institutionalism in Comparative Politics. In Steven Steinmo, Kathleen Thelen, and Frank Longstreth, eds.,

Structuring Politics: Historical Institutionalism in Comparative Analysis. New York: Cambridge University Press.

Thomas, Clive S., and Ronald J. Hrbrenar. 2004. Interest Groups in the States. In Virginia Gray and Russell L. Hanson, eds., *Politics in the American States: A Comparative Analysis.* Washington, DC: Congressional Quarterly Press.

Tonry, Michael. 1996. *Sentencing Matters.* New York: Oxford University Press.

Tonry, Michael. 1995. *Malign Neglect: Race, Crime and Punishment in America.* New York: Oxford University Press.

Torbet, Patricia, and Linda Syzmanski. 1998. *State Legislative Responses to Violent Juvenile Crime, 1996–7 Update.* Washington DC: Office of Juvenile Justice and Delinquency Prevention. Department of Justice.

Treadway, Jack. 2005. *Elections in Pennsylvania: A Century of Partisan Conflict in the Keystone State.* University Park: Pennsylvania State University Press.

Truman, David. 1951. *The Governmental Process: Political Interests and Public Opinion.* New York: Knopf.

Wacquant, Loïc. 2005. The Great Penal Leap Backward: Incarceration in America from Nixon to Clinton. In John Pratt, ed., *The New Punitiveness: Current Trends, Theories, Perspectives.* London: Willan Press.

Walker, Jack L. 1991. *Mobilizing Interest Groups in America.* Ann Arbor: University of Michigan Press.

Walker, Samuel. 2001. *Police Accountability: The Role of Civilian Oversight.* Belmont, CA: Wadsworth.

Walker, Samuel. 1999. *The Police in America: An Introduction.* Boston: McGraw-Hill.

Walker, Samuel, Cassia Spohn, and Miriam DeLone. 2004. *The Color of Justice: Race, Ethnicity and Crime in America.* Belmont, CA: Wadsworth.

Weitzer, Ronald, and S. A. Tuch. 2005. Racially Biased Policing: Determinants of Citizen Perceptions. *Social Forces* 83 (3): 1009–1030.

Wells-Barnett, Ida B. 1893. *Southern Horrors: Lynch Law in All Its Phases.* New York: *New York Age.*

Western, Bruce. 2006. *Punishment and Inequality in America.* New York: Russell Sage.

Western, Bruce. 2004. *Imprisoning America: The Social Effects of Mass Incarceration.* New York: Russell Sage.

Western, Bruce, Jeffrey R. Kling, and David F. Weiman. 2001. *The Labor Market Consequences of Incarceration.* Princeton, NJ: Princeton University Press.

Williams, M. R., and J. E. Holcomb. 2001. Racial Disparity and Death Sentences in Ohio. *Journal of Criminal Justice* 29 (3): 207–218.

Wilson, James Q. 1989. *Bureaucracy: What Government Agencies Do and Why They Do It.* New York: Basic Books.

Wilson, James Q. 1975. *Thinking about Crime.* New York: Basic Books.

Wilson, James Q. 1978. *The Investigators: Managing FBI and Narcotics Agents.* New York: Basic Books.

Windelsham, Lord. 1998. *Politics, Punishment and Populism.* New York: Oxford University Press.

Yates, Jeff. 1997. Racial Incarceration Disparity among the States. *Social Science Quarterly* 78: 1001–1010.

Young, Iris Marion. 2000. *Inclusion and Democracy*. New York: Oxford University Press.

Zahniser, Keith A. 2005. *Steel City Gospel: Protestant Laity and Reform in Progressive-Era Pittsburgh*. New York: Routledge.

Zimring, Franklin E. 2005. Penal Policy and Penal Legislation in Recent American Experience. *Stanford Law Review* 58: 323–338.

Zimring, Franklin, and Gordon Hawkins. 1997. *Crime Is Not the Problem: Lethal Violence in America*. New York: Oxford University Press.

Zimring, Franklin E., and Gordon Hawkins. 1996. Legislating Federal Crime and Its Consequences: Toward a Principled Basis for Federal Criminal Legislation. *Annals of the American Academy of Political and Social Science* 543 (15): 16–26.

Zimring, Franklin E., Gordon Hawkins, and Samuel Kamin. 2001. *Punishment and Democracy: Three Strikes and You're Out in California*. New York: Oxford University Press.

INDEX